The Long March

THE LONG MARCH

HOW THE CULTURAL REVOLUTION OF THE 1960S CHANGED AMERICA

Roger Kimball

ENCOUNTER BOOKS

San Francisco

ENCOUNTER BOOKS

Published by Encounter Books, an activity of Encounter for Culture and Education, Inc., a nonprofit tax-exempt corporation.

Encounter Books website address: www.encounterbooks.com

Manufactured in the United States.

The paper used in this publication meets the minimum requirements of ANSI/NISO Z39.48-1992 (R 1997) (Permanence of Paper).

Library of Congress Cataloging-in-Publication Data:
Kimball, Roger, 1953– .
    The long march : how the cultural revolution of the 1960s changed America / Roger Kimball
        p. cm.
    Includes bibliographic references and index.
    ISBN 1-893554-09-0 (cloth : alk.)
    1. United States—Civilization—1945– 2. United States—Intellectual life—20th century. 3. Nineteen sixties. 4. Nineteen seventies. 5. Radicalism—United States—History—20th century. 6. Subculture—United States—History—20th century. 7. Social change—United States—History—20th century. 8. Social values—United States—History—20th century. I. Title.
E169.12 .K467 2000
973.92—dc21   00-022211

To Hilton Kramer

Contents

The Long March

Introduction
What is a Cultural Revolution?

Was the phenomenon in fact so extraordinary as contemporaries supposed? Was it as unprecedented, as profoundly subversive and world-changing as they thought? What was its true significance, its real nature, and what were the permanent effects of this strange and terrifying revolution? What exactly did it destroy, and what did it create?
—Alexis de Tocqueville, *The Old Regime and the Revolution*, 1856

The effect of liberty to individuals is, that they may do what they please: We ought to see what it will please them to do, before we risque congratulations, which may be soon turned into complaints.
—Edmund Burke, *Reflections on the Revolution in France*, 1790

Afloat but rudderless

In May 1994, *The New York Times* reported in its science pages on the unhappy fate of one Phineas P. Gage, a foreman for the New England Railroad. In 1848, Gage was helping to lay track across Vermont. His job involved drilling holes in large rocks, into which he would pour blasting powder and lay down a fuse. He would then cover the explosives with sand, tamping it all down with a long metal

3

rod. One day, he inadvertently triggered an explosion. The metal rod went hurtling through his skull, entering just under his left eye and landing some yards away. Amazingly, Gage survived the assault. He was stunned but able to walk away. And although he lost an eye, he seemed otherwise to recover.

It soon became clear, however, that Gage was a sharply diminished man. His intellectual powers were apparently unimpaired; but what the writer for the *Times* called his "moral center" had been destroyed. Before the accident, Gage "had been an intelligent, socially responsible, hard-working fellow. . . . But in the weeks after the tamping rod pierced his brain, he began using profane language, lied to his friends and could not be trusted to honor his commitments." Phineas Gage had become a moral cripple, utterly unable to make ethical decisions.

Pondering the state of contemporary American cultural life, I have often recalled the sad story of Phineas Gage. Like him, our culture seems to have suffered some ghastly accident that has left it afloat but rudderless: physically intact, its "moral center" a shambles. The cause of this disaster was not an explosion of gunpowder, but a more protracted and spiritually convulsive detonation—one that trembled with gathering force through North America and Western Europe from the mid-1950s through the early 1970s and tore apart, perhaps irrevocably, the moral and intellectual fabric of our society. Even now, at the dawn of a new millennium, we are far from done tabulating its effects.

The Long March: How the Cultural Revolution of the 1960s Changed America contributes to that task. It is part cultural history, part spiritual damage report. It looks behind the received wisdom about "the Sixties" to the animating ideas, passions, and personalities that made that long decade a synonym for excess and moral breakdown. Above all, *The*

Long March aims to show how the paroxysms of the 1960s continue to reverberate throughout our culture. The Age of Aquarius did not end when the last electric guitar was unplugged at Woodstock. It lives on in our values and habits, in our tastes, pleasures, and aspirations. It lives on especially in our educational and cultural institutions, and in the degraded pop culture that permeates our lives like a corrosive fog. Looking afresh at the architects of America's cultural revolution, *The Long March* provides a series of cautionary tales, an annotated guidebook of wrong turns, dead ends, and unacknowledged spiritual hazards.

What is most obvious is often the easiest to overlook. To a casual observer, Phineas Gage might have appeared almost normal. So it is with our culture. Such blindness is a common by-product of cultural and moral upheaval. In his book on the *ancien régime* and the French Revolution (1856), Alexis de Tocqueville wrote that "great revolutions which succeed make the causes which produced them disappear, and thus become incomprehensible because of their own success." Acceptance breeds invisibility, the ultimate token of triumph. For an American writing at the end of the 1990s, Tocqueville's words fit our current cultural and political situation seamlessly. Although sometimes tempted to ignore it, we are living in the aftermath of a momentous social and moral assault. As David Frum observes in *How We Got Here*, his new book about the 1970s, we are the heirs of "the most total social transformation that the United States has lived through since the coming of industrialism, a transformation (a revolution!) that has not ended yet." Even now it is difficult to gauge the extent of that transformation. In 1991, looking back over his long and distinguished career in an essay called "A Life of Learning," the philosopher Paul Oskar Kristeller sounded a similar melancholy note. "We have witnessed," he wrote, "what amounts to a cultural revolution, comparable to the one in China if not worse, and whereas the Chinese have to some extent overcome their cultural revolution, I see many signs that ours is getting worse all the time, and no indication that it will be overcome in the foreseeable future."

What is a cultural revolution?

"Revolution," of course, is a strong word, one that covers a multitude of disparate activities and phenomena. And it is well at the outset to note that a cultural revolution is not the same thing as an intellectual or artistic revolution, though the three things often go together. The writings of Copernicus fomented a far-reaching intellectual revolution, as did, for example, the writings of Darwin. The development of one-point perspective in the Renaissance sparked a fertile artistic revolution in Italy and elsewhere. When Virginia Woolf, referring to a London exhibition of Post-Impressionist painting organized by her friend and fellow Bloomsbury figure Roger Fry, wrote that "in or about December 1910, human character changed. . . . All human relations . . . shifted," she was indulging in comic exaggeration. And yet Post-Impressionism did mark a revolution in artistic culture, just as the writing of Joyce and Eliot did in literary culture.

But a cultural revolution differs from an intellectual or artistic revolution. And it also differs from a political revolution—though, again, the two sometimes go together. A cultural revolution, whatever the political ambitions of its architects, results first of all in a metamorphosis in values and the conduct of life. In this context, it is also worth noting the differences between those political revolutions that aim at establishing a limited, constitutional government and those that—notwithstanding the proliferation of slogans about freedom and liberation—actually aim at or result in tyranny. The Glorious Revolution in England in 1688 and the American Revolution at the end of the eighteenth century are the chief—perhaps the only—examples of the former; the latter, regrettably, are much more common: the French Revolution and the Russian Revolution provide archetypes of actual tyranny staging a coup under the banner of imagined liberation. As the Marxists say, "it is no accident" that proponents of cultural revolution overwhelmingly favor the latter.

In a democratic society like ours, where free elections are guaranteed, political revolution is almost unthinkable in practical terms. Consequently, utopian efforts to transform society have been channeled into cultural and moral life. In America, scattered if much-publicized episodes of violence have wrought far less damage than the moral and intellectual assaults that do not destroy buildings but corrupt sensibilities and blight souls. The success of America's recent cultural revolution can be measured not in toppled governments but in shattered values. If we often forget what great changes this revolution brought in its wake, that, too, is a sign of its success: having changed ourselves, we no longer perceive the extent of our transformation.

In his reflections on the life of learning, Kristeller was concerned primarily with the degradation of intellectual standards that this cultural revolution brought about. "One sign of our situation," he noted, "is the low level of our public and even of our academic discussion. The frequent disregard for facts or evidence, or rational discourse and arguments, and even of consistency, is appalling." Who can disagree?

As Kristeller suggests, however, the intellectual wreckage visited upon our educational institutions and traditions of scholarship is only part of the story. There are also social, political, and moral dimensions to America's cultural revolution—or perhaps it would be more accurate to say that the spiritual deformations we have witnessed are global, and affect every aspect of life. Writing about America's cultural revolution in *The Totalitarian Temptation*, Jean-François Revel noted that "a revolution is not simply a new political orientation. It works through the depths of society. It writes the play in which political leaders will act much later."

The movement for sexual "liberation" (not to say outright debauchery) occupies a prominent place in the etiology of this revolution, as does the mainstreaming of the drug culture and its attendant pathologies. Indeed, the two are related. Both are expressions of the narcissistic hedonism that was an important ingredient of the counterculture from its development in the 1950s. The Marxist philosopher Herbert Marcuse was not joking when, in *Eros and Civilization*—one of many inspirational tracts for the movement—he extolled the salvational properties of "primary narcissism" as an effective protest against the "repressive order of procreative sexuality." "The images of Orpheus and Narcissus reconcile Eros and Thanatos," Marcuse wrote.

> They recall the experience of a world that is not to be mastered and controlled but to be liberated: . . . the redemption of pleasure, the halt of time, the absorption of death; silence, sleep, night, paradise—the Nirvana principle not as death but as life.

The succeeding decades showed beyond cavil that the pursuit of "the redemption of pleasure, the halt of time" was narcissistic in a far more common sense than Marcuse suggested. It turned out to be a form of death-in-life, not "paradise." But of course this was something that neither this guru of liberation nor his many followers ever acknowledged or perhaps even recognized.

One of the most conspicuous, and conspicuously jejune, features of America's cultural revolution has been the union of such hedonism with a species of radical (or radical-chic) politics. This union fostered a situation in which, as the famous slogan put it, "the personal is the political." The politics in question was seldom more than a congeries of radical clichés, serious only in that it helped to disrupt society and blight a good many lives. In that sense, to be sure, it proved to be very serious indeed. Apocalyptic rhetoric notwithstanding, the behavior of the "revolutionaries" of the counterculture consistently exhibited that most common of bourgeois passions, anti-bourgeois animus—expressed, as always, safely within the swaddling clothes of bourgeois security. As Allan Bloom remarked in *The Closing of the American Mind*, the cultural revolution proved to be so successful on college campuses partly because of "the bourgeois' need to feel that he is not bourgeois, to have dangerous experiments with the unlimited. . . . Anti-bourgeois ire is the opiate of the Last Man." It almost goes without saying that, like all narcotics, the opiate of anti-bourgeois ire was both addictive and debilitating.

The triumph of babydom

Like Falstaff's dishonesty, the adolescent quality of these developments was "gross as a mountain, open, palpable." If America's cultural revolution was anything, it was an attack on maturity: more, it was a glorification of youth, of immaturity. As the Yippie leader Jerry Rubin put it, "We're permanent adolescents." The real victory of the "youth culture" of the Sixties lay not in the fact that its demands were met but in the fact that its values and attitudes were adopted by the culture at large. Rubin again: "Satisfy our demands, and we've got twelve more. The more demands you satisfy, the more we got." Everywhere one looks one sees the elevation of youth—that is to say, of immaturity—over experience. It may seem like a small thing that nearly everyone of whatever age dresses in blue jeans now; but the universalization of that sartorial badge of the counterculture speaks volumes. At the end of *The Revolt of the Masses*, his prescient 1930 essay on the direction of culture, José Ortega y Gasset noted that "Though it may appear incredible, 'youth' has become a *chantage* [blackmail]; we are in truth living in a time when this adopts two complementary attitudes, violence and caricature."

The idealization of youth has resulted not only in the spread of adolescent values and passions: it has also led to the eclipse of adult virtues like circumspection, responsibility, and restraint. Writing about the cultural revolution in his book *The Undoing of Thought*, the French philosopher Alain Finkielkraut described this eclipse as "the triumph of babydom over thought."

> Two decades have been enough for deviance to become the norm, . . . and for the adolescent life-style to set the pace for society as a whole. Youth is fashionable. The cinema and advertising focus primarily on a public of fifteen to twenty year olds. Thousands of portable radios sing, almost all to the same guitar strains, of our good fortune to be done with conversation. And the drive against growing old is quite open. . . . Today youth is the categorical imperative of all the generations. . . . People in their forties are teenagers who have not grown up. . . . It is no longer the case that adolescents take refuge in their collective identity, in order to get away from the world; rather it is an infatuated world

which pursues adolescence. . . . The long process of the conversion to hedonism and consumerism of Western societies has culminated today in the worship of juvenile values. The bourgeois is dead, long live the adolescent.

The effect of these developments on cultural life in America has been immense. One of the most far-reaching and destructive effects has been the simultaneous glorification and degradation of popular culture. Even as the most ephemeral and intellectually vacuous products of pop culture—rock videos, comic books, television sit-coms—are enlisted as fit subjects for the college curriculum, so, too, has the character of popular culture itself become ever more vulgar, vicious, and degrading.

A watershed moment came with the apotheosis of The Beatles in the mid-1960s. Now, there is no denying that John Lennon and Paul McCartney were talented song writers, or that The Beatles (and their technicians) brought a new sophistication and inventiveness to rock music. It is also worth noting that in their proclamations of peace and love (blissed-out on drugs, but still) The Beatles stood in stark contrast to the more diabolical pronouncements of many other rock stars preaching a nihilistic gospel of (as the The Rolling Stones put it) "Let it Bleed" or "Sympathy for the Devil." Nevertheless, The Beatles, like other rock musicians, were unmistakably prophets of Dionysian excess; and they were all the more effective on account of their occasional tunefulness and their cuddly image. The dangerous Dionysianism, however, was overlooked in the rush to acclaim them geniuses. Even today, some of the claims made for The Beatles are breathtaking. The literary critic Richard Poirier was hardly the only academic to make a fool of himself slobbering over the Fab Four. But his observation that "sometimes they are like Monteverdi and sometimes their songs are even better than Schumann's" in the *Partisan Review* in 1967 did establish a standard of fatuity that has rarely been surpassed.

Unfortunately, the more popular culture has been raised up—the more vigorously it has been championed by the cultural elite—the lower popular culture has sunk. In comparison with the pop music of today, The Beatles almost do seem like Monteverdi. Almost. At the same time, though—and this is one of the most insidious effects of the whole process—the integrity of high culture itself has been severely compromised by the mindless elevation of pop culture. The academic enfranchisement of popular culture has meant not only that trash has been mistaken for great art, but also that great art has been treated as if it were trash. When Allen Ginsberg (for example) is upheld in the classroom as a "great poet" comparable to Shakespeare, the very idea of greatness is rendered unintelligible and high art ceases to function as an ideal. To quote Alain Finkielkraut again:

> It is not just that high culture must be demystified, brought remorselessly down to the level of the sort of everyday gestures which ordinary people perform in obscurity; sport, fashion, and leisure now lay claim to high cultural status. . . . [I]f you cannot accept that the author of the *Essais* [i.e., Montaigne] and a television personality, or a meditation designed to uplift the spirit and a spectacle calculated to brutalize, belong in the same cultural bracket; if you refuse, even though one is white and the other black, to equate Beethoven and Bob Marley—then you belong, quite irredeemably, to the party of the bastards (*salauds*) and the kill-joys.

In addition to its general coarsening effect on cultural

life, this triumph of vulgarity has helped to pave the way for the success of the twin banes of political correctness and radical multiculturalism. The abandonment of intrinsic standards of achievement creates (in Hermann Broch's phrase) a "value vacuum" in which everything is sucked through the sieve of politics and the ideology of victimhood.* Thus it is that vanguard opinion champions the idea of "art" as a realm of morally unassailable privilege even as it undermines the realities that make artistic achievement possible: technique, a commitment to beauty, a grounding in tradition. Art retains its status as a source of spiritual uplift, however dubious, yet it also functions as an exercise of politics by other means. Hence Robert Mapplethorpe's brutal and disgusting photographs of the sado-masochistic sexual underground are beyond criticism because they are "art," while at the same time they are held up as important "challenges" to the repressive, bourgeois regime of "mandatory heterosexuality" and the like.

From confrontation to insinuation

Today's college students were barely ten years old when the Berlin Wall was dismantled; they had not yet been born when Saigon fell. To the present generation, the Sixties and all it represented seem like nostalgic snapshots from a bygone era, an era that is presented as The Last Good Time. Yet despite the placidity of our own prosperous times, the

---

* William Henry's largely overlooked book *In Defense of Elitism* (1994) has many intelligent (and horrifying) things to say about the "battle between elitism and egalitarianism" that has been waged in American society since World War II—a battle in which, he points out, "egalitarianism has been winning far too thoroughly."

radical, emancipationist assaults of the Sixties are not confined to the past. Indeed, the effects of those assaults are in evidence throughout the culture. If, as Francis Fukuyama and others argue, some social indicators—falling crime rates and welfare rolls, arrested divorce rates—are encouraging, there is much else about contemporary life that must continue to alarm us.

Robert Bork's description of our situation as a "slouching towards Gomorrah" is melodramatic but not, I think, inaccurate. "The Sixties," Judge Bork wrote,

> may be seen in the universities as a mini–French Revolution that seemed to fail but did not. The radicals were not defeated by a conservative or traditionally liberal opposition but by their own graduation from the universities. And theirs was merely a temporary defeat. They and their ideology are all around us now.

That ideology has insinuated itself, disastrously, into the curricula of our schools and colleges; it has significantly altered the texture of sexual relations and family life; it has played havoc with the authority of churches and other repositories of moral wisdom; it has undermined the claims of civic virtue and our national self-understanding; it has degraded the media, the entertainment industry, and popular culture; it has helped to subvert museums and other institutions entrusted with preserving and transmitting high culture. It has even, most poignantly, addled our hearts and innermost assumptions about what counts as the good life: it has perverted our dreams as much as it has prevented us from attaining them.

In the Sixties and Seventies, after fantasies of overt political revolution faded, many student radicals urged their followers to undertake the "long march through the institutions." The phrase, popularized by the German New Leftist Rudi Dutschke, is often attributed to the Italian Marxist philosopher Antonio Gramsci—an unimpeachable authority for countercultural standard-bearers. But of course the phrase also carries the aura of an even higher authority: that of Mao Tse-tung and *his* long march and cultural revolution.

In the context of Western societies, "the long march through the institutions" signified—in the words of Herbert Marcuse—"working against the established institutions while working in them." It was primarily by this means—by insinuation and infiltration rather than confrontation—that the countercultural dreams of radicals like Marcuse have triumphed. Bellbottoms, long hair, and incense were dispensable props; crucial was the hedonistic antinomianism they symbolized. In this sense, countercultural radicalism has come more and more to define the dominant culture even as the memory of student strikes and demonstrations fades under the distorting glaze of nostalgia. For examples, you need look no further than the curriculum of your local school or college, at what is on offer at the nearest museum or so-called "public" radio station: indeed, you need look no further than your workplace, your church (if you still go to church), or your family to see evidence of the damage wrought by the long march of the counterculture. The radical ethos of the Sixties can be felt throughout public and private life, from the most ordinary domestic situations all the way up to the Presidency of the United States. (The Clinton presidency, a monument to sordidness, has also been a drama depicting how one representative figure succeeded in *his* long march through the institutions.) Writing recently about "the nasty things that were done in the late Sixties and transmitted to us," the political philosopher Harvey Mansfield noted that today they are neither so outrageous nor so violent as at first. The poison has worked its way into our souls, the effects becoming less visible to us as they become more ordinary. Even those who reject the Sixties unconsciously concede more than they know to the vicious principle of liberation that once was shouted into the street microphone.

The Long March is in part a reckoning of those concessions. It is also an effort to show why Mansfield was right to speak of the "vicious" principle of liberation. The principle of liberation is vicious when it is a blind for servitude. The grisly political history of this century has reminded us of the extent to which the totalitarian impulse appeals to liberation in its effort to expunge genuine liberty. Again and again we have seen the promise of liberation dissolve into outright tyranny. The totalitarian impulse occupies a prominent place in most revolutionary movements, cultural as well as political. America's war of independence from Britain, again, is unique, or near enough, in consistently eschewing the totalitarian option. From the very beginning, the Founding Fathers understood, as John Adams put it, that "neither morals, nor riches, nor discipline of armies, nor all these together will do without a constitution." How different this was from the Marxist-inspired tyranny visited upon Russia in 1917 or the megalomaniacal Rousseauvian variety that tore France apart in 1789. Indeed, the political fantasies of Jean-Jacques Rousseau have a great deal to answer for. For two centuries, his sentimentalizing utopian rhetoric has provided despots of all description with a means of pursuing conformity while praising freedom.

It is a neat trick. Words like "freedom" and "virtue" were ever on Rousseau's lips. But freedom for him was a chilly abstraction; it applied to mankind as an *idea*, not to in-

dividual men. "I think I know man," Rousseau sadly observed near the end of his life, "but as for men, I know
them not." In the *Confessions*, he claimed to be "drunk on
virtue." And indeed, it turned out that "virtue" for Rousseau had nothing to do with acting or behaving in a certain
way toward others. On the contrary, the criterion of virtue
was his subjective feeling of goodness. For Rousseau, as for
the countercultural radicals who followed him, "feeling
good about yourself" was synonymous with moral rectitude. Actually *behaving* well was irrelevant if not, indeed,
a sign of "inauthenticity" because it suggested a concern for
conventional approval. Virtue in this Rousseauvian sense is
scarcely distinguishable from moral intoxication.

The antinomian temptation

Translated into the political sphere, Rousseau's ideas about
freedom and virtue are a recipe for totalitarianism. "Those
who dare to undertake the institution of a people," Rousseau wrote in the *Social Contract*, "must feel themselves
capable, as it were, of changing human nature, . . . of altering the constitution of man for the purpose of strengthen-
ing it." As the philosopher Roger Scruton observed in an
essay on the French Revolution, "the revolutionary consciousness lives by abstract ideas, and regards people as the
material upon which to conduct its intellectual experiments." Man is "born free," Rousseau famously wrote, but
is "everywhere in chains." Alas, most men did not, according to him, truly understand the nature or extent of their
servitude. It was his job to enlighten them—to *force* them,
as he put it in one chilling epithet, to be free. Such
"freedom" is accomplished, Rousseau thought, by bringing
individual wills into conformity with what he called the

"general will"—surely one of the most tyrannical political principles ever enunciated. "If you would have the general will accomplished," he wrote, "bring all the particular wills into conformity with it; in other words, as virtue is nothing more than this conformity of the particular wills, establish the reign of virtue."

Establishing the reign of virtue is no easy task, as Rousseau's avid disciple Maximilien Robespierre discovered to his chagrin. All those "particular wills"—i.e., individual men and women with their diverse aims and desires—are so recalcitrant and so ungrateful for one's efforts to make them virtuous. Still, one does what one can to convince them to conform. And the guillotine, of course, is a great expedient. Robespierre was no political philosopher. But he understood the nature of Rousseau's idea of virtue with startling clarity, as he showed when he spoke of "virtue and its emanation, terror." It is a remark worthy of Lenin, and a grim foreshadowing of the Marxist-Leninist rhetoric that informed a great deal of Sixties radicalism.

I mention Rousseau here because, acknowledged or not, he is an important intellectual and moral grandfather of so much that happened in the cultural revolution of the 1960s. (Important "fathers" include Nietzsche, Marx, and Freud.) Rousseau's narcissism and megalomania, his paranoia, his fantastic political ideas and sense of absolute entitlement, his sentimentalizing nature-worship, even his twisted, hypertrophied eroticism: all reappeared updated in the tumult of the 1960s. And so did the underlying totalitarian impulse that informs Rousseau's notion of freedom.

In "Dreams of Plenitude, Nightmares of Scarcity" (1969), the sociologist Edward Shils summarized the chief components of the revolution he saw unfolding around him in the universities and elsewhere in American life. "The moral revolution," Shils wrote, consists in a demand for a total transformation—a transformation from a totality of undifferentiated evil to a totality of undifferentiated perfection. Evil consists in the deadening of sentiment through institutions and more particularly through the exercise of and subordination to authority. Perfection consists in the freedom of feeling and the fulfillment of desires. . . . A good community is like Rousseau's; the common will harmonizes individual wills. . . . The common will is not the resultant of the rationally arrived at assent of its members; it is not actually a *shared* decision making. . . . It is the transformation of sentiment and desire into reality in a community in which all realize their wills simultaneously. Anything less is repressive.

Two decades later, in "Totalitarians and Antinomians," Shils elaborated on the theme of absolute fulfillment in his description of the "antinomian temptation." At the center of that temptation was the fantasy of absolute freedom, unfettered by law, custom, or the promptings of morality.

The highest ideal of antinomianism is a life of complete self-determination, free of the burden of tradition and conventions, free of the constraints imposed by institutional rules and laws and of the stipulations of authority operating within the setting of institutions.

"Free," in other words, from the very things that underwrite freedom, that give it content, that prevent it from collapsing into that merely rhetorical freedom that always turns out to be another name for servitude.

The glorification of such spurious freedom is closely connected with another misuse of language—one of the most destructive: the description of irresponsible political naïveté as a form of "idealism." Nor is it only naïveté that gets the extenuating absolution of "idealism." So do all manner of crimes, blunders, and instances of brutality: all can be morally sanitized by the simple expedient of being rebaptized as examples of (perhaps misguided) "idealism." The one essential qualification is that the perpetrator be identified with the political Left. In her book *On Revolution*, Hannah Arendt—who was certainly no enemy of the Left herself—cannily observed that

> one has often been struck by the peculiar selflessness of the revolutionists, which should not be confused with "idealism" or heroism. Virtue has indeed been equated with selflessness ever since Robespierre preached a virtue that was borrowed from Rousseau, and it is the equation which has put, as it were, its indelible stamp upon the revolutionary man and his innermost conviction that the value of a policy may be gauged by the extent to which it will contradict all particular interests, and that the value of a man may be judged by the extent to which he acts against his own interest and against his own will.

In fact, the "peculiar selflessness" that Arendt describes often turns out to be little more than an abdication of individual responsibility abetted by utter self-absorption. It is a phenomenon that, among other things, helps to explain the queasy-making spectacle of left-wing Western intellectuals falling over themselves in a vain effort to excuse, mitigate, or sometimes simply deny the crimes of the Soviet Union and other murderous left-wing regimes throughout the Cold War and beyond. Perhaps we can admit that Stalin (or Mao or Pol Pot or Fidel or whoever) was repressive (or maybe that is just an ugly rumor propagated by the United States); perhaps he "went too far"; maybe some measures were "extreme"; this or that policy was "misjudged"; . . . but omelettes require breaking a few eggs, . . . and besides what glorious ideas are equality, community, the brotherhood of man . . . going beyond capitalistic greed, mere selfish individualism, repressive patriarchal society based on inequitable division of labor, etc., etc. The odor of piety that attends these rituals of exculpation is almost as disagreeable as the aura of grotesque unreality that emanates from them.

One sees the same thing in another key in the left-liberal response to America's cultural revolution. Whatever criticisms might be made of the counterculture, they are quickly neutralized by invoking the totem of "idealism." For example, one is regularly told that youth in the 1960s and 1970s, whatever its extravagances and sillinesses, had a "passionate belief" (the beliefs of radicals are never less than "passionate") in a "better world," in a "more humane society," in "equality." The guiding assumption is that "passion" redeems moral vacuity, rendering it noble or at least exempting it from censure. This assumption, which is part of the Romantic background of the counterculture, is profoundly mistaken and destructive.

As T. S. Eliot observed in 1934, the belief that there is "something admirable in violent emotion for its own sake, whatever the emotion or whatever the object," is "a cardinal point of faith in a romantic age." It is also, he noted, "a symptom of decadence." For it is "by no means self-evident," Eliot wrote,

> that human beings are most real when they are most violently excited; violent physical passions do not in themselves differentiate men from each other, but rather tend to reduce them to the same state; and the passion has significance only in relation to the character and behavior of the man at other moments of his life and in other contexts.

Furthermore, strong passion is only interesting or significant in strong men, those who abandon themselves without resistance to excitements which tend to deprive them of reason, become merely instruments of feeling and lose their humanity; and unless there is moral resistance and conflict there is no meaning.

"Passion," like "idealism," is a nostrum that the Left prescribes in order to relieve itself from the burdens of moral accountability.

Virtue gone mad

G. K. Chesterton once observed that in the modern world "the virtues have gone mad because they have been isolated from each other and are wandering alone. Thus some scientists care for truth; and their truth is pitiless. Thus some humanitarians only care for pity; and their pity . . . is often untruthful." Something similar can be said about the virtues of freedom and idealism. Freedom is an important virtue. But it is not the only virtue. And apart from other virtues—apart from prudence, say, and duty and responsibility, all of which define and limit freedom—freedom becomes a parody of itself. It becomes, in a word, unfree. And so it is with idealism. Idealism remains a virtue only to the extent that the causes to which it devotes itself are worthy of the devotion they attract. The more abstract the cause, the more vacuous the idealism.

In a subtle essay called "Countercultures," first published in 1994, the political commentator Irving Kristol noted that the counterculture of the 1960s was in part a reaction against a society that had become increasingly secular, routinized, and crassly materialistic. In this respect, too, the counterculture can be understood as part of our Romantic inheritance, a plea for freedom and transcendence in a society increasingly dominated by the secular forces of Enlightenment rationality. Indeed, revolts of this tenor have been a staple of Romanticism since the nineteenth century: Dostoevski's "underground man," who seeks refuge from the imperatives of reason in willful arbitrariness, is only one example (a rather grim one) among countless others.

The danger, Kristol notes, is that the counterculture, in its attack on secular materialism, "will bring down—will discredit—human things that are of permanent importance. A spiritual rebellion against the constrictions of secular humanism could end up . . . in a celebration of irrationalism and a derogation of reason itself." At a time when the radical tenets of the counterculture have become so thoroughly established and institutionalized in cultural life—when they have, in fact, come more and more to define the tastes, habits, and attitudes of the dominant culture—unmasking illegitimate claims to "liberation" and bogus feats of idealism emerges as a prime critical task.

For over two hundred years, the Left has had an effective but unearned monopoly on the rhetoric of virtue. *The Long March* scrutinizes that unearned monopoly and attempts to expose the spuriousness of radical claims to liberation. As with most revolutions, the counterculture's call for total freedom quickly turned into a demand for total control. The phenomenon of "political correctness," with its speech codes and other efforts to enforce ideological conformity, was one predictable result of this transformation. What began at the University of California at Berkeley with the Free Speech Movement (called by some the "Filthy Speech Movement") soon degenerated into an effort to abridge freedom by dictating what could and could not be said about any number of politically sensitive issues.

Books and other commentary about the 1960s and the "culture wars" have been appearing almost as fast as one can turn their pages. Many have been critical. Some are encomia. Thus we find the celebrated Marxist professor Fredric Jameson evoking the "widely shared feeling that in the 60s, for a time, everything was possible; that this period, in other words, was a moment of universal liberation, a global unbinding of energies." If that feeling has faded, it was, Jameson said in good Marxist fashion, because of "the world wide economic crisis" which has led to "powerful restorations of the social order and a renewal of the repressive power of the various state apparatuses." If you have the temerity to ask "What economic crisis? What repressive power?," then it just shows that you do not have sufficient contempt for reality to make a good academic Marxist.

To move a little closer to planet earth, *The New York Times*, in December 1994, published an editorial called "In Praise of the Counterculture." Obviously chastened by the Republican sweep in the 1994 Congressional race—how long ago that seems now!—the *Times* set out to challenge the "pejorative" use of the term "counterculture." It was Newt Gingrich, then the Republican Speaker of the House, who really set the *Times* off. In a phrase that was quickly taken up by the press, Gingrich described Bill and Hillary Clinton as "counterculture McGoverniks." The editorialist for the *Times* seized on the term and castigated "puritans" like Gingrich who dared to criticize the "summery, hedonistic ethos" of the 1960s.

Connoisseurs of cant will find much to savor in the *Times*'s brief document, beginning with the common but misleading use of the epithet "puritan" as a synonym for "priggish." As the novelist and essayist Marilynne Robinson astutely noted, "the way we think of the Puritans seems . . .

a serviceable model for important aspects of the phenomenon we call Puritanism." In other words, castigating someone as a "puritan" is a "great example of our collective eagerness to disparage without knowledge or information about the thing disparaged, when the reward is the pleasure of sharing an attitude one knows is socially approved." Then, too, there was the proposition that the 1960s "produced a renewal of the Thoreauvian ideal of the clear, defiant voice of the dissenting citizen." What the *Times*'s editorialist didn't say, of course, is that "the clear, defiant voice of the dissenting citizen" is to be applauded only when it conforms to the left-liberal orthodoxy as understood by *The New York Times*. "Only a few periods in American history," the *Times* informed its readers,

> have seen such a rich fulfillment of the informing ideals of personal freedom and creativity that lie at the heart of the American intellectual tradition. . . . The 60's spawned a new morality-based politics that emphasized the individual's responsibility to speak out against injustice and corruption.

In the following chapters, I discuss some of the chief works, personalities, and events that constituted this so-called "rich fulfillment of the informing ideals of personal freedom and creativity," these supposed triumphs of "individual responsibility" and a "new morality-based politics." At the moment, it is enough to note the tenor of the *Times*'s encomium, its invocation of liberation, its assumption of a superior virtue that is barely distinguishable from a knowing if "summery" hedonism.

Critics of the counterculture have not been slow to attack the phenomena that the *Times* extolled. Many palpable hits have been scored, and by now there exists a rich literature enumerating the excesses and absurdities of 1960s

radicalism. Useful though much of that literature is, however, there has been no attempt to trace the overall course
of America's cultural revolution. Because America's cultural
revolution cannot be understood apart from the seductive
personalities that articulated its goals, *The Long March* contains, in addition to historical narrative and analysis, several
biographical sketches of influential figures whose lives and
work helped to advance the agenda of the counterculture.
The questions with which Tocqueville began his book
about the *ancien régime* and the French Revolution are also
the questions that guide my inquiry: "What was its true
significance, its real nature, and what were the permanent
effects of this strange and terrifying revolution? What exactly did it destroy, and what did it create?"

The aim of *The Long March* is to show how many of the
ideals of the counterculture have quietly triumphed in the
afterlife of the Sixties and what that triumph has meant for
America's cultural and intellectual life.

Mainstreaming radicalism

One part of this story has already been told in my book
*Tenured Radicals: How Politics Has Corrupted Our Higher
Education.** In *The Long March* I attempt a more encom-
passing and far-reaching inquiry. It is possible to trace the
origins of certain aspects of the counterculture back to the
late nineteenth century and figures like Marx and Nietzsche, or to locate its origins in the upheavals of the Jazz

---

* *Tenured Radicals* was originally published in 1990 by Harper & Row.
HarperCollins brought out a paperback edition, with a new post-
script, in 1991. In 1998, a thoroughly revised and updated edition of
Tenured Radicals was published in paperback by Ivan R. Dee.

Age of the 1920s. But those periods, important though they have been historically, furnish antecedents rather than the real origins of the cultural revolution of the 1960s and 1970s. The distinctive energies and origins of that revolution, though doubtless fed by countless additional influences, lie in the 1950s and the emergence of the Beats. Accordingly, I begin my story then, focusing in particular on such representative figures as the poet Allen Ginsberg and the novelist William S. Burroughs. The Beats are crucial to an understanding of America's cultural revolution not least because in their lives, their proclamations, and (for lack of a more accurate term) their "work" they anticipated so many of the pathologies of the Sixties and Seventies. Their programmatic anti-Americanism, their avid celebration of drug abuse, their squalid, promiscuous sex lives, their pseudo-spirituality, their attack on rationality and their degradation of intellectual standards, their aggressive narcissism and juvenile political posturing: in all this and more, the Beats were every bit as "advanced" as any Sixties radical.

If the Beats differed from their successors (or *became* their successors: those Beat figures who survived long enough–Ginsberg above all, but also Burroughs–may be said to have outlived their former selves to become prominent countercultural idols), it had to do less with their attitudes and behavior than with the attitudes and behavior of the culture at large. As the Sixties unfolded, attitudes that had characterized a tiny minority on the fringes of culture were more and more accepted into the mainstream. By the early 1970s, they had *become* the mainstream.

In this process of spiritual colonization, the Beats were aided by a number of intellectual fellow travelers, many of whom, though not Beats themselves, eagerly championed the Beat sensibility and, throughout the 1950s, provided the moral alibis with which the excesses of the Beats were explained and justified. In various ways, establishment writers like Norman O. Brown (*Life Against Death*), C. Wright Mills (*White Collar, The Power Elite*), John Kenneth Galbraith (*The Affluent Society*), Paul Goodman (*Growing Up Absurd*), Michael Harrington (*The Other America*), Herbert Marcuse (*One-Dimensional Man, Eros and Civilization*), and William Whyte, Jr. (*The Organization Man*) "softened up" the culture at large, preparing it to assimilate—in many respects, to emulate—the Beats, their attitudes toward life, art, and above all toward the United States.

Every revolution has its myths. One of the myths dearest to the counterculture is that America in the 1950s was a sterile, soulless society, obsessed with money, stunted emotionally, negligible culturally and intellectually, brutal and hamfisted in its politics and social policy. Never mind that, when it came to cultural and intellectual achievement, America in the 1950s looks like fifth-century Athens in comparison with what came afterward. The idea of America as a materialistic wasteland, barren of cultural achievement, was central to the cosmology of the Beats and, in differing ways, it was an image these writers and intellectuals strenuously reinforced. It will be instructive to sample some of these writings: Goodman's lugubrious *Growing Up Absurd*, for example, whose image of America as an evil, soul-destroying "Organized System" had an immense influence when it was first published in 1960, and Brown's *Life Against Death* (1959), whose toxic cocktail of Freud and Marx inebriated many influential figures and so helped pave the way for the legitimization of hedonism that swept through the country in the years ahead.

As the 1950s wore on, anti-Americanism became a necessary badge of authenticity for writers and intellectuals; more and more, the cultural establishment demanded the pose of anti-establishment animus. Among those railing against the evils of America—or "Amerika," as it was often spelled in the 1960s—the novelist Norman Mailer occupies a special place. Today, Norman Mailer is regarded by many as a grotesque, almost comic figure, alternately repulsive and pathetic. There was a time, however, when Mailer was widely considered to be not only a serious novelist but also a deep thinker. I am assured by an older friend that in the mid-1960s the publication of Mailer's novels was a celebrated event, awaited with the same sort of breathless anticipation that greeted the installments of Dickens's novels a century before. My friend, like many intelligent people at the time, stood in line to acquire a copy of *An American Dream* when it was first published in 1965. Such behavior is not *only* an object lesson in the myopia of contemporary taste. Mailer was enormously popular because he, like other countercultural spokesmen, touched a nerve. The revolution of which he was a part offered—or seemed to offer—new freedoms and new insights. In their different ways, what Mailer and his countercultural confrères promised was that irresistible "life of complete self-determination, free of the burden of tradition and conventions" that Edward Shils spoke of above. What Shils called the "antinomian temptation" is a hardy perennial. It stands at the heart of the counterculture and helps to explain why it exercised such a mesmerizing influence and found such an eager audience.

Prominent in Mailer's writings are a fascination with violence and an adolescent obsession with sex. Both feature centrally in his once-notorious essay "The White Negro," first published in 1957. Fulminating in that essay against "the totalitarian tissues of American society," Mailer praises the "hipster" as someone who, having "absorbed the existentialist synapses of the Negro," accepts "the meaninglessness of life" and deliberately encourages the "psychopath" in himself. Devoted to jazz, drugs, violence, and sex, the hipster would think nothing of "beat[ing] in the brains of a candy-store keeper." As Mailer explains, "the psychopath murders—if he has the courage—out of the necessity to purge his violence," a catharsis that for him is inextricably bound up with "apocalyptic" sex.

> At bottom, the drama of the psychopath is that he seeks love. Not love as the search for a mate, but love as the search for an orgasm more apocalyptic than the one that preceded it. Orgasm is his therapy—he knows at the seed of his being that good orgasm opens his possibilities and bad orgasm imprisons him.

Looking back on it several years later, Mailer said that he considered "The White Negro" "one of the best things I have ever done." It is certainly one of his most characteristic productions.

The career of Norman Mailer is one that figures prominently in *The Long March*; another is that of Susan Sontag. From the moment she burst upon the scene in the early 1960s with her essays "Against Interpretation" and "Notes on 'Camp,'" Sontag has been a model of radical chic. Indeed, from her declaration that "the white race *is* the cancer of human history" in the mid-Sixties to her travels to Bosnia to stage an all-female production of *Waiting for Godot* in the 1990s, Sontag has been a living compendium of radical clichés and stereotypes. In a report from Castro's Cuba in 1969, for example, she moves from declaring that "America is a cancerous society" to observing that "rock, grass, better orgasms, freaky clothes, grooving on nature— really grooving on anything—unfits, maladapts a person for the American way of life" to assuring her readers that "no Cuban writer has been or is in jail, or is failing to get his

work published." Like Mailer, Sontag may be a preposterous figure at bottom. But, again like Mailer, what
prevents her from being simply a source of unintended
comedy is the extent to which her aestheticizing political
radicalism not only was taken seriously but also came to
represent a major current of elite cultural opinion.

No account of America's cultural revolution would be
complete without some discussion of the Vietnam War.
More than any other event, it legitimated anti-Americanism
and helped insinuate radical feeling into the mainstream of
cultural life. The literature on American involvement in
Vietnam and the counterculture is enormous, but what is
relevant to *The Long March* is not so much the history of
the war itself or even the protest against it as the way the
war helped to "normalize" a spectrum of radical sentiments.
The early history of *The New York Review of Books* (which
began publishing in 1963) belongs here, in part for its
reporting on the Vietnam War, in part for its increasingly
enthusiastic embrace of other items on the menu of cultural
radicalism. The disastrous effect of the war—or, more
precisely, of the protests against the war—on our institutions of higher education also deserves attention. What I
am interested in providing here is not a history of student
activism against the war: that, too, is an oft-told story. My
focus is rather on a handful of exemplary case studies that
show how the capitulation of certain key university presidents helped to sanction (and therefore recommend to the
society at large) a whole set of radical attitudes, not only
about the war and America's role in it, but also about art,
education, and morality.

One prominent part of that radicalism concerns race.
The destructive effects of America's cultural revolution on
race relations in this country cannot be overestimated. In
the transformation of the civil-rights movement from a

non-violent crusade for equal rights into an agitation for black power, we see not only a new segregationism but also a blueprint for the "victim politics" and demands for political correctness that have so disfigured American culture in the 1980s and 1990s. The unhappy metamorphosis of James Baldwin—from a novelist who insisted that he was not "merely a Negro writer" but an American one, to a figure who embraced the racialist politics of the black-power movement—epitomized this trend. I focus below on violent heirs to Baldwin like the Black Panther Eldridge Cleaver, whose assertion in his book *Soul on Ice* that rape is "an insurrectionary act" "trampling upon the white man's law" won abject praise from any number of *bien pensant* white radicals.

It has been in the life of art and the life of the mind, however, that the counterculture has had its most devastating effects. To an extent that would have been difficult to imagine thirty years ago, art and education have become handmaidens of political radicalism. Standards in both have plummeted. The art world has more and more jettisoned any concern with beauty and has become a playground for bogus "transgressive" gestures. Colleges and universities, aping this exhausted radicalism, have given themselves up to an uneasy mixture of politically correct causes and the rebarbative rhetoric of deconstruction, poststructuralism, and "cultural studies." The story of what has happened to our institutions of high culture since the Sixties is a story of almost uninterrupted degradation and pandering to forces inimical to culture. In the pages that follow, I outline this chronicle of decline, focusing particularly on the destruction of the humanities in higher education and the surrender of art to the perverting imperatives of politics.

Weapons of emotional anarchy

If the politicization of art and education represents one large part of the counterculture's legacy, the coarsening of feeling and sensibility is another. No phenomenon has done more to advance this coarsening than rock music. It is impossible to exaggerate the importance of rock music to the agenda of the cultural revolution. It is also impossible to overstate its soul-deadening destructiveness. The most reviled part of Allan Bloom's book *The Closing of the American Mind* was his chapter criticizing the effects of rock. But Bloom was right in insisting that rock music is a potent weapon in the arsenal of emotional anarchy. The triumph of rock was not only an aesthetic disaster of gigantic proportions: it was also a moral disaster whose effects are nearly impossible to calculate precisely because they are so pervasive.

Writing recently in *The Wall Street Journal*, Diana West warned about the "the leviathan of popular culture" that was assaulting even the last redoubts of childhood. West described the parties that her six-and-a-half-year-old twin daughters are routinely invited to, events at which they are invited to "jump, jam & party" to the pop music of "Britney Spears and the Backstreet Boys, idols du jour of the lipgloss and lunchbox set." Although, as West notes, this brand of "hip hop" is "nothing like gangsta rap," she is right to be worried:

A child weaned on what you might call "pop hop"—with its rudimentary percussive insistence and its keening self-pity —will not emerge unaffected. Such music is inimical to childhood innocence, and it eventually deafens the ear to better melodic forms, from Mozart to Lehár to Gershwin, in which meter is a vehicle for song, not an end in itself. It's tough enough when your gawky adolescent has the bad taste to ask for the latest pop nightmare, but why introduce it, with the inevitable lexicon of coupling and separation, to an impressionable six-year-old?

Why indeed?

As West realizes, inseparable from the culture of rock music, even in its more sanitized versions, is the celebration of drugs and the demand for sexual liberation. The three go together. They are the counterculture's primary instruments of ecstasy, its chief weapons against the obligations of traditional culture. It is still not clear which has done the most damage. Although drugs have cut short thousands of lives and permanently maimed countless more, I suspect that the real competition is between rock music and the sexual revolution. Both promised boundless freedom; both involved the entire culture in moral chaos. Figures like Timothy Leary, the prophet of LSD, and Charles Reich, author of *The Greening of America*, epitomized this side of the counterculture, and I discuss both in detail below.

At the end of *Life Against Death*, Norman O. Brown assured his readers that "the path of sublimation, which mankind has religiously followed since the foundation of the first cities, is no way out of the human neurosis, but, on the contrary, leads to its aggravation." According to Brown, what was needed was "a union with others and with the world around us based not on anxiety and aggression but on narcissism and erotic exuberance." Brown was writing in the late 1950s. The subsequent decades put his thesis to the test. Whether the consequences of embracing such narcissism and exuberance lessened or aggravated "the human neurosis" is an open question, to say the least. But this much is clear: the long march of America's cultural revolution has everywhere departed from "the path of sublimation."

Near the beginning of her book *On Revolution*, Hannah
Arendt quotes the conservative thinker Joseph de Maistre
who, looking back on the French Revolution in 1796, observed that "La contrerévolution ne sera point une révolution contraire, mais le contraire de la révolution": "The
counterrevolution will not be a revolution in reverse, but
the reverse of revolution." She dismisses this as "an empty
witticism." But is it? Given the spiritual malaise brought on
by the long march of America's cultural revolution, we may
conclude that the way forward lies not in any sort of new
revolution but, on the contrary, in the patient recovery of
lost virtues. As *The Long March* attempts to show, the an-
tidote to a cultural revolution is not counterrevolution but
recuperation.

Chapter 1
A Gospel of Emancipation

We'll get you through your children.
—Allen Ginsberg, 1958

*The core of the heresy of the Free Spirit lay in the adept's attitude
towards himself: he believed that he had attained a perfection so
absolute that he was incapable of sin.*

*Disclaiming book-learning and theological subtleties, they rejoiced
in direct knowledge of God—indeed, they felt themselves united with
the divine essence in a most intimate union. And this in turn liberated
them from all restraints. Every impulse was experienced as a divine
command; now they could surround themselves with worldly possessions
. . . now, too, they could lie or steal or fornicate without qualms of
conscience. For since inwardly the soul was wholly absorbed into God,
external acts were of no account.*
—Norman Cohn, *The Pursuit of the Millennium*, 1957

A toxic cultural movement

In November 1995, an exhibition called "Beat Culture
and the New America: 1950–1965" opened at The Whitney Museum of American Art. Considered as an art exhibition, this traveling mélange of some two hundred objects
hardly existed. In more ways than one, walking through the

exhibition was like touring a junk shop.* Forgettable and justly forgotten paintings, sculptures, and films were intermixed with innumerable books, photographs, magazines, and other literary detritus, all scattered about the Whitney's exhibition spaces while the drug-inspired jazz of Miles Davis droned on in the background: that is what "Beat Culture and the New America" had to offer. The two or three objects of even minimal aesthetic accomplishment on view—some paintings by Jackson Pollock and Franz Kline—were not products of the Beat sensibility at all but merely happened to be created at the same time that the Beats got going.

Although aesthetically nugatory, "Beat Culture and the New America" was an exhibition of considerable significance—but not in quite the way that Lisa Phillips, its curator, intended. Casting a retrospective glance at the sordid world of Allen Ginsberg, Jack Kerouac, William S. Burroughs, Lawrence Ferlinghetti, and other Beat icons, the exhibition unwittingly furnished a kind of pathologist's report on one of the most toxic cultural movements in American history.

In this sense, at least, the Whitney deserved our gratitude for sponsoring "Beat Culture." The romance that has surrounded the Beat generation since the mid-Sixties has acted as a kind of sentimental glaze, obscuring its fundamentally nihilistic impulse under a heap of bogus rhetoric about liberation, spontaneity, and "startling oases of creativity." Notwithstanding their recent media make-over, the Beats were not Promethean iconoclasts. They were drug-abusing sexual predators and infantilized narcissists whose shame-

---

* Other stops for "Beat Culture and the New America" were the Walker Art Center, Minneapolis, and the M. H. de Young Memorial Museum, the Fine Arts Museums of San Francisco.

lessness helped dupe a confused and gullible public into believing that their utterances were works of genius. We have to thank Lisa Phillips and the Whitney for inadvertently reminding us of this with such vividness. If nothing else, "Beat Culture and the New America" showed that the Beats were not simply artistic charlatans; they were—and, in the case of those who are still with us, they remain— moral simpletons whose destructive influence helped fuel the cultural catastrophe with which we are now living.

Not, of course, that the folks at the Whitney saw it this way. But then the Whitney Museum has long been a splendid example of cultural breakdown. In his foreword to the catalogue, David Ross, at that time the Whitney's director, complained that the "depth and seriousness of Beat culture" was insufficiently appreciated by many postwar journalists, whose "reactionary" response led them to dismiss the Beats as "loony beret-wearing weirdos, conspiratorial communists, amoral homosexuals, filthy drug-addicted hipsters, or merely pathetic wannabe artists."

One nice thing about David Ross was his predictability. On the subject of Beat culture, one knew in advance that he would deplore "McCarthyism" and the Fifties generally, and that he would then trot out a number of clichés about race-class-gender, ending with a flourish about the importance of federal funding for the arts. And right on cue he told us that the Beats suffered from "politicians looking for convenient scapegoats," that they "opened up a closed-down culture," and that later "artists struggling with their emerging sexual identities found the Beat world a nurturing place, where desire could be freely expressed and pleasure openly extolled." Finally, he registered his relief that he can "still cite the National Endowment for the Arts as a public champion of important exhibitions such as this one."

Lisa Phillips sang a similar song, but waxed even more lyrical. In "Beat Culture: America Revisioned," her essay for the catalogue, Phillips spoke of the "enduring achievement" and "now legendary literary accomplishments" of the Beats, whose "vanguard and antimaterialist" stance set them against the "conformity and consensus of official culture" and the "smug optimism of the Eisenhower years." In one remarkable passage, she explains how

> during the Cold War, in the aftermath of World War II, a new generation emerged in America, known as the Beat generation. Disillusioned with the progress of science and Western technocracy, the Beats embarked on a quest for a new set of values out of which to build a new faith, [and] a new tribal ethic was born. Although once rejected by mainstream society as outlaws, rebels, and morally dangerous, today the Beats are recognized as icons of America's counterculture and as one of the most influential cultural movements of the century. Their literary works, which aroused great controversy and academic disdain when first published in the fifties, are now part of the canon of American literature taught in universities around the country. Their archives are selling for vast sums, . . . and first editions of their books are highly sought after. Perhaps most important, the Beats continue to inspire younger generations of artists with their directness, courage, and intensity of vision.

There is a great deal one could say about this paragraph, beginning with that supposed disillusionment with "the progress of science and Western technocracy." The Beats regularly denounced (in the words of that proto-Beat, Henry Miller) the "air-conditioned nightmare," but they freely availed themselves of the fruits of modern science and technology—electricity, jet travel, penicillin, not to mention other drugs. Nevertheless, there is one frighteningly accurate statement in Phillips's inventory: namely, that the Beats "are now part of the canon of American literature taught in universities around the country." As she later observed, "the Beat rebellion gave form to an invisible turning point in American culture at mid-century."

David Ross and Lisa Phillips celebrated this development as a giant step forward for freedom and creativity. In fact, the institutionalization of the Beat ethic has been a moral, aesthetic, and intellectual disaster of the first order. (It has also been a disaster for fashion and manners, but that is a separate subject.) We owe to the 1960s the ultimate institutionalization of immoralist radicalism: the institutionalization of drugs, pseudo-spirituality, promiscuous sex, virulent anti-Americanism, naïve anti-capitalism, and the precipitous decline of artistic and intellectual standards. But the 1960s and 1970s only codified and extended into the middle class the radical spirit of the Beats, who, in more normal times, would have remained what they were in the beginning: members of a fringe movement that provided stand-up comics with material.

The church of the Beats

Looking back on it now, it seems peculiarly appropriate that the only real job that the Beat poet Allen Ginsberg ever had—for more than a few weeks, anyway—was in market research. He clearly had a tremendous gift in that direction. For although he later ridiculed his time on Madison Avenue ("We spent $150,000 to learn that most people didn't want furry teeth," he scoffed)—as indeed he ridiculed every other aspect of middle-class, bourgeois life—his own career as a poet and spiritual guru depended crucially on his talent as a tireless self-promoter. It was the one talent, in fact, that he indisputably possessed in great abundance.

Readers only vaguely familiar with Ginsberg's life and work will doubtless find this surprising. When he died at seventy of liver cancer in April 1997, Allen Ginsberg was almost universally celebrated as a major literary figure—and one who, moreover, exercised a benign if sometimes "controversial" influence on the cultural and ethical life of his times. A smiling, sybaritic hippie, lost in clouds of incense and marijuana, chanting mantras, seducing young men, he disparaged the United States while preaching nonviolence and love, and taking off his clothes in public at every opportunity. Among other things, Ginsberg was an active supporter of the North American Man Boy Love Alliance (NAMBLA), an organization devoted to encouraging homosexual pedophilia: "I don't know exactly how to define what's underage," Ginsberg once said—adding that he himself "had never made it with anyone under fifteen." It says a lot about our culture—or perhaps it is one more testimony to Ginsberg's marketing skills—that such a man should be exalted by the mainstream press as a beneficent or at least harmlessly amusing presence. As Norman Podhoretz noted in his recent memoir, "in later life, Ginsberg would adopt a sweet and gentle persona, but there was nothing either sweet or gentle about the Allen Ginsberg" of the late 1940s and early 1950s.

The few dissenting voices[*] at the time of his death were drowned out in a chorus—one might say a "Howl," after Ginsberg's best-known poem—of fulsome eulogy. In a front-page obituary, *The New York Times* hailed Ginsberg as

---

[*] Among the dissenting voices was my reflection, "A Baneful Influence," *The New Criterion*, May 1997, pages 1–2.

"the poet laureate of the Beat Generation," "one of America's most celebrated poets," whose "irrepressible personality . . . provided a bridge between the Underground and the Transcendental." An hour-long PBS television documentary paraded a long list of luminaries, from Joan Baez to Norman Mailer, to extol his "courage," his literary and spiritual daring, and (a favorite epithet) his "gentleness." Not to be outdone, the well-known poetry critic and Harvard professor Helen Vendler wrote in the September–October 1997 issue of *Harvard Magazine* about Ginsberg's "great gifts to world culture," "the moral base of his poetry," and her "own profound gratitude for his work and the life out of which it came." ("He allowed me my own rage, social criticism, and coarseness," she claimed, no doubt correctly.)

Ginsberg's friend William S. Burroughs, II, Beat novelist and sometime heroin addict, whose paternal grandfather invented the adding machine, got a similarly enthusiastic send-off when he died at eighty-three in August 1997. No one spoke of his "gentleness," of course. "Gentleness" was definitely not part of Burroughs's reputation as the author of *Junkie*, *Naked Lunch*, and other surrealistic hymns to violence, drug abuse, and extreme sexual degradation. "Bill was never keen on the love-and-peace side of the sixties," one fan noted. "The only way I'd like to see a policeman given a flower," Burroughs sneered, "is in a flowerpot from a high window." The first line of the obituary that appeared in *The Village Voice* summed up Burroughs: "Addict, killer, pederast." Even so, a memorialist in *New York* magazine assured readers that, whatever his pathologies and fondness for guns, Burroughs was really "a sweet, funny, and lonely man. Just lovely." And naturally there were plenty of encomia to Burroughs's "courage," "candor," and "strange genius," his exalted place (in the words of the *Los Angeles*

Times) as "a seminal figure of the Beat Generation." "Seminal," indeed: "He spent years experimenting with drugs as well as with sex," *The New York Times* cheerfully reported, "which he engaged in with men, women, and children."

The enthusiastic praise that Ginsberg and Burroughs elicited on the occasion of their deaths was not just valedictory piffle, white lies that surround the dead like a second shroud. During his lifetime, Ginsberg was showered with just about every literary award and honor it was possible to win, short of the Nobel Prize, including the National Book Award, election to the American Academy of Arts and Letters, even, in 1993, the Chevalier de l'Ordre des Arts et Lettres. This enemy of "materialism" and the corporate culture of "Amerika" had his eight-hundred-page *Collected Poems* published by Harper & Row (now HarperCollins) and received more than one million dollars for his papers from Stanford University.

Burroughs, who lacked Ginsberg's charm and craving for publicity, did not prosper to the same extent. As an heir to a fortune built by American ingenuity, he didn't need to. But Burroughs, too, lived to see himself lionized, both as an important literary figure and as a hero and role model for countless rock musicians, from The Beatles to David Bowie. Having begun as outlaws from the establishment, literary and otherwise, Ginsberg and Burroughs were taken up by a grateful academic establishment desperate to play a role in the countercultural carnival. Innumerable papers, monographs, and dissertations have appeared to praise and interpret their works, and both men were the subject of fawning biographies in the early 1990s.

The third celebrated member of the Beat triumvirate was Jack Kerouac. It was he who coined the phrase "Beat Generation," and who, one is reminded again and again in the literature about the Beats, suggested the title of *Naked*

Lunch to Burroughs. Kerouac managed to drink himself to death in 1969 at the age of forty-seven. Consequently, he missed out on a lot of what we might call the pre-posthumous adulation showered on his friends Ginsberg and Burroughs when the culture caught up with their radicalism in the 1970s. Moreover, Kerouac became an increasingly problematic figure for fans of the counterculture: by the end of his life he had returned to the Roman Catholic faith, espoused conservative political views, and supported the war in Vietnam.

Nevertheless Kerouac, too, was subsequently lionized by the establishment he once affected to scorn. Not only are all (or virtually all) his works still in print, but Viking recently honored him with a fat *Portable Jack Kerouac*, a tribute once reserved for genuinely accomplished writers. There is a scholarly edition of his letters from 1940–1956 (with no doubt more to come) and a special fortieth-anniversary reissue of Kerouac's most famous book, *On the Road*, first published in 1957. There are also the usual academic studies and at least one star-struck biography. His home city of Lowell, Massachusetts, even saw fit to name a new park after him in 1987.

About the Beats generally, an "Appreciation" of Burroughs in *The Washington Post* admirably summed up the current state of received opinion. The obituarist quotes from a book of Burroughs's dreams: "I attend a party and dinner at Columbia. Allen Ginsberg is there and rich. He has founded some sort of church." The obituarist comments: "This was no dream; this was reality. . . . [Today,] the church of the Beats is stronger than ever, unquestionably the most significant literary congregation in America since the Lost Generation of Hemingway and Fitzgerald."

Flirting with the underworld

Well, that is partly true. The Beats *were* tremendously significant, but chiefly in the way that they provided a preview
in the 1950s of the cultural, intellectual, and moral disasters
that would fully flower in the late 1960s. The ideas of the
Beats, their sensibility, contained *in ovo* all the characteristics we think of as defining the cultural revolution of the
Sixties and Seventies. The adolescent longing for liberation
from conventional manners and intellectual standards; the
polymorphous sexuality; the narcissism; the destructive
absorption in drugs; the undercurrent of criminality; the
irrationalism; the naïve political radicalism and reflexive
anti-Americanism; the adulation of pop music as a kind of
spiritual weapon; the Romantic elevation of art as an alternative to rather than as an illumination of normal reality;
the pseudo-spirituality, especially the spurious infatuation
with Eastern religions: in all this and more the Beats
provided a vivid glimpse of what was to come.

The chief difference between the Beat Generation and the
Sixties was the ambient cultural climate: when the Beats first
emerged, in the mid-Fifties, the culture still offered some
resistance to the poisonous antinomianism the Beats advocated. But by the time the Sixties established themselves,
virtually all resistance had been broken down. It was then
that the message of the Beats gained mass appeal. Reaction
to the Vietnam War probably did more than anything else to
enfranchise their antinomianism, though the introduction
of the birth-control pill certainly did a great deal to further
the cause of the sexual revolution, a prime item on the
agenda of the Beats. In short order, the unconventional became the established convention; the perverse was embraced
as normal; the unspeakable was broadcast everywhere; the
outrageous was met with enthusiastic applause.

In a word, the establishment of the Beat "church" was significant as a chapter in the moral and cultural degradation of our society. Regarded as a *literary* phenomenon, however, what the Beats produced exists chiefly as a kind of artistic antimatter. It would not be quite right to say that its value is nil, for that might imply an innocuous neutrality. What the Beats have bequeathed us is *actively* bad, a corrupting as well as a corrupt phenomenon. To borrow an image from the Australian philosopher David Stove, the Beats created a "disaster-area, and not of the merely passive kind, like a bombed building, or an area that has been flooded. It is the active kind, like a badly-leaking nuclear reactor, or an outbreak of foot-and-mouth disease in cattle." Two things have kept what the Beats wrote in circulation: the academic maw, with its insatiable appetite for verbal fodder of any kind, and the unhealthy craving for instances of psychopathology that the Beats not only exemplified but also helped to foster in their work and in their lives.

Of the Beat triumvirate, Kerouac was probably both the most pathetic and least noxious character. Psychologically, he was a mess—as indeed were Ginsberg and Burroughs. But, unlike them, Kerouac never mastered the knack of sanctifying his pathologies and inducing others to bow down in obeisance. The three met in 1944, when Ginsberg was a student at Columbia College. In 1945, they lived together, with a shifting cast of low-life friends, in an apartment leased by Joan Vollmer, a drug-addicted student at Columbia's School of Journalism whom Burroughs, despite his homosexuality, married.

Having explained that "it was not long after Bill's sixteenth birthday that he conducted his first experiments with mind altering drugs," Burroughs's biographer Barry Miles gives us a good sense of the Beat life on 115th Street. (Incidentally, why is it that drug abuse is always described

as an "experiment," as if some important scientific enterprise were at stake instead of hedonistic self-indulgence?)

> Bill continued his experiments with drugs, joined by Allen,
> Jack, and Joan. Joan had developed a liking for benzedrine,
> which was easily available in nasal inhalers, and she quickly
> became addicted. Jack took so much that his health suf-
> fered; he became very run down and developed phlebitis in
> his legs. Ginsberg found that benzedrine made him write
> "stanzas of gibberish" and used it less than the others. . . .
> Bill's friend [Herbert] Huncke took to using the 115th
> Street apartment as a place for storing stolen goods, once
> even leaving a stolen car parked outside. Bill was shooting
> up quite openly in front of everyone.

Burroughs, who had graduated from Harvard a decade
earlier, was in and out of jail, living a drug-sodden existence
in New York on an allowance from his parents. As Miles
explains, "$200 a month, . . . which in 1946 was plenty to
live on, was not enough to feed his habit. Bill began helping Phil White roll drunks on the subway."

Although not as susceptible to criminal machinations as
was Burroughs, Kerouac, too, was a denizen of this world,
as was Ginsberg. It was the botched world of an ivy-leaguer
flirting with the underworld from a position of privilege.
Like Ginsberg, Kerouac had attended Columbia in the early
1940s, but dropped out in 1942. He enlisted in the Navy in
1943, was discharged for psychiatric reasons a few months
later, and drifted back to New York. He was married three
times: twice for a matter of months, the last time in 1966
when he was already lost in an alcoholic fog. He had a
daughter by his second wife, but hysterically denied pater-
nity and refused to pay a penny for child support until the
child was ten years old (at which point the court ordered

him to pay twelve dollars a week until the child was twenty-one). When not "on the road," he spent most of his adult life living with his mother.

Although predominantly heterosexual, Kerouac also had sex with Ginsberg and Burroughs (who in turn had sex with each other). For all of them, sex functioned chiefly as a prop to wounded narcissism. For Ginsberg and especially for Burroughs, this transformed sex into an obsessive, predatory activity in which an endless stream of "partners" —male or female, young or old—became little more than discardable accessories to masturbation and fantasies of absolute transcendence. Kerouac's insecurities hobbled this aspect of his narcissism, making him somewhat less promiscuous but also distinctly more helpless than Ginsberg or Burroughs.

Kerouac famously wrote *On the Road* in less than three weeks on a single continuous roll of paper: 175,000 words in twenty days. In this he was abiding by the procedures he had outlined in his once-famous manifesto, "The Essentials of Spontaneous Prose" (1953). Here are two samples:

LAG IN PROCEDURE. No pause to think of proper word but the infantile pileup of scatological buildup till satisfaction is gained, which will turn out to be a great appending rhythm to a thought and be in accordance with Great Law of timing.

CENTER OF INTEREST. Begin not from preconceived idea of what to say about image but from jewel center of interest in subject of image at *moment* of writing, and write outwards swimming in sea of language to peripheral release and exhaustion—Do not afterthink except for poetic or P.S. reasons. Never afterthink to "improve" or defray impressions, as, the best writing is always the most painful personal

wrung-out tossed from cradle warm protective mind—tap
from yourself the song of yourself, *blow!—now!—your* way
is your only way—"good"—or—"bad"—always honest,
("ludicrous"), spontaneous, "confessional," interesting, because not "crafted."

It is possible that such stuff once seemed fresh. Nowadays,
it reads as sub-Romantic adolescent nonsense, the kind of
thing you *hope* high school teachers are busy discouraging.
On the Road, too, is a period piece: it is the literary equivalent of the huge fins on a 1950s Cadillac, though not as
impressive. Kerouac's impassive "this-happened, then-this-
happened, then-this-happened" prose is a caricature of
Hemingwayesque precision: a barren rather than a pregnant sparseness.

> We drove to Terry's family shack. It was situated on the old
> road that ran between the vineyards. It was dark when we
> got there. They left me off a quarter-mile away and drove to
> the door. Light poured out of the door; Terry's six other
> brothers were playing their guitars and singing.

In short, an insomniac's dearest wish. Truman Capote had
the last word on Kerouac's prose when he observed that "it
isn't writing at all—it's typing."

"Starving hysterical naked"

It is impossible to look so kindly on Ginsberg's or Bur-
roughs's literary work—or so indulgently on their lives.
Significantly, the most famous work of both writers—
Ginsberg's *Howl and Other Poems* (1956) and Burroughs's
Naked Lunch (1959)—first came to public notice through

the obscenity suits that they provoked. (Of course, the legal actions against both works failed. And like all court decisions that promote pornography, the decisions clearing both works of obscenity are invariably described as "landmark" decisions by their partisans.)

As was seen clearly when the works first appeared, their primary claim is not literary but ethical or moral. More precisely, both issued a defiant challenge to prevailing moral standards, *Howl* in its glorification of drugs, madness, and promiscuous sex, *Naked Lunch* in its grisly depiction of depravity, sexual torture, and heroin-induced dementia. The challenge, alas, encountered no effective resistance. In one of the many flattering obituaries that appeared about Burroughs, a long-time associate is quoted as saying that "William Burroughs opened the door for supporters of freedom of expression." Obituaries of Ginsberg were full of similar testimony: the poet as crusader for free speech. In fact, both writers contributed heavily to the debasement of the debate over free speech by implicating it irrevocably in the defense of pornography. If they "opened the door" on anything, it was on the academic and social enfranchisement of pornography as a morally neutral matter of "lifestyle."

Most of Ginsberg's poetry is little better than doggerel. "Hūm Bom!" (1984) is typical.

I
Whom bomb?
We bomb them!
Whom bomb?
We bomb them!
Whom bomb?
We bomb them!
Whom bomb?
We bomb them!

Whom bomb?
You bomb you!
Whom bomb?
You bomb you!

And so on, for two pages. Ginsberg's style is often praised as "Whitmanesque" by its fans, but that is a calumny upon Whitman. It is true that, like Whitman, Ginsberg makes abundant use of anaphora, repeating certain phrases again and again for rhetorical effect. But what was fresh and individual in 1855, when Whitman published the first edition of *Leaves of Grass*, seems, in Ginsberg's hands, mannered, pretentious, hectoring. There's much more wind than Whitman in Ginsberg's verse. In the breathless effervescence of *Song of Myself*, Whitman transformed megalomania into poetry: the merely personal is lost in an almost mystic apprehension of nature. In Ginsberg, the megalomania is always personal. His preachy verse lurches from the sickly sentimental to the pornographic ("Sweet Boy Gimme Yr Ass") to the politically tendentious ("Verses Written for Student Antidraft Registration Rally 1980"). There are several poems to drugs: "Lysergic Acid," "A Methedrine Vision in Hollywood," "Mescaline," etc., and lots of four-letter words and pornographic descriptions of sex acts.

Come on go down on me your throat
swallowing my shaft to the base tongue
cock solid suck—
I'll do the same your stiff prick's soft skin, lick your ass—
Come on Come on, open up, legs apart here this pillow
under your buttock
Come on take it here's vaseline the hard on here's
your old ass lying easy up in the air—here's
a hot prick at yr soft mouth asshole—just relax and let it in—

Is it any wonder that Helen Vendler, with "profound gratitude," should have spoken of Ginsberg's "great gifts to world culture" and "the moral base of his poetry"?

"Kaddish" (1959), after "Howl" Ginsberg's best-known poem, is meant to be an elegy for his mother, who died in an asylum in 1956 shortly after Ginsberg authorized that she be given a lobotomy. Some people have claimed to find the poem a moving filial tribute. I confess that it impresses me as a long, shapeless, stream-of-consciousness rant. Ginsberg settles various family scores and says a lot of disgusting things about his mother that, because of the "Whitman-esque" bad writing, are supposed to be touching.

As for "Howl," I am sometimes tempted to agree with the characterization of the wit who described it as "the greatest comic poem in the language." In the end, however, "Howl" has had far too damaging an effect to be considered merely an unwitting comic performance. In addition to being Ginsberg's most famous poem, "Howl" also epitomizes a central mendacity of the entire Beat enterprise. In essence, the poem is a paean to madness and drug abuse as the only really authentic responses to life in a repressive society, i.e., our society, the United States circa 1956:

> I saw the best minds of my generation destroyed by madness,
>   starving hysterical naked,
> dragging themselves through the negro streets at dawn
>   looking for an angry fix,
> angelheaded hipsters burning for the ancient heavenly
>   connection to the starry dynamo in the machinery of night.

Of course, far from being "the best minds" of his generation—is it really necessary to say this?—"the angel-headed hipsters" whom Ginsberg saw destroyed were the unhappy misfits of a prosperous and overindulgent society.

In romanticizing the madness of those he met in the psychiatric institution where he was incarcerated for eight months in the late 1940s or later when he became a prophet of psychedelia, Ginsberg deliberately falsified their suffering. As Norman Podhoretz observed in *Ex-Friends*, Ginsberg's suggestion that madness provides access to a higher reality is "heartless nonsense." "There was," Podhoretz notes, "something cruel about drafting such pitiable creatures into the service of an ideological aggression against the kind of normal life to which they would have given everything to return. And it was all the more heartless for parading itself as compassion."

This glorification of madness, drug abuse, criminality, and excess is a defining current of the Beat sensibility. Burroughs's biographer Barry Miles tells us that all the Beats "shared a passionate desire to 'widen the area of consciousness,'" and cites their insatiable appetite for drugs as one piece of evidence of this desire. In 1966, Ginsberg even testified before Congress about the "mind expanding" potential of psychedelics. But in fact, as the philosopher Harvey Mansfield has observed in his essay "The Legacy of the Late Sixties," the idea that drugs are an aid to "mind expansion" is "an illusion so pathetic that one can hardly credit that it was once held." It is a prime example of what the historian Christopher Lasch (in *The Culture of Narcissism*) once called "The Banality of Pseudo-Self-Awareness." The central appeal of drugs, as Mansfield noted, "is that of infinite power together with infinite desire." It is not an accident that a celebration of drugs went hand in hand with the sexual revolution and the tremendous upsurge in juvenile political radicalism. Here is Timothy Leary describing Ginsberg's reaction to a dose of psilocybin in 1960:

Allen, completely naked except for his glasses, waved a

finger in the air. "I'm the Messiah," he proclaimed. "I've come down to preach love to the world. We're going to walk through the streets and teach people to stop hating. . . . We'll call Kerouac on Long Island, and Kennedy and Khrushchev and Bill Burroughs in Paris and Norman Mailer. . . . We'll get them all hooked up in a big cosmic electronic love talk. War is just a hang-up."

"And then," Leary noted in a memoir, "we started planning the psychedelic revolution."

There is something highly comic in this spectacle, of course—especially in the prospect of calling on Norman Mailer to help with the envisioned love march. But there is nothing at all funny about the many shattered lives that the Beats' glorification of excess left in its wake. William Everson, a second-tier Beat propagandist and poet, has written that the rise of the Beats marked the "reemergence in the twentieth century of the Dionysian spirit." In a sense this is right. But as the Greeks knew, Dionysus is not necessarily a friendly deity. It would be closer to the truth to say that the rise of the Beats marked the elevation of criminal irresponsibility in American society to a new position of romance and respectability. The Beats inaugurated the long march through the moral territory of American culture. Who knows how many lives were blighted along the way as a result of their proselytizing on behalf of drugs and promiscuous sex?

A religious writer?

Burroughs's even creepier world, marked by paranoia and unrelieved sordidness, has left a number of individual casualties we know about quite well. It would be difficult to overstate the loathsomeness of Burroughs's opinions. Asked about Christianity, he said: "I'm violently anti-Christian. It was the worst disaster that ever occurred on a disaster-prone planet, the most virulent spiritual poison. . . . Fundamentalists are dangerous lunatics. There's really no place for them in an over-crowded life boat. They're a menace."

Burroughs apparently thought women were a menace, too. He once advised Peter Orlovsky, Ginsberg's boyfriend, to "take a tip from me, kid, and steer clear of 'em. They got poison dripping all over 'em." In an interview from 1969, Burroughs explained that "I think love is a virus. I think love is a con put down by the female sex. I don't think it's a solution to anything. . . . I think they [women] were a basic mistake, and the whole dualistic universe evolved from this error." Ginsberg recalled that Burroughs, in a fit of paranoia, believed that women were extraterrestrial agents and that "maybe you had to exterminate all the women, or get rid of them one way or another. Evolve some sort of male that could give birth by parthenogenesis."

Barry Miles claims that Burroughs later "modified" his feelings about women. Perhaps he did. In any event, in 1951 Burroughs was living in Mexico with his wife, Joan, and the young son he had fathered. Unable to procure her favorite amphetamines, Joan was drinking a quart of tequila a day—which, Burroughs's biographer tells us, cost four cents, "the cost of a boy," whose services Burroughs availed himself of regularly. Burroughs's drug of choice at the time seems to have been yage (a hallucinogen that Ginsberg indulged in frequently as well). He was also drinking heavily. One afternoon, he and Joan were very drunk at a friend's apartment. "Bill opened his travel bag," Miles recounts in his biography, "and pulled out the gun." Burroughs then said,

"It's about time for our William Tell act. Put a glass on your head." They had never performed a William Tell act before but Joan, who was also very drunk, laughed and balanced a six-ounce water glass on her head. Bill fired. Joan slumped in her chair and the glass fell to the floor, undamaged. The bullet had entered Joan's brain at the temple. She was pronounced dead on arrival at Red Cross Hospital.

Burroughs jumped bail and fled Mexico rather than stand trial. He later said that it was his wife's death that made him a writer, forcing him into "a lifelong struggle, in which I have no choice except to write myself out." Another choice might have been to lead a responsible life and take care of the son he had fathered and the daughter he had inherited from his wife's previous marriage. But Burroughs abandoned them both to other family members. His son survived until 1981, when he finally managed to drink himself to death at the age of thirty-three. Burroughs claimed to have felt badly about that, too.

There is not much to be said about Burroughs's writing. It consists of semiliterate ravings by a very sick mind, a kaleidoscope of surrealistic depictions of drug-taking, violent, often misogynistic fantasy, and sexual depravity. Here is a random sample:

> A horde of lust-mad American women rush in. Dripping cunts, from farm and dude ranch, factory brothel, country club, penthouse and suburb, motel and yacht and cocktail bar, strip off riding clothes, ski togs, evening dresses, levis, tea gowns, print dresses, slacks, bathing suits and kimonos. They scream and yipe and howl, leap on the guests like bitch dogs in heat with rabies. They claw at the hanged boys shrieking: "You fairy! You bastard! Fuck me! Fuck me! Fuck me!"

One of Burroughs's favorite scenarios was to picture young boys being simultaneously hanged and sodomized:

> Suddenly the Mugwump pushes the boy forward into space, free of his cock. He steadies the boy with hands on the hip bones, reaches up with his stylized hieroglyph hands and snaps the boy's neck. A shudder passes through the boy's body. His penis rises in three great surges pulling his pelvis up, ejaculates immediately. . . .
>
> The Mugwump pulls the boy back onto his cock. . . .

Et cetera.

No wonder great claims have been made for Burroughs's writing, particularly *Naked Lunch*. One academic essay compares Burroughs's book with Wittgenstein's *Tractatus Logico-Philosophicus*: "the sex and sadism," this writer tells us, "spring not from the diseased mind's explosion into a chaos of violence and obscenity but from the major conventions of a literary *genre* and from the world-view suggested by the procedures of philosophical analysis and implied in the early work of Wittgenstein." During the obscenity trial over publication of the book, Norman Mailer testified that Burroughs was in his opinion "a religious writer." Only slightly less ridiculous was the claim made by the critic and novelist Mary McCarthy in 1963 that there were "many points of comparison" between Jonathan Swift and Burroughs, and that, "like a classical satirist, Burroughs is dead serious—a reformer." McCarthy was wrong. Burroughs was not a reformer. Unlike Swift, he had no ideal to oppose to the degradation his books depicted. On the contrary, he was a cynical opportunist who realized that calling his work "satire" could help exempt it from legal action.

The legacy of the Beats

One of the most remarkable things about the Beat generation was the extent to which its spokesmen managed to con
a gullible public into accepting their publicity. They told
the world that they were rebelling against a drab, repressive
society, and the world believed them. In fact, when the
Beats hove into view, in the late Forties and early Fifties,
American society was vibrantly alive. In the aftermath of
World War II, it was confident, prosperous, and dynamic,
helping to rebuild a shattered Europe and rising to contain
the newly militant Soviet threat. Notwithstanding the dis-
traction of Senator McCarthy and his hearings, domestic
life in the United States had never offered young people
more real freedom, economically, socially, or intellectually.
Universities were newly galvanized and cultural life generally was marked by a seriousness of purpose and level of
accomplishment that have never been regained.

The Beats disparaged all this, preferring fantasies of absolute liberation to the real freedoms that surrounded
them. Like the medieval heretics that Norman Cohn wrote
about in *The Pursuit of the Millennium*, the Beats cultivated
an extreme narcissism that bordered on self-deification and
that "liberated them from all restraints" and allowed them
to experience every impulse as "a divine command." What
Norman Podhoretz observed of Ginsberg was also true of
the Beats generally: they "conjured up a world of complete
freedom from the limits imposed by [bourgeois] responsibilities." Podhoretz added, "It was a world that promised
endless erotic possibility together with the excitements of
an expanded consciousness constantly open to new dimensions of being: more adventure, more sex, more intensity,
more *life*." Alas, the promise was illusory. Instead of an "expanded consciousness," the Beats purchased madness, ruin-

ation, and, for many, an early death. Their attack on bourgeois responsibility led not to greater freedom but to greater chaos. The erotic paradise they envisioned turned out to be rife with misery.

In a memorable image, Immanuel Kant spoke of a dove that, soaring above the ground and feeling the resistance of the air, imagines that "its flight would be easier still in empty space." The dream of absolute fulfillment cultivated by the Beats is just as illusory. The Beats, like their successors in the Sixties, have often been described as "idealists." But fantasies of total gratification are not the product of idealism. They arise from a narcissism that, finding the world unequal to its desires, retreats into a realm of heedless self-absorption. Modesty, convention, and self-restraint then appear as the enemies rather than as the allies of humanity. In this sense, the Beat generation marks a step away from civilization. As the nineteenth-century English writer Walter Bagehot observed, savages, contemporary or prehistoric, prefer "short spasms of greedy pleasure to mild and equable enjoyment; . . . they [cannot] postpone the present to the future."

Ginsberg, Burroughs, and Kerouac were all on the side of the savage. That their penny-ante gnosticism was not only perpetuated but mythologized and spread abroad as a gospel of emancipation is something for which we have the Sixties to thank—or to blame. The Beats did a remarkable job of marketing their perversions and self-indulgences. But just as America's cultural revolution drew on the example of the Beats to propagate its radical antinomianism, so the Beats required the Sixties to complete their own apotheosis and long march through the soul of American life. Ginsberg turned out to be depressingly prescient when, after a heated argument with Norman Podhoretz in 1958, he yelled, "We'll get you through your children!" For countless American families, that turned out to be only too true.

Chapter 2
Norman Mailer's American Dream

The sour truth is that I am imprisoned with a perception which will settle for nothing less than making a revolution in the consciousness of our time.
—Norman Mailer, *Advertisements for Myself*, 1959

Men of great power and magnificent ambition, men who become Presidents or champions of the world, are, if one could look into their heads, men very much like Mailer.
—Richard Poirier, *Norman Mailer*, 1972

Despite the central importance of truth in his fictional ethic he had the characteristic intellectual's belief that, in his own case, truth must be the willing servant of his ego.
—Paul Johnson, on Ernest Hemingway, 1988

An established antiestablishment guru

Of course, the Beats were not the only figures who harbingered the "worship of juvenile values" and helped prepare the way for the long march of America's cultural revolution. They had many collaborators. Indeed, the Beats, by being ostentatiously bohemian, insinuated themselves and their values into American life only gradually. It took a decade or more for America fully to catch up with the adolescent ethos they represented. Other figures, although equally preposterous, were embraced with far greater alacrity by the establishment culture. And because they were taken more seriously to begin with, the toxic ideas they promulgated found a large, eager, and influential audience even earlier.

One such figure was Norman Mailer, novelist, wife-stabber, political activist, sometime candidate for mayor of New York, and perpetual *enfant terrible*. Mailer epitomized a certain species of macho, adolescent radicalism that helped to inure the wider public to displays of violence, anti-American tirades, and sexual braggadocio.

It didn't start out that way. Born in Long Branch, New Jersey, in 1923, Mailer was brought up in Brooklyn, "a nice Jewish boy," as he once put it, from a middle-class family of first-generation immigrants. It was a background from which he has been endeavoring to escape ever since. "Mailer," Norman Podhoretz observed in his memoir *Ex-Friends*, "would spend the rest of his life overcoming the stigma of this reputation as a 'nice Jewish boy' by doing as an adult all the hooliganish things he had failed to do in childhood and adolescence." After a dutiful childhood, Mailer matriculated at Harvard in 1939. His parents had made a "big sacrifice" to send their intense, studious son to the elite institution, and he was "not going to let them down." Although he did some writing in college, he majored in aeronautical engineering, graduating in 1942. In 1944, he married for the first of (so far) six times; and then from 1944 to 1946, he served with the U.S. Army in the Philippines and Japan.

In 1948, when he was only twenty-five, Mailer's war novel, *The Naked and the Dead*, was published. For most critics of war fiction, *The Naked and the Dead* ranks somewhere between the novels of Herman Wouk (e.g., *The Caine Mutiny*) and James Jones (*From Here to Eternity*). It is more pretentious, but less well-crafted, and its narrative develops less momentum. Its heavy-handed psychologizing and use of four-letter words were thought smart in 1948; most contemporary readers will find them quaint if not downright embarrassing. Nevertheless, *The Naked and the Dead* was an immediate and immense success. The novel catapulted its young author to an atmosphere of wealth, adulation, and celebrity from which he has yet to descend. Whatever else can be said about it, the reception of *The Naked and the Dead* is an object lesson in the perils—what it might please Norman Mailer to call the "existential" perils of early success. Mailer himself has never recovered.

For readers who did not witness his elevation to the role of literary-political culture hero, it is difficult to appreciate the awe with which Norman Mailer was regarded by the literary and academic establishment from the 1950s through the 1960s and into the 1970s. A typical paean is Diana Trilling's convoluted 1962 essay on "The Radical Moralism of Norman Mailer," which concludes by comparing Mailer to the prophet Moses "with a stopover at Marx." "His moral imagination," Mrs. Trilling assured her readers, "is the imagination not of art but of theology, theology in action." Which means . . . ? Very little, alas, although talk of "theology in action" (as distinct, perhaps, from "theology asleep"?) doubtless sparked interesting vibrations in susceptible souls. As Mailer more or less admitted in what is probably his best-known collection, *Advertisements for Myself* (1959)—a title that could be used again for his complete works—he was a sucker for mystification: "mate the absurd with the apocalyptic, and I was captive."

No one, not even Susan Sontag, combined critical regard, popular celebrity, and radical chic politics with quite the same insouciance as did Mailer. From the late 1940s until the 1980s, he showed himself to be extraordinarily deft at persuading credulous intellectuals to collaborate in his megalomania. Although he modeled his persona on some of the less attractive features of Ernest Hemingway—booze, boxing, bullfighting, and broads—he managed to update that pathetic, shopworn *machismo* with some significant postwar embellishments: reefer, radicalism, and Reich, for starters. There was also the matter of another "R": royalties. Mailer's first royalty check for *The Naked and the Dead* was $40,000 —eminently respectable even today, but an enormous sum in the late 1940s. The glittering example of Mailer's commercial success was obviously the cynosure that many aspiring writers set out to follow: his neat trick was to combine cachet with large amounts of cash.

In 1955, Mailer helped to found *The Village Voice*, which, though always riven by internal dissension, quickly became a megaphone barking New Left thought, such as it was, into the mainstream culture. By the mid-1960s, he had emerged as an established antiestablishment guru. In *Scriptures for a Generation*, a left-leaning synopsis of radical texts from the Sixties, the critic Philip Beidler observed that

> there is no doubt that Mailer as a literary intellectual wished to assume the mantle of '60s youth-illuminatus, at once existential prophet and pied piper. Accordingly, his career across the decade revealed a relentless, almost obsessive wish to be the voice of '60s adversarial culture in its broadest sense: a voice uniting the radical intelligentsia *and* dissenting youth in a new project of revolutionary consciousness spilling over from bohemian lofts and campus enclaves into the streets of the nation at large.

The spectacular success of works like *The Armies of the Night*

(1968)—Mailer's bloated, "non-fiction novel" about the 1967 march on the Pentagon and his own role in the demonstration—bore witness to his gifts for literary demagoguery. Subtitled *History as a Novel, the Novel as History*, the book followed Truman Capote's example in *In Cold Blood* (1966), deliberately blurring fact and fiction, a procedure gratefully seized upon by a public eager to sacrifice truth to the demands of ideological zeal. Indeed, it was a procedure that characterized the intellectual—or, more accurately, the anti-intellectual—temper of a generation battened on mind-altering drugs and taught to regard any appeal to facts as an unacceptably "authoritarian" threat. Among anti–Vietnam War radicals—which is to say, among nine out of ten establishment intellectuals—Mailer's exercise in narcissistic psychohistory was greeted with ecstatic hosannas, and duly picked up both the Pulitzer Prize and the National Book Award. Sample adulation from the critic Richard Gilman: "Mailer has opened up new possibilities for the literary imagination and new room for us to breathe in the crush of actuality." From the writer Nat Hentoff: "Mailer has won clear claim to being the best writer in America."

Getting away with murder

In fact, like almost all of Mailer's books, *The Armies of the Night* is badly written—almost preposterously so. It has often been observed that Mailer's early literary heroes were Hemingway and John Dos Passos. But his own writing totally lacks Hemingway's lapidary craftsmanship and Dos Passos's cinematic control. When *The Armies of the Night* was serialized in *Harper's*,* to the great excitement of the

---

* *Commentary* also published an excerpt.

editor, Willie Morris, a young copy editor complained about Mailer's prose and, as one witness recollects, asked, "I wonder what he writes like when he's sober?" The unfortunate copy editor was promptly fired. But she was right: *The Armies of the Night* is a hyperbolic, self-indulgent mess that looks sillier and more naïve with every year that passes. Its famous third-person narrative strikes one now as a facile gimmick: "Mailer discovered he was jealous. Not of the talent. [Robert] Lowell's talent was very large, but then Mailer was a bulldog about the value of his own talent. . . . Nonetheless, to Mailer it was now *mano a mano.*" That "*mano a mano*" is about as close to Hemingway as Mailer gets.

The adulation that greeted *The Armies of the Night* underscores an important fact about Mailer's success. It is part of Mailer's genius to have been able to calibrate his appetites and deficiencies precisely to the appetites and deficiencies of the moment. His obsessions have been celebrated as brave insights because they have mirrored the defining obsessions of the time. For a moment—but only for a moment—they appear to be revelatory insights. Well into the 1970s, anyway, Mailer instinctively knew exactly what register of rhetorical excess would galvanize the left-wing intellectual establishment. This talent made him an important figure in the long march of America's cultural revolution. It has proved to be immensely profitable, financially and in terms of prestige. By the time Mailer came to write *The Prisoner of Sex* (1971), he was widely rumored to be up for a Nobel Prize, a rumor that absorbed his full attention for the first thirty pages of that execrable book.

This is not to say that Mailer has escaped criticism. His second and third novels, *The Deer Park* (1955) and *Barbary Shore* (1961), were widely attacked, as indeed was *An Amer-*

ican Dream (1965). *An American Dream* was the infamous novel in which the hero, Stephen Rojack, a savvy, tough-guy intellectual—just like Norman Mailer, you see—starts out by strangling his wife. He then walks downstairs and buggers his wife's accommodating German maid, a former Nazi who declares, "I do not know why you have trouble with your wife. You are an absolute genius, Mr. Rojack." (Buggery—another "B" to put alongside booze, boxing, bullfighting, and broads—was to become an obsession with Mailer.) There are numerous Mailerian fingerprints in the novel. President Kennedy ("Jack") calls to convey his condolences; Rojack's wife is rumored to have had affairs with men high up in the British, American, and Soviet spy agencies; even Marilyn Monroe—who was to become another of Mailer's notorious obsessions—makes a posthumous cameo appearance: when Rojack fantasizes about having a telephone conversation with a dead character, he reports that "the girls are swell. Marilyn says to say hello." But the chief point of the book is that Rojack gets away with the murder. Such, Mailer wants us to believe, is the real if unacknowledged "American dream."

For those in the know about Mailer, the novel carried an additional *frisson*. A few years before, at a party he threw to announce his mayoral candidacy on the "Existentialist" ticket, Mailer got drunk and stabbed his wife Adele (number two), nearly killing her. (In 1969, Mailer ran for mayor again, this time on the "Secessionist" ticket, which included proposals that New York City become the fifty-first state and that disputes among young criminals be settled by jousting tournaments in Central Park.) Adele declined to press charges, and so Mailer escaped this outrage with a fortnight in Bellevue for observation.

Mailer's obsession with violence against women seems to have had a long gestation. Carl Rollyson opens his biography of Mailer with the story of John Maloney, a drunkard and a friend of Mailer and William Styron. In 1954, Maloney stabbed his mistress and fled. He was later jailed but released when charges were dropped. Styron recalled that at the time Mailer said to him: "God, I wish I had the courage to stab a woman like that. That was a real gutsy act." That tells one all one needs to know about Norman Mailer's idea of "courage."

What is perhaps most alarming about Mailer's violence against his wife was that it seems to have titillated more than it repelled his circle of friends. In any event it brought very little condemnation. "Among 'uptown intellectuals,'" Irving Howe wrote "there was this feeling of shock and dismay, and I don't remember anyone judging him. The feeling was that he'd been driven to this by compulsiveness, by madness. He was seen as a victim." Readers who wonder how stabbing his wife could make Mailer a "victim"—and who ask themselves, further, what Mailer's being a victim would then make Adele—clearly do not have what it takes to be an "uptown intellectual." In Dawn Powell's 1962 novel *The Golden Spur*, there is a character who observes that "Artists get away with more human nature than anybody else." Powell had a painter in mind, but Norman Mailer illustrates the point even more graphically than the loutish character of Powell's imagination.

The Walter Mitty of sex

If Mailer's attempted murder of his wife met with little censure, *An American Dream* did not escape so easily. It had its admirers. But the critic Stanley Edgar Hyman, in a devastating review called "Norman Mailer's Yummy Rump," spoke for many when he judged it "a dreadful novel," "infinitely more pretentious than the competition," a book whose "awfulness is really indescribable."

Something similar, in truth, can be said about all of Mailer's books. It is hard to say which is the most pretentious. As of this writing, the palm must probably go to *The Gospel According to the Son* (1997), Mailer's effort at rewriting the Gospel story in the first person. It is after all a tall order to write not simply about but *as* Jesus. "I'm one of the 50 or 100 novelists in the world who could rewrite the New Testament," Mailer said when the book came out, explaining that "I have a slight understanding of what it's like to be half a man and half something else, something larger." But breathtaking though Mailer is about *The Gospel According to the Son*, the apogee of his pretentiousness probably came with *Ancient Evenings* (1983). This phantasmagoric tale features reincarnation and is set in Egypt around 2000 BC. Mailer really indulges his fondness for buggery in this "novel," picturing it—along with various other sex acts—taking place between and among various characters as they mutate in and out of existence. Actually having a body does not, for Mailer, seem to be a prerequisite for any form of sexual congress. The one thing that can be said for *Ancient Evenings* is that it displays Mailer's great gifts for unintentional comedy. He is funniest when he waxes solemn:

> "Let me tell you again. There is the magic we invoke, and the magic that calls upon us. Do you recall that Isis dropped the fourteenth piece of the body of Osiris in the salts of Yeb, and saw battles to come between Horus and Set? That was a warning to find a proper sacrifice or there would be no peace. She heard Her own voice tell Her to slaughter a bull, but as she killed the beast, Her voice also told Her that the sacrifice was not great enough to compensate for the evil powers of Set. She must add the blood

of a more painful loss. She must cut off her own head, and replace it with the bull's face." Menenhetet now giggled.

And who can blame him?

Ancient Evenings illustrates why readers who came to Norman Mailer in the 1970s and 1980s have a difficult time understanding the reverence with which he was once regarded by literary intellectuals. Who could take the author of this book seriously?

> "Even in the first years I knew Him, I do not believe He had many thoughts which were not of battle, prayer, Nefertiti, or His other true taste—the buttocks of brave men.
>
> "After the Battle of Kadesh, however, He was like an oasis that finds new water beneath its palms and divides to a hundred trees where before there were three. Our good Pharaoh came back from Kadesh with more hunger for the sweet meat of women than any man I knew in all of my four lives. He must have gained the seed of the Hittites He killed, for his loins were like the rising of the Nile, and He could not look at a pretty woman without having her. But then, He could like ugly women as well."

Menenhetet is still giggling.

The truth is that Norman Mailer very quickly became a parody of himself. Since the Sixties was itself a ghastly caricature of political radicalism, few people at the time seemed to notice just how ridiculous Mailer's preening exhibitionism and blustering political and sexual pronouncements were. But as the years passed and Mailer became more and more indiscriminate in his enthusiasms, Mailer the existential sage was gradually revealed as Mailer the buffoon.

The point of no return was probably *Marilyn* (1973),

a picture-book-cum-biography of the actress Marilyn
Monroe. It is difficult to say with confidence which of
Mailer's books is really his worst: he has managed to be
truly awful in several distinct ways. But *Marilyn* is certainly
his silliest book (to date). Over the years, Mailer's fascination with the Star Who Slept With the Kennedys developed
into another of his obsessions. In John Simon's definitive
description, what Mailer gave us with *Marilyn* was "a new
genre called transcendental masturbation or metaphysical
wet dreaming."

In real life, Marilyn Monroe was an unhappy sexpot, a
sometimes amusing but distinctly mediocre comic actress
whose air-headedness was almost as much of an attraction
as her pneumatic bustline. The unhappy truth, as Clive
James observed, is that Marilyn Monroe "was good at
being inarticulately abstracted for the same reason that
midgets are good at being short." According to Mailer,
though, Marilyn Monroe was a combination of Aphrodite
and Ellen Terry. On the one hand, he says, Monroe was a
"superb" actress who "possessed the talent to play Cor-
delia"; she was "Madame Bovary and Nana all in one";
"one might literally have to invent the idea of a soul in
order to approach her." On the other hand, she was "a very
Stradivarius of sex," "the angel of Sex": "she had learned by
Mind," Mailer writes, "to move sex forward—sex was not
unlike an advance of little infantrymen of libido sent up to
the surface of her skin. She was a general of sex before she
knew anything of sexual war."

No one in our sex-obsessed culture is likely to underestimate the importance of sexual gratification in the lives of
most people. But Mailer advanced the idea that sexual
gratification was the existential center of life. In the world
according to Mailer, every activity revolves around sex. In
Marilyn, he remarks in passing that "it is a rule of thumb

today: one cannot buy a Polaroid in a drugstore without announcing to the world, one chance in two, the camera will be used to record a copulation of family or friends." One chance in two? Writing about Mailer in *Commentary*, Joseph Epstein observed that "it is a sign of the deep poverty of Norman Mailer's imagination that the only climax he can imagine in any human relationship is really just that—a sexual climax." It is all the more ironical, then, that Mailer should display such a profound misunderstanding of sex. It is his one true subject, but he has got it all wrong.

Indeed, if Marilyn Monroe is "the angel of Sex," Norman Mailer is its Walter Mitty. He constructs absurd melodramas of sexual conquest and then casts himself as their inevitable hero. His ubiquitous descriptions of sex are wince-makingly embarrassing. In "The Time of Her Time," for example—a fictional sketch that concludes *Advertisements for Myself* and of which Mailer was particularly proud—the hero refers to his penis as "the avenger" and is taken to saying things like "For her, getting it from me, it must have been impressive." In *The Prisoner of Sex*, which Mailer intended as an answer to *Sexual Politics*, Kate Millet's once-famous feminist screed, we read about "the power of the semen going over the hill" as well as "the ovum [that] in its turn would be ready as any priestess to greet the arcane and dismiss the common, ready as a whore to welcome a wad or get rid of a penniless prick, ready as an empress to find a lord or turn her face to the wall." The moral of this, perhaps, is that an egg's work is never done.

Mailer's penchant for bombast makes him a difficult writer to parody; one can never be sure that he hasn't said something even more ridiculous than the caricature. Still, Elizabeth Hardwick caught something essential about Mailer in the parody she wrote (under the pseudonym

Xavier Prynne) of *The Presidential Papers* (1963) for *The New York Review of Books*:

> This 6th note was ignored by LBJ, but attacked by the Black Negroes and the FBI. One admits that a lot of it is lousy—I was having personal troubles at the time—but I still think it lousy but good. The Bitch Goddess didn't quite get into bed with me this round, but at least she didn't get into bed with Bill Styron either, up in his plush Connecticut retreat. All the Bitch did was blow into my ear—one of those mysterious pre-psychotic Jackie Kennedy whispers. My answer to the FBI would run this way: *The existential orgasm would make atomic war and even atomic testing impossible* . . .

The problem with this virtuoso performance is that it is virtually indistinguishable from the writing it set out to spoof. Its perfection as an exercise in mimicry renders it void as parody.

Gambling with a portion of society

The unwitting comic dimension of Mailer's writing is large. But its many sinister elements far overshadow its humor. Norman Mailer may be unintentionally funny; he is deliberately repulsive. He is an important figure in the story of America's cultural revolution not because people found him ridiculous but, on the contrary, because many influential people took the ideas of this ridiculous man seriously.

Mailer has written a great deal about politics. Yet in the end, he regards politics the way he regards everything else, as a coefficient of sex. As he put it in *Advertisements for Myself*, "the only revolution which will be meaningful and natural for the twentieth century will be the sexual revolution one senses everywhere." Even his identity as an "existentialist" is filtered through sexual anxiety: "a man is in a more existential position than a woman," Mailer assures us: "he has to get an erection."

In fact, in Mailer's writing, the term "existential" and its cognates are little more than hortatory epithets, devoid of anything except sexual wish-fulfillment. He begins his essay "The White Negro" by telling his readers that "the American existentialist" is "the hipster," and then goes on to say that "to be an existentialist, one must be able to feel oneself —one must know one's desires, one's rages, one's anguish, one must be aware of the character of one's frustration and know what would satisfy it." Elsewhere he writes that "we find ourselves in an existential situation whenever we are in a situation where we cannot foretell the end." In other words, Mailer's conception of existentialism is scarcely more substantial (though it is a lot less amusing) than Delmore Schwartz's wry observation that existentialism means that no one else can take a bath for you.

It is in his ideas about sex, especially as he relates them to the rest of life, that Mailer has been most influential and most destructive. It would be difficult to overstate the crudeness of his position. In 1973, in one of the countless interviews he has given, Mailer was asked for his opinion about legalized abortion. Mailer thought well enough of his answer to reprint it in *Pieces and Pontifications* (1982):

I think when a woman goes through an abortion, even legalized abortion, she goes through hell. There's no use hoping otherwise. For what is she doing? Sometimes she has to be saying to herself, "You're killing the memory of a beautiful fuck." I don't think abortion is a great strain when the act was some miserable little screech, or some squeak oozed up through the trapdoor, a little rat which got in, a worm who slithered under the threshold. That sort of abortion costs a woman little more than discomfort. Unless there are medical consequences years later.

But if a woman has a great fuck, and then has to abort, it embitters her.

Of course, it is possible that Mailer was being deliberately outrageous in his response to the interviewer's question. Nevertheless, this is the declaration of a moral cretin.

It is one of the moral peculiarities of Mailer's writings about sex that he seems barely able to distinguish it from violent physical conflict. His depictions of lovemaking are almost always cast in terms of struggle and domination. There is scarcely any room for warmth or tenderness. Desire reveals itself first of all as a desire for conquest. No doubt this is one reason that sodomy features so prominently in his writings. Sex in Mailer is not so much an act of union as brute subordination. This is part of what makes it, for Mailer, so "existential." As a macho existentialist, Mailer sees, or pretends to see, everything as a battle, a "war." Indeed, despite his virulent anti–Vietnam War stand, "war" is one of Mailer's abiding passions. It's part of his Hemingway pose: he likes to bluster about life being a continual struggle—*mano a mano* as he might put it—with the void.

In "A Public Notice on Waiting for Godot," in which Mailer has the effrontery to tell us that he regards Samuel Beckett as "a minor artist," he writes that "man's nature, man's dignity, is that he acts, lives, loves, and finally destroys himself seeking to penetrate the mystery of existence, and unless we partake in some way, as some part of this human exploration (and war) then we are no more than the pimps of society and the betrayers of our Self." Destroys himself? Pimps of society? "Betrayers of our

Self"? Mailer is clearly the captive of a debased and self-aggrandizing Romanticism. He manufactures melodramas to ventilate the tedium of his comfortable, bourgeois existence. It is a familiar adolescent gambit. But Mailer has managed to prolong his pubescent rage into his seventies. It is what has made him so productive of comic relief. It is also what underlies his fascination with violence.

Many critics believe that *The Executioner's Song* (1979) is Mailer's best book. Subtitled *A True Life Novel*, it tells the *In Cold Blood*–type story of the arrest and execution by firing squad of Gary Gilmore, a psychopathic killer who spent most of his thirty-odd years in jail. Written in a clipped, unembellished style, the book contains some of Mailer's most urgent and compelling prose. Considered as a moral document, however, *The Executioner's Song* is profoundly repulsive. For Mailer does not simply delve into and display the humanity of the tortured killer he writes about: He offers him up as a kind of hero, a courageous "outsider" who deserves our sympathy as a Victim of Society and our respect as an implacable rebel. Gary Gilmore, he said, was "another major American protagonist," a man who was "malignant at his worst and heroic at his best," implacable in his desire for (his clinching virtue) "revenge upon the American system."

After Gilmore had been executed, Mailer's attention was captured by Jack Abbott, a violent convict and self-declared Communist who began writing Mailer long "existential" letters about life in prison. Mailer loved them. He helped Abbott have them published, first in *The New York Review of Books* and then as a book, called *In the Belly of the Beast* (1981). In his introduction, Mailer described Abbott as "an intellectual, a radical, a potential leader, a man obsessed with a vision of more elevated human relations in a better world that revolution could forge." It seems clear that

Mailer's interest helped to expedite Abbott's release from prison: "Culture," Mailer declared at one point, "is worth a little risk." Abbott had scarcely set foot in New York when he stabbed and killed Richard Adan, a twenty-two-year-old Cuban-American waiter. Mailer testified on Abbott's behalf at the ensuing murder trial. Asked about Adan's family at a press conference following his testimony, Mailer said: "I'm willing to gamble with a portion of society to save this man's talent." A reporter from *The New York Post* then asked "who he was willing to see sacrificed. Waiters? Cubans?" Questions to which Mailer had no response but bluster: "What are you all feeling so righteous about, may I ask?" Clearly, he did not know the answer to his own question.

The drama of the psychopath

Mailer's flirtation with criminals like Gary Gilmore and Jack Abbott must be seen as the fulfillment of his celebration of the "psychopath" as an existential hero. In "The White Negro," first published in *Dissent* in 1957, and reprinted in *Advertisements for Myself*, Mailer definitively articulated an ethic that underlies not only his own view of the world in all his later writings, but also the view that would inform the cultural revolution of the 1960s. In tone, "The White Negro" is a panoply of "existentialist" rant. In content, it is a manifesto on behalf of moral nihilism. Mailer speaks casually about "the totalitarian tissues of American society" and invokes "the psychic havoc of the concentration camps and the atom bomb upon the unconscious mind of almost everyone alive in these years." The only authentic response to this dire situation, he says, is "to divorce oneself from society" and "to encourage the psychopath in oneself." This is the strategy of "the hipster," who has "absorbed the existentialist synapses of the Negro, and [who] for practical purposes could be considered a white Negro." (Mailer's stereotypical portrayal of blacks as beastlike sexual athletes is one of the many distasteful things about the essay.)

> One is Hip or one is Square, . . . one is a rebel or one conforms, one is a frontiersman in the Wild West of American night life, or else a Square cell, trapped in the totalitarian tissues of American society, doomed willy-nilly to conform if one is to succeed.

The rest of "The White Negro" is a glorification of the hipster and his ethic of promiscuous sex, drug-taking, and criminal violence. The hipster, Mailer explains, is part of "an elite with the potential ruthlessness of an elite, and a language most adolescents can understand instinctively, for the hipster's intense view of existence matches their experience and their desire to rebel."

Mailer conjures up the image—it is what made the essay infamous—of eighteen-year-old hoodlums who "beat in the brains of a candy-store keeper." For Mailer such behavior is acceptable, even laudable, because the psychopath, by murdering, demonstrates his "courage" and "purge[s] his violence." To the objection that it does not take much courage to kill someone older and weaker, Mailer explains that

> one murders not only a weak fifty-year-old man but an institution as well, one violates private property, one enters into a new relation with the police and introduces a dangerous element into one's life. The hoodlum is therefore daring the unknown, and so no matter how brutal the act, it is not altogether cowardly.

Mailer goes on to explain that "at bottom, the drama of the psychopath is that he seeks love." Not, however, "love as the search for a mate, but love as the search for an orgasm more apocalyptic than the one which preceded it. Orgasm is his therapy—he knows at the seed of his being that good orgasm opens his possibilities and bad orgasm imprisons him." This is one reason that the hipster adores jazz: "jazz," Mailer tells us, "is orgasm, it is the music of orgasm, good orgasm and bad, and so it spoke across a nation." The hipster's quest "for absolute sexual freedom" entails the necessity of "becoming a sexual outlaw."

It is not only sexual morality that the hipster discards.

> Hip abdicates from any conventional moral responsibility because it would argue that the results of our actions are unforeseeable, and so we cannot know if we do good or bad. . . . The only Hip morality . . . is to do what one feels whenever and wherever it is possible, and . . . to be engaged in one primal battle: to open the limits of the possible for oneself, for oneself alone, because that is one's need.

Could poor Phineas Gage, his "moral center" destroyed by dynamite, have put it more bluntly?

"The White Negro" adumbrates practically everything that went wrong with American society under the assault of left-wing radicalism in the 1960s, from the addiction to violence, drugs, pop music, and sexual polymorphism, to the moral idiocy, jejune anti-Americanism, and mindless glorification of narcissistic irresponsibility and extreme states of experience. It was, as David Horowitz notes in his autobiography *Radical Son*, "the seminal manifesto of New Left nihilism. . . . In New Left thinking, criminals were only 'primitive rebels.'" Although many critics took issue with Mailer's exoneration of violence, the real message of the essay—if it feels good, do it!—was just then beginning to sweep the country with irresistible force. "The White Negro," along with some of Mailer's other essays from the late 1950s, represented an important opening salvo in the war on convention, restraint, and traditional morality. This, not his literary accomplishment, was the ultimate secret of Mailer's broad appeal. Mailer, as Joseph Epstein observed, "was one of the key men responsible for releasing the Dionysian strain in American life." He promised his readers what they longed to hear: that ultimate, self-centered ecstasy was theirs for the taking. Mailer once said that he would "settle for nothing less than making a revolution in the consciousness of our time." He did not make the revolution, but he assuredly became one of its most egregious abettors.

Chapter 3
Susan Sontag & the New Sensibility

Everyone who feels bored cries out for change. With this demand I am in complete sympathy, but it is necessary to act in accordance with some settled principle. . . . Nil admirari [nothing is to be marveled at] is . . . the real philosophy. No moment must be permitted so great a significance that it cannot be forgotten when convenient; each moment ought, however, to have so much significance that it can be recollected at will. . . . From the beginning one should keep the enjoyment under control, never spreading every sail to the wind in any resolve; one ought to devote oneself to pleasure with a certain suspicion, a certain wariness, if one desires to give the lie to the proverb which says that no one can eat his cake and have it too.
—Søren Kierkegaard, *Either/Or*, 1843

Like all great aesthetes, Barthes was an expert at having it both ways.
—Susan Sontag, "On Roland Barthes," 1981

Dethroning the serious

Norman Mailer was not the only upscale intellectual striving to make "a revolution in the consciousness of our time." Musing about the glories of Fidel Castro and the Cuban revolution in 1969, that archetypical New-Left writer Susan Sontag noted in passing that "perhaps the foremost difference between New and Old Left is that New Left people are busier with cultural revolution than with anything else." She was right. The endless demonstrations, sit-ins, rallies, petitions, marches, and "non-negotiable demands" that were such a prominent feature of the 1960s and 1970s had myriad political ramifications. Nevertheless, the result of the counterculture's political activism was not to topple a regime but to transform morals—using "morals" broadly, as Matthew Arnold did in his famous essay on Wordsworth, to encompass "whatever bears upon the question, 'how to live.'" Art, too, had a moral function. "Poetry," Arnold suggested, "is at bottom a criticism of life."

It is against this Arnoldian compact of morals and culture that the long march of America's cultural revolution has scored its greatest victories. In a famous epithet, Arnold described the task of culture as "*a disinterested endeavour to learn and propagate the best that is known and thought in the world.*" The "new sensibility" of the Sixties and Seventies set out not simply to lower intellectual, aesthetic, and moral standards, but also to undermine the shared intellectual and moral foundations upon which such standards must rest. Distinctions between high and low, good and bad, noble and base, were suddenly rendered otiose, beside the point. The revolution brought with it a process of blurring or (more accurately) of inverting that made its partisans believe that critical discrimination was an antiquarian pursuit.

As a consequence, the long march of America's cultural revolution resulted in a corruption of taste that was at the same time the triumph of a certain species of aestheticizing decadence. Today, the results of that victory are recognizable everywhere—above all in the garbage dumps of popular culture, but also throughout those cultural institutions that traditionally had been entrusted with perpetuating the ideas and achievements that Arnold celebrated:

academia, the fine-arts museums, theaters, orchestras, even churches and other repositories of moral wisdom.

No one has more lovingly delineated, or more perfectly epitomized, the mandarin ambiguities of this situation than Susan Sontag, the critic, novelist, playwright, filmmaker, theatrical director, professional aesthete, and full-time political radical. Sontag descended on the New York intellectual scene in the mid-1960s with a handful of remarkable essays: "Notes on 'Camp'" (1964) and "On Style" (1965) in *Partisan Review*; "Against Interpretation" (1964) in *Evergreen Review*; "One Culture and the New Sensibility" (1965), an abridged version of which first appeared in *Mademoiselle*; and several essays and reviews in the newly launched *New York Review of Books*. (Sontag contributed a short review of Simone Weil's essays for the *Review*'s inaugural issue in 1963.) Almost overnight these essays electrified intellectual debate and catapulted their author to celebrity.

Not that Sontag's efforts were unanimously praised. The critic John Simon, to take just one example, wondered in a sharp letter to *Partisan Review* whether Sontag's "Notes on 'Camp'" was itself "only a piece of 'camp.'" No, the important things were the attentiveness, speed, and intensity of the response. Pro or con, Sontag's essays galvanized debate: indeed, they contributed mightily to changing the very climate of intellectual debate. Her demand, at the end of "Against Interpretation," that "in place of a hermeneutics we need an erotics of art"; her praise of camp, the "whole point" of which "is to dethrone the serious"; her encomium to the "new sensibility" of the Sixties, whose acolytes, she observed, "have broken, whether they know it or not, with the Matthew Arnold notion of culture, finding it historically and humanly obsolescent": in these and other such pronouncements Sontag offered not arguments but a mood, a tone, an atmosphere.

Never mind that a lot of it was literally nonsense: it was nevertheless *irresistible* nonsense. It somehow didn't matter, for example, that the whole notion of "an erotics of art" was ridiculous. Everyone likes sex, and talking about "erotics" seems so much sexier than talking about "sex"; and of course everyone likes art: How was it that no one had thought of putting them together in this clever way before? Who would bother with something so boring as mere "interpretation"—which, Sontag had suggested, was these days "reactionary, impertinent, cowardly, stifling," "the revenge of the intellect upon art"—when we could have (or pretend to have) an erotics instead?

It was a remarkable performance, all the more so as Sontag was then barely thirty years old. In truth, there had always been something precocious—not to say hasty—about her. Born in New York City in 1933, she had been brought up mostly in Arizona and California. (Her father died in 1938; Sontag is her stepfather's name.) She began skipping grades when she was six. Graduating from high school when she was barely sixteen, Sontag went first to the University of California at Berkeley and then, in the fall of 1949, to the University of Chicago. In December of 1950, when she was seventeen, she met the critic Philip Rieff (author of *The Triumph of the Therapeutic* [1966], among other works). Rieff, then a twenty-eight-year-old instructor, was giving a course that Sontag audited. As she was leaving after the first class, Sontag recalled, "He was standing at the door and he grabbed my arm and asked my name. I apologized and told him I had only come to audit. 'No, what's your name?' he persisted. 'Will you have lunch with me?'" Married ten days later, the couple in due course found themselves, in 1952, with a son—who would grow up to be the left-wing writer David Rieff—and a divorce in 1958. (Sontag later told an interviewer: "You know, I think rock & roll is the reason I got divorced.") Meanwhile, having picked up a bachelor's degree at Chicago after three years, Sontag also spent time studying at Harvard—where she took a master's degree in philosophy—and at Oxford and the Sorbonne. Armed with a battery of French names that few people knew about here, she returned to New York in 1959, worked briefly at *Commentary* and elsewhere before taking up, in 1960, a teaching position at Columbia in (*mirabile dictu*) the department of religion.

The art of intellectual impersonation

But all this was prolegomenon. Looking back on it now, it seems obvious that throughout those years Sontag was constructing, burnishing, perfecting what to call it? A style, partly; a tone, assuredly; but in the end, perhaps, it might be best described as an *altitude*: chic, lofty, disdainful. By the time she began publishing in highbrow journals like *Partisan Review* and *The New York Review of Books*, Sontag had made herself the mistress of a new brand of cultural hauteur. It was ferociously intellectual without necessarily being intelligent; it deployed, but did not rely upon, arguments. Its invariable direction was *de haut en bas*. In her early essays, "formal" and "formalist" were among Sontag's favorite words. She endlessly repeated that works of art must be judged for their formal properties, not their "content." If we judge Sontag's own essays in "formal" terms, they may appear as models of fashionable daring; but judged in terms of content, they are little more than a repository of intellectual clichés—witness the insistence, as if it were something original, on judging art for its formal excellence and not its "message," one of the hoariest of modern half-truths. "The satisfactions of *Paradise Lost*," she writes in "On Style," "do not lie in its views on God and man, but in the superior kinds of energy, vitality, expressiveness which are incarnated in the poem." What she doesn't say is that the energy, vitality, and expressiveness of Milton's poem are unintelligible apart from the truths it aspires to articulate. If this were not the case, *Paradise Lost* might just as well be about baked beans as about "justify[ing] the ways of God to men." In "Susie Creamcheese Makes Love Not War," a devastating—and devastatingly funny—review of the Sontag *oeuvre* as of 1982, the critic Marvin Mudrick noted that Sontag was

> a critic whose every half-baked idea is a reject or thrift-shop markdown from the pastry cooks of post–World War II French intellectualism. . . . [W]hat matters [to her] isn't truth or sincerity or consistency or reality; what matters is 'style' or getting away with it.[*]

What we are dealing with in Sontag's work is only partly a matter of *intellectual* style. Sontag was creating a *Gesamtkunstwerk*, a total work of art, and it had sartorial as well as cerebral leitmotifs. We get a hint of this in the introduction

---

[*] Mudrick is especially good on Sontag's use of the word "exemplary": "Barthes's ideas have an exemplary coherence"; "Some lives are exemplary, others not"; Rimbaud and Duchamp made "exemplary renunciations" in giving up art for, respectively, gun-running and chess; "Silence exists as a *decision*—in the exemplary suicide of the artist . . ."; etc. Dilating on Sontag's effusions about silence—"the silence of eternity prepares for a thought beyond thought, which must appear from the perspective of traditional thinking . . . as no thought at all"—Mudrick usefully points out the similarity between Sontag and that other sage of silence, Kahlil Gibran: "Has silence or talk about it," Mudrick asks, "ever anywhere else been so very . . . *exemplary?*"

to a collection of interviews with Sontag published in 1995. The editor quotes a description of an author's photograph depicting Sontag "in black trousers, black polo-neck and wearing cowboy boots. She is stretched out on a window-sill with a pile of books and papers under her arm. The seriousness is lightened by the faint flicker of pleasure: this is an image which pleases the author. At home, with books, wearing black." It is not said whether this was before or after the publication of *Texas Boots*, David Rieff's celebration of cowboy boots. In any event, it is clear that a less physically attractive woman could never have aspired to be Susan Sontag.*

It is hardly surprising that one of Sontag's indisputable contributions has been to the art of pretension—or perhaps it should be called intellectual impersonation. It is not every day, after all, that a writer, asked when his interest in "the moral" began, will reply as did Sontag that

> I believe that it began when I was three years old. In other aspects, I am not very clear about when I was young, which is a source of strength and a problem at the same time. I remember that I would think much on the things that I think about now before I was ten years old.

---

* Norman Podhoretz has suggested that the "*rapidity*" of Sontag's rise was due partly to her filling the role of "Dark Lady of American Letters," vacated when Mary McCarthy was "promoted to the more dignified status of *Grande Dame* as a reward for her years of brilliant service. The next Dark Lady would have to be, like her, clever, learned, good-looking, capable of writing [New York–intellectual] family-type criticism as well as fiction with a strong trace of naughtiness." The "ante on naughtiness," Podhoretz notes, had gone up since McCarthy's day: "in an era of what Sherry Abel has called the 'fishnet bluestocking,' hints of perversion and orgies had to be there."

It is almost enough to make one join Sontag in her campaign "against interpretation."

In one early essay, Sontag described the bombastic performance events known as "happenings" as "an art of radical juxtaposition." The same can be said of her essays, singly and taken together. What she produces are not essays, really, but verbal collages. *Against Interpretation* (1966), her first collection, contains pieces on Sartre *and* science fiction novels, the literary criticism of the Marxist Georg Lukács *and* a paean to Jack Smith's *Flaming Creatures*, a cult film in which, as Sontag cheerfully puts it, "a couple of women and a much larger number of men, most of them clad in flamboyant thrift-shop women's clothes, frolic about, pose and posture, dance with one another, and enact various scenes of voluptuousness, sexual frenzy, romance, and vampirism," including scenes of masturbation, gang rape, and oral sex. Sontag castigates the "indifference or hostility" of "the mature intellectual and artistic community" to this "small but valuable work" in the tradition of "the cinema of shock." She praises the "extraordinary charge and beauty of [Smith's] images" and—a signature Sontag touch —the film's "exhilarating freedom from moralism." Sontag is very big on that "exhilarating freedom from moralism." Acknowledging that "by ordinary standards"—but not, of course, by *her* standards—*Flaming Creatures* is composed of themes that are "perverse, decadent," she insists that really the film "is about joy and innocence," not least because it is "both too full of pathos and too ingenuous to be prurient."

This sort of thing was catnip to the intellectual establishment of the mid 1960s. Not that any of it was new, exactly. *Nostalgie de la boue* has long been a defining disease of bourgeois intellectuals, and has been effectively peddled by many before the advent of S. Sontag. But few if any writers commanded Sontag's air of perfect knowingness, which managed to combine commendation, indifference, and disdain with breathtaking virtuosity.

In his review of *Under the Sign of Saturn*, a collection of Sontag's essays published in 1980, John Simon noted that "nothing succeeds better than highbrow endorsement of lowbrow tastes." Sontag was a master at that game. Her great trick was not merely to endorse lowbrow tastes, but to create the illusion that for the truly sophisticated all intellectual, artistic, and moral distinctions of merit were *infra dig*, dispensable, *de trop*. This is one reason that she championed the camp sensibility. Camp is the enemy of earnestness. "Camp," Sontag observed, "is the consistently aesthetic experience of the world. It incarnates a victory of 'style' over 'content,' 'aesthetics' over 'morality,' of irony over tragedy." Camp, she went on to say, "is a solvent of morality," concluding with one of her famous paradoxes: "The ultimate Camp statement: it's good *because* it's awful." (She immediately added: "of course, one can't always say that. Only under certain conditions"—thus letting you know that not just anyone is allowed to indulge in contradiction and win praise for it.)

Beyond good and evil

One of Sontag's characteristic productions was "The Pornographic Imagination" (1967), which appears in *Styles of Radical Will* (1969), her second collection. In essence, it is a defense of pornography—though not, of course, as something merely salacious; Sontag doesn't champion pornography the way its usual clients do: for its content, for the lubricious stimulation it supplies. Instead, she champions pornography for its "formal" resources as a means of "transcendence." It is hardly news that sexual ecstasy has often poached on religious rhetoric and vice versa; nor is it news that pornography often employs religious metaphors. That is part of its perversity—indeed its blasphemy. But Sontag decides to take pornography seriously as a solution to the spiritual desolations of modern secular culture. Writing about Pauline Réage's pornographic *Story of O*, for example, she solemnly tells us that

> O is an adept; whatever the cost in pain and fear, she is grateful for the opportunity to be initiated into a mystery. That mystery is the loss of self. O learns, she suffers, she changes. Step by step she becomes more what she is, a process identical with the emptying out of herself. In the vision of the world presented by *The Story of O*, the highest good is the transcendence of personality.

Which is about as accurate as saying that the Marquis de Sade's books are essentially about physical exercise.

One of Sontag's great gifts has been her ability to enlist her politics in the service of her aestheticism. For her, it is the work of a moment to move from admiring pornography—or at least "the pornographic imagination"—to castigating American capitalism. Accordingly, toward the end of her essay she speaks of

> the traumatic failure of capitalist society to provide authentic outlets for the perennial human flair for high-temperature visionary obsession, to satisfy the appetite for exalted self-transcending modes of concentration and seriousness. The need of human beings to transcend "the person" is no less profound than the need to be a person, an individual.

"The Pornographic Imagination," like most of Sontag's

essays, is full of powerful phrases, seductive insights, and extraordinary balderdash. Sontag dilates on pornography's "peculiar access to some truth." What she doesn't say is that *The Story of O* (for example) presents not an instance of mystical fulfillment but a graphic depiction of human degradation. Only someone who had allowed "form" to triumph over "content" could have ignored this. In a way, "The Pornographic Imagination" is itself the perfect camp gesture: for if camp aims to "dethrone the serious" it is also, as Sontag points out, "deadly serious" about the demotic and the trivial. Sontag is a master at both ploys. Having immersed herself in the rhetoric of traditional humanistic learning, she is expert at using it against itself. This of course is a large part of what has made her writing so successful among would-be "avant-garde" intellectuals: playing with the empty forms of traditional moral and aesthetic thought, she is able to appear simultaneously unsettling and edifying, daringly "beyond good and evil" and yet passionately *engagé*. In the long march through the institutions, Sontag has been an emissary of trivialization, deploying the tools of humanism to sabotage the humanistic enterprise.

"The Pornographic Imagination" also exhibits the seductive Sontag hauteur in full flower. After telling us that pornography can be an exciting version of personal transcendence, she immediately remarks that "not everyone is in the same condition as knowers or potential knowers. Perhaps most people don't need 'a wider scale of experience.' It may be that, without subtle and extensive psychic preparation, any widening of experience and consciousness is destructive for most people." Not for you and me, Dear Reader: we are among the elect. We deserve that "wider scale of experience"; but as for the rest, as for "most people," well . . .

It doesn't always work. As a writer, Sontag is essentially a coiner of epigrams. At their best they are witty, well phrased, provocative. A few are even true: "Nietzsche was a histrionic thinker but not a lover of the histrionic." But Sontag's striving for effect (unlike Nietzsche, she *is* a lover of the histrionic) regularly leads her into muddle. What, for example, can it mean to say that "the AIDS epidemic serves as an ideal projection for First World political paranoia" or that "risk-free sexuality is an inevitable reinvention of the culture of capitalism"? Nothing, really, although such statements do communicate an unperturbable aura of left-wing contempt for common sense. In "One Culture and the New Sensibility" Sontag enthusiastically reasons that "if art is understood as a form of discipline of the feelings and a programming of sensations, then the feeling (or sensation) given off by a Rauschenberg painting might be like that of a song by the Supremes." But of course the idea that art is a "programming of the sensations" (a phrase, alas, of which Sontag is particularly fond) is wrong, incoherent, or both, as is the idea that feelings or sensations might be "given off" by any song or painting, even one by Rauschenberg (odors, yes; sensations, no). As often happens, her passion for synesthesia and effacing boundaries leads her into nonsense.

Charity dictates that we pass lightly over Sontag's fiction and drama. Most of it reminds one of Woody Allen's parody of Kafka: "Should I marry K.? Only if she tells me the other letters of her name"—that sort of thing. Here's a representative sample from *I, etcetera* (a book whose title might be reused for Sontag's collected works): "Dearest M. I cannot telephone. I am six years old. My grief falls like snowflakes on the warm soil of your indifference. You are inhaling your own pain." Indeed, readers looking for the comic side of Sontag's *oeuvre* will want to dip into her fic-

tion: *The Benefactor* (1963) and *Death Kit* (1967) are particularly fine, provided they are read as parodies of intellectual
solemnity. In *Either/Or*, Kierkegaard advised the aspiring
aesthete to look for "a very different kind of enjoyment
from that which the author has been so kind as to plan for
you." It is advice that is particularly relevant when approaching Sontag's "creative writing."

"The cancer of human history"

If one wanted to sum up Sontag's allure in a single phrase,
it would be difficult to do better than Tom Wolfe's "radical
chic." In her manner, her opinions, her politics, Sontag has
always been a walking inventory of radical chic attitudes.
Writing about Camus' notebooks in 1963, she naturally
patronizes him as having been "acclaimed beyond his
purely literary merits," assuring us that, unlike Sartre (but
like George Orwell), he was not "a thinker of importance."
In 1963, Sartre was still an Approved Radical Figure, whose
Communist sympathies and virulent anti-Americanism
made him beloved of American intellectuals. Camus, who
had had the temerity to criticize Communism, was distinctly non-ARF and had to be taken down a peg or two.

And then there were Sontag's own political activities.
Cuba and North Vietnam in 1968, China in 1973, Sarajevo
in 1993 (where she went to direct a production of *Waiting
for Godot*—surely one of the consummate radical chic gestures of all time). Few people have managed to combine
naïve idealization of foreign tyranny with violent hatred of
their own country to such deplorable effect. She has always
talked like a political radical but lived like an aesthete. At
the annual PEN writers' conference in 1986, Sontag declared
that "the task of the writer is to promote dissidence." But it

it turns out that, for her, only dissidence conducted against American interests counts. Consider the notorious essay she wrote about "the right way" for Americans to "love the Cuban revolution." Sontag begins with some ritualistic denunciations of American culture as "inorganic, dead, coercive, authoritarian." Item: "America is a cancerous society with a runaway rate of productivity that inundates the country with increasingly unnecessary commodities, services, gadgets, images, information." One of the few spots of light, she tells us, is Eldridge Cleaver's *Soul on Ice*, which teaches that "America's psychic survival entails her transformation through a political revolution." (It also teaches that, for blacks, rape can be a noble "insurrectionary act," a "defying and trampling on the white man's laws," but Sontag doesn't bother with that detail.)

According to her, "the power structure derives its credibility, its legitimacy, its energies from the dehumanization of the individuals who operate it. The people staffing IBM and General Motors, and the Pentagon, and United Fruit are the living dead." Since the counterculture is not strong enough to overthrow IBM, the Pentagon, etc., it must opt for subversion. "Rock, grass, better orgasms, freaky clothes, grooving on nature—really grooving on anything—unfits, maladapts a person for the American way of life." And here is where the Cubans come in: they enjoy this desirable "new sensibility" naturally, possessing as they do a "southern spontaneity which we feel our own too white, death-ridden culture denies us. . . . The Cubans know a lot about spontaneity, gaiety, sensuality and freaking out. They are not linear, desiccated creatures of print culture."

Indeed not: supine, desiccated creatures of a Communist tyranny would be more like it, though patronizing honky talk about "southern spontaneity" doubtless made things seem much better when this was written. In the great contest for writing the most fatuous line of political drivel, Sontag is always a contender. This essay contains at least two gems: after ten years, she writes, "the Cuban revolution is astonishingly free of repression and bureaucratization"; even better perhaps, is this passing remark delivered in parentheses: "No Cuban writer has been or is in jail, or is failing to get his work published." Readers wishing to make a reality check should consult Paul Hollander's classic study *Political Pilgrims: Western Intellectuals in Search of the Good Society*, which cites Sontag's claim and then lists, in two or three pages, some of the many writers and artists who have been jailed, tortured, or executed by Castro's spontaneous gaiety.*

Sontag concocted a similar fairy tale when she went to Vietnam in 1968 courtesy of the North Vietnamese government. Her long essay "Trip to Hanoi" (1968) is another classic in the literature of political mendacity. Connoisseurs of the genre will especially savor Sontag's observation that the real problem for the North Vietnamese is that they "aren't good enough haters." Their fondness for Americans, she explains, keeps getting in the way of the war effort.

They genuinely care about the welfare of the hundreds of captured American pilots and give them bigger rations than

---

* Hollander quotes from "Dissent in Cuba," a 1979 essay by Carlos Ripoll: "Armando Valladares, a poet and painter, has been imprisoned for the last 19 years. . . . The young poet Miguel Sales was given a 25-year sentence in 1974 after he was found preparing to flee Cuba with his wife and infant daughter. . . . Another poet, Angel Cuadra, . . . served two-thirds of a 15-year sentence. . . . Cuban penal legislation prescribes sentences of up to eight years for those who 'create, distribute or possess' written or oral 'propaganda' 'against the socialist state.'" Et cetera.

the Vietnamese population gets, "because they're bigger than we are," as a Vietnamese army officer told me, "and they're used to more meat than we are." People in North Vietnam really do believe in the goodness of man . . . and in the perennial possibility of rehabilitating the morally fallen.

It would be interesting to know what Senator John Mc-Cain, a prisoner of war who was brutally tortured by the North Vietnamese, had to say about this little fantasia.

Sontag acknowledges that her account tended somewhat to idealize North Vietnam; but that was only because she "found, through direct experience, North Vietnam to to be a place which, in many respects, *deserves* to be idealized." Unlike any country in Western Europe, you understand, and above all unlike the United States. "The Vietnamese are 'whole' human beings, not 'split' as we are." In 1967, shortly before her trip to Hanoi, Sontag had this to say about the United States:

> A small nation of handsome people . . . is being brutally and self-righteously slaughtered . . . by the richest and most grotesquely overarmed, most powerful country in the world. America has become a criminal, sinister country— swollen with priggishness, numbed by affluence, bemused by the monstrous conceit that it has the mandate to dispose of the destiny of the world.

In "What's Happening in America (1966)," Sontag tells readers that what America "deserves" is to have its wealth "taken away" by the Third World. In one particularly notorious passage, she writes that "the truth is that Mozart, Pascal, Boolean algebra, Shakespeare, parliamentary government, baroque churches, Newton, the emancipation of women, Kant, Marx, and Balanchine ballets don't redeem what this particular civilization has wrought upon the world. The white race *is* the cancer of human history." After a bout with cancer in the 1970s, Sontag emended that last observation because on reflection she had come to believe that it was unfair—to cancer.

A tourist of reality

What can one say? Sontag excoriates American capitalism for its "runaway rate of productivity." But she has had no scruples about enjoying the fruits of that productivity: a Rockefeller Foundation grant in 1964, a Merrill Foundation grant in 1965, a Guggenheim Foundation Fellowship in 1966, etc., etc., culminating in 1990 with a MacArthur Foundation "genius" award.

It is not simply in such mundane terms, however, that Sontag wants to have it both ways. Inveterate aestheticism entails intractable intellectual and moral frivolity. Some years after instructing us on the "right way" to love the Cuban revolution, she finally blasted the Castro regime for its brutal treatment of certain approved writers. But her condemnation meant little more than her initial enthusiasm. It was, as she herself might put it, merely "formal": the content didn't count. It was the same at the famous Town Hall symposium in 1982 when Sontag stunned the audience with reflections like this:

> Imagine, if you will, someone who read only the *Reader's Digest* between 1950 and 1970, and someone in the same period who read only *The Nation* or the *New Statesman.* Which reader would have been better informed about the realities of Communism? The answer, I think, should give us pause. Can it be that our enemies were right?

97

Sontag had plenty of throat-clearing qualifications about how she, too, "detest[ed] the Reagan Administration"— about "Reagan the union-buster, Reagan the puppet master of the butchers in El Salvador," etc.—but she nonetheless concluded her remarks with the famous announcement that "Communism *is* fascism." How piquant that Susan Sontag should finally face up to this elementary truth!

Or did she? Immediately after making that declaration she went on to add that if "Communism is itself a variant . . . of fascism," it is nevertheless "Fascism with a human face." In her essay "On Style," Sontag had assured her readers that Leni Riefenstahl's Nazi films "transcend the categories of propaganda or even reportage": the content of the films—i.e., their endorsement of Nazi ideology—has come "to play a purely formal role." Ten years later, in an essay called "Fascinating Fascism" (1974), she says the opposite: that the "very conception" of *Triumph of the Will* "negates the possibility of the filmmaker's having an aesthetic conception independent of propaganda." Taxed by an interviewer with the contradiction, Sontag replied that "both statements illustrate the richness of the form-content distinction, as long as one is careful always to use it against itself." "Rich" is indeed the *mot juste*.

In her book *On Photography* (1977), Sontag says that photography transforms people into "tourists of reality." It is a neat phrase: vivid, arresting, overstated. But as she has shown over and over, Sontag herself is just such a tourist. One day she embraces camp, the next day she warns about the "perils of over-generalizing the aesthetic view of life." As the critic Hilton Kramer observed in his review of *The Susan Sontag Reader*, "it is not that Sontag was ever prepared to abandon her stand on aestheticism and all its implications. It was only that she did not want it to cost her anything." Sontag once noted that "the relation between boredom and Camp taste cannot be overestimated." One suspects that boredom underlies a good deal of her unhappy radicalism. Discontented with "the Matthew Arnold notion of culture," she abandoned the question of "how to live" and became instead a harbinger of aesthetic nihilism and radical chic politics.

When Sontag began writing, in the early 1960s, the kind of programmatic contempt she exhibited for the Arnoldian humanistic tradition was still a fringe phenomenon. Although warning signs were beginning to flash, the major cultural institutions in America had not yet caught up with the "new sensibility" she both embodied and proclaimed: a sensibility that rejected seriousness while embracing amoralism and histrionic political radicalism. All that was about to change. Within a very few years, "the Matthew Arnold idea of culture" was everywhere in rout. The universities—institutions pre-eminently charged with perpetuating the Arnoldian inheritance—were the scenes of the most violent confrontations and abject betrayals of principle. They provided the perfect breeding ground for the anti-American radicalism extolled by figures like Sontag. When the dust had cleared, the universities were still standing, their faculties and departments intact. But the long march of the cultural revolution had largely transformed them from bastions of Arnoldian humanism into repositories of politically correct sentiment in which intellectual standards had collapsed. As Sontag herself put it, "one important consequence of the new sensibility (with its abandonment of the Matthew Arnold idea of culture) . . . [is] that the distinction between 'high' and 'low' culture seems less and less meaningful." What we had witnessed was the spectacle of wholesale capitulation—a liberal capitulation to the grim yet smirking radicalism whose goal was the destruction of an intellectual tradition and, ultimately, a way of life.

Chapter 4
The Liberal Capitulation

*Do you know that we are tremendously powerful already? . . . Listen.
I've reckoned them all up: a teacher who laughs with children at their
God and at their cradle is on our side. The lawyer who defends an
educated murderer because he is more cultured than his victims . . . is
one of us. . . . The juries who acquit every criminal are ours. The
prosecutor who trembles at a trial for fear he should not seem advanced
enough is ours, ours. Among officials and literary men we have lots,
lots. . . . Do you know how many we shall catch by little, ready-made
ideas? When I left Russia, Littré's doctrine that crime is insanity was
all the rage; I came back to find that crime is no longer insanity, but
simply common sense, almost a duty; anyway, a gallant protest.*
—Dostoevski, *The Possessed*, 1872

*There is nothing I have said or will say which will not be modified by
changing circumstances.*
—James A. Perkins, president of Cornell University, 1963–1969

A cultural Pearl Harbor

Although neither the "new sensibility" championed by
Susan Sontag nor the ethos of the hipster advocated by
Norman Mailer first arose on college campuses, both soon
found a warm welcome in the halls of academe. Like the

gospel according to the Beats, the messages purveyed by Mailer and Sontag were deeply inimical to everything that the traditional university stood for—what Susan Sontag had referred to contemptuously as "the Matthew Arnold notion of culture." When Norman Mailer wrote that the only authentic response to "the totalitarian tissues" of contemporary American life was "to divorce oneself from society" and "to encourage the psychopath in oneself," he found an eager audience among professors and students who were as mesmerized as was Mailer by what he called the "strategy of the hipster." Indeed, perhaps no phenomenon more vividly epitomizes the long march of America's cultural revolution than the student uprisings that swept across college and university campuses from the mid-1960s through the early 1970s. What began in 1964 with demonstrations by members of the Free Speech Movement at the University of California at Berkeley soon engulfed hundreds of campuses and made front-page news everywhere.

The ostensible political issues—the Vietnam conflict, curricular reform, housing arrangements for racial minorities, university investment policies, and so on—were quickly assimilated to a much broader emancipationist program that had vast moral as well as intellectual implications. Students may have marched to protest the presence of the ROTC on campus, university rules governing political activism, or U.S. policy in Southeast Asia. But in the end such issues were mere rallying points for a revolution in sensibility, a revolution that brought together radical politics, drug abuse, sexual libertinage, an obsession with rock music, exotic forms of spiritual titillation, a generalized antibourgeois animus, and an attack on the intellectual and moral foundations of the entire humanistic enterprise. Recall Susan Sontag's paean to Castro's Cuba, in which she wrote that "Rock, grass, better orgasms, freaky clothes, grooving on nature—really grooving on anything—unfits, maladapts a person for the American way of life." By the end of the 1960s, that message was nowhere more enthusiastically embraced than on American college campuses.

It is difficult at this distance to recapture the suddenness and fury of those insurrectionary episodes. The consternation of early press accounts—at the beginning, even *The New York Times* was aghast—shows that the assault, like a kind of cultural Pearl Harbor, caught the nation totally unprepared. As the philosopher (and then president of Boston University) John Silber ruefully noted in 1974, "from the first seizure of a campus building at the University of California at Berkeley on 2 December 1964," the transformation of public opinion about American universities "took just four years."* Our present complacency, as we look back on those events, is one measure of how successful the revolution turned out to be. The whole cultural climate of America, including the climate of higher education, was transformed by that blitzkrieg of radical activism. What had been a society defined and guided by allegiance to classic liberal ideals—the ideal, for example, that distinguished sharply between disinterested academic inquiry and political activism—suddenly found itself at the mercy of a distinctly illiberal radicalism. The Middlebury English professor Jay Parini put the point candidly in an article for *The Chronicle of Higher Education* in 1988:

> After the Vietnam War, a lot of us didn't just crawl back into our literary cubicles; we stepped into academic posi-

---

* Silber is careful not to blame Clark Kerr, then in charge of the University of California "multiversity," for the disaster. "After all," Silber observed, "higher education in this country has no Distant Early Warning system, unless it be California itself."

tions. With the war over, our visibility was lost, and it seemed for a while—to the unobservant—that we had disappeared. Now we have tenure, and the work of reshaping the universities has begun in earnest.

That work has been proceeding apace. If American universities these days are rarely scenes of serious student agitation, that is partly—perhaps primarily—because there is little that the radicals demanded that they did not get: Afro-American studies programs? Women's studies, gay studies, gender and transgender studies? Segregated classrooms and dormitories and even entire colleges set up for supposedly victimized minorities? Open admissions? Yes to all, and also to dumbing down the curriculum, destroying academic standards, bringing politics into the center of the humanistic enterprise. Was there anything that the radicals wanted that college administrations were not eager to grant them? Consider, to take just one example, the near universality of so-called "affirmative action"—i.e., preferential treatment based on race, sex, or some other approved badge of minority or victim status. That this bit of Orwellian Newspeak has passed largely unchallenged into the language is itself an enormous victory for the forces challenging the traditional, liberal idea of the university. Yes, there have recently been some efforts—notably in California—to roll back affirmative action and to rename it for what it is: a systematic regime of preferential treatment. But these efforts have taken place against the grain and against the opposition of the entire liberal establishment from *The New York Times* to the president of nearly every major college and university.

This is hardly surprising. The phrase "affirmative action" is too good to give up on. For one thing, it has allowed radicals the luxury of institutionalizing racial and sexual discrimination under the banner of liberal virtue. Henceforth, discriminating against certain classes of people can be taken as a means of ending discrimination. In the academy, the result of this mendacity has been to politicize not only college admissions policies, but also hiring and promotion practices for the faculty, decisions about the curriculum, grading, methods of teaching, and student life. In every case, bedrock liberal principles—that preferment ought to be based on achievement, that everyone is equal before the law—were shamelessly abandoned in the face of political pressure. Perhaps the greatest victory of this sort for the radicals was to popularize the idea that *everything* is political—a conviction that eats away at the very heart of classical liberalism. Henceforth, the *merits* of an argument—its probability or truth value or explanatory power—must be subordinated to the tests of political rectitude. Lenin's famous formula of power politics—what mattered, he said, was "Who whom"—made a gigantic comeback on American campuses, where the only absolute was that truth is relative.

Liberalism lost

The complex story of student protest movements in this country yields a series of cautionary tales. One of the central dramas concerns the fate of liberalism itself. The disheartening spectacle of liberal university administrators abasing themselves and their institutions before law-breaking radicals signalled not simply a failure of nerve. Even more troubling, it expressed a profound crisis in the fundamental principles upon which higher education in Western democratic societies had always rested. Whether this bespoke an essential weakness in liberal ideology or only a failure of particular men faced with difficult decisions is perhaps an open question. Critics of liberalism will note that liberalism's tendency to let tolerance and openness trump every other virtue renders it peculiarly impotent when faced with substantive moral dilemmas: absolutized, "tolerance" and "openness" become indistinguishable from moral paralysis. What we know for a certainty is that the liberal capitulation of university administrators in the Sixties and Seventies helped enormously to establish—and to institutionalize—the radical ethos of the counterculture.

The basic outlines of this capitulation were present from the beginning. As the sociologist Nathan Glazer observed in his 1965 essay "What Happened at Berkeley," the agitation for "free speech" that erupted at Berkeley in 1964 contained all the elements of a well-organized political coup.

> Those of us who watched the Free Speech Movement (FSM) daily set up its loud-speakers on the steps of the administration building to denounce the president, the chancellor, the newspapers, the Regents, the faculty, and the structure and organization of society in general and universities in particular, could only admire the public-relations skill exhibited in the choice of a name for the student movement.

The catalytic issue at Berkeley was the disposition of a twenty-six-foot strip of land at the entrance to the campus. Students, who believed that the land was owned by the City of Berkeley, had been using it for political purposes, soliciting funds, distributing political literature, and the like. When campus officials announced that the strip of land was in fact university property and therefore subject to university regulations regarding political activity, the results were student protests and the birth of the Free Speech Movement. The ensuing confrontation produced endless rallies, marches, protests, and vigils, some of which involved upwards of seven thousand people and which brought the university to the edge of collapse.

The slogan was "free speech." But the real issue, Glazer pointed out, was not free speech—the students already enjoyed that right—but "the student demand that the university allow them facilities for full political action and give up its right to discipline them for what it consider[ed] improper use of these facilities." In other words, the demand for "free speech" was really a demand that the university transform itself from an academic community into an operating base for political radicalism.

In a speech called "An End to History," Mario Savio, a philosophy student who was one of the prime movers of the FSM, claimed that the chief issues were "racial injustice" and "automation." A pamphlet distributed in January 1965 by the FSM elaborated on such themes: since "politics and education are inseparable," the "main purpose of the university" should not be "passing along the morality of the middle class, nor the morality of the white man, nor even the morality of the potpourri we call 'western society.'"

The authors of this pamphlet were a bit fuzzy about what they thought the "main purpose" of the university should be. Rebelling against the "excessive greed" and "machinery" of the educational establishment was clearly a prominent ingredient.

For anyone not caught up in their rhetoric, however, such animadversions tended mostly to reinforce a point that the sociologist Seymour Martin Lipset made in his introductory essay to *The Berkeley Student Revolt*. "A high incidence of intense student political activity," Lipset noted, "is in some sense an indication of the failure of a university as an academic community, particularly since in most cases such activity involves a rejection of the intellectual leadership of the faculty, a denigration of scholarship to a more lowly status than that of politics within the university itself." To the extent that a campus is politicized, Lipset concluded, "academic freedom is threatened, if not destroyed." In his reflections on "well poisoning" in academe, John Silber made a similar point. In the 1960s and early 1970s, Silber noted,

> Academics developed a novel meaning for the term "political crime," which had once meant an action rendered criminal solely by its political content but which now came to mean a crime—however vicious—justified by its political motivation. This new definition of "political crime" found swift adoption not merely on college campuses but throughout the world, as hijackers, kidnappers, killers, and Watergate "plumbers" justified their contempt for law through inappropriate appeal to political motivation. . . .
>
> Not only was political crime given a novel meaning; the concept of academic freedom was transformed. Once, it entailed an immunity for what is said and done by dedicated, thoughtful, conscientious scholars in pursuit of truth or the truest account. Now it came to entail, rather, an immunity for whatever is said and done, responsibly or carelessly, within or without the walls of academia, by persons unconcerned for the truth; who, reckless, incompetent, frivolous or even malevolent, promulgate ideas for which they can claim no expertise, or even commit deeds for which they can claim no sanction of law.

This is what Silber referred to as "the absolute concept of academic freedom," according to which "the academic can say whatever he pleases about whatever he pleases, whenever and wherever he pleases, and be fully immune from unpleasant consequences."

Living as we do at a time when virtually all cultural institutions have been politicized by the radical imperatives of the counterculture, it may be difficult to appreciate how thoroughly traditional Lipset's encomium to academic independence and Silber's reflections on academic freedom are. It was not so long ago, in fact, that an insistence on the autonomy of intellectual work in the academy was a prime tenet of liberal orthodoxy. The diplomat and historian George F. Kennan, for example, gave expression to this conviction in his once-famous essay "Rebels Without a Program," published in 1968 at the height of the radical assault on the universities:

> There is an ideal that has long been basic to the learning process as we have known it. . . . It is the ideal of the association of the process of learning with a certain remoteness from the contemporary scene—a certain detachment and seclusion, a certain voluntary withdrawal and renunciation of participation in contemporary life in the interests of the achievement of a better perspective on that life when the period of withdrawal is over.

That this ideal of scholarly seclusion had lately been abrogated on campuses across the country was something that Kennan regarded with profound concern. "The fact of the matter," he noted, "is that the state of being *enragé* is simply incompatible with fruitful study."

Kennan's essay is a sad, lucid, and searching piece of work, full of penetrating observations on the moral and spiritual depredations of the counterculture. About the glorification of drugs as an aid to expanded consciousness, for example, he bluntly castigates the "error" of believing that

> the human being has marvelous resources within himself

that can be released and made available to him merely by the passive submission to certain sorts of stimuli. . . . There is no pose more fraudulent . . . than that of the individual who pretends to have been exalted and rendered more impressive by his communion with some sort of inner voice whose revelations he is unable to describe or to enact.

Kennan admits that he pities the devotees of free love and boundless revolution. But he also acknowledges that pity is sometimes difficult to muster "because they themselves are so pitiless."

There is, in this cultivation of an absolute freedom, and above all in the very self-destructiveness with which it often expresses itself, a selfishness, a hardheartedness, a callousness, an irresponsibility, an indifference to the feelings of others, that is its own condemnation. No one ever destroys just himself alone. Such is the network of intimacy in which every one of us is somehow embraced, that whoever destroys himself destroys to some extent others as well. Many of these people prattle about the principle of love; but their behavior betrays this principle in the most elementary way. Love . . . is itself an obligation, and as such is incompatible with the quest for a perfect freedom.

We shall return to Kennan's essay below. Here it is worth noting to what extent it represents a species of liberalism that has been undone by its accommodation with countercultural radicalism. Today, no academic liberal would be caught dead repeating Kennan's analysis. In this sense, his essay serves as a marker of how much liberalism has lost.

The battles precipitating that loss were being waged in the months before and after Kennan published "Rebels Without a Program" in 1968. At Harvard, radical students seized buildings and issued a series of "non-negotiable demands." At Columbia, a dean was held hostage, the president's office was occupied, and his files were looted. In response to this mayhem, the Frankfurt School psychologist Erich Fromm—author of *The Art of Loving* and *Escape from Freedom*—happily declared that this was "a revolution in the name of life" in the midst of a culture of "zombies."

Similar outrages were occurring at campuses large and small, distinguished and undistinguished, all across the country. Taking over buildings and smashing up property had, as *Time* magazine put it in April 1969, become a "deplorable custom." The general pattern that emerged was irresponsible, self-aggrandizing license on the part of students; fretful collaboration on the part of faculties; and pusillanimous capitulation on the part of administrators. Of course, there were a few exceptions. But for the most part, as John Silber observed, it was a matter of "Operation Pander." The inaction of university presidents, Silber wrote,

> was established and quickly set a pattern for vacillation emulated by administrators across the nation, just as the mindless behavior of Mark Rudd [the head of the Students for a Democratic Society at Columbia] and his band of militants found student imitators as Rudd travelled across the country lecturing on desecration as art.

Among the hundreds of incidents, events at Cornell University in April 1969 and Yale University in April 1970 stand out. There were more violent and destructive protests elsewhere. But nowhere was the behavior of administrators and faculty more craven. The protagonists of both events deserve a special place in the annals of liberal capitulation.

Operation Pander

For pusillanimity and sheer collapse of principle, James A. Perkins, then the president of Cornell, must take the palm. Perkins had come from the Carnegie Foundation in 1963 to assume the presidency of Cornell. A Quaker, Perkins was, as *Newsweek* put it at the time, "the liberal president of a liberal institution." He came brimful of good intentions and simplistic misunderstandings of human nature. As Donald Alexander Downs notes in *Cornell '69: Liberalism and the Crisis of the American University*, "no one personified what was at stake as much as James Perkins. Sporting a résumé studded with all-star national and international appointments, the tall, elegant Perkins was a quintessential progressive liberal of his era."

One of Perkins's first orders of business was to create a Committee on Special Educational Projects to recruit black students whose SAT scores were well below (175 points below, as it happened) the average of Cornell's entering class. Perkins wanted to show what a bit of liberal education could do by way of social engineering. So what if these black students, many of whom were from urban ghetto areas, came totally unequipped to take advantage of an ivy-league education? What was the accident of human nature in the face of liberal nostrums about the transforming power of education? All it took were a few liberal clichés about the importance of innovation and creativity to overcome any objections on that score.

The results of Perkins's experiment ran entirely according to script. The number of black students at Cornell rapidly rose from 25 to about 250. Seeking solidarity, they banded together to form an Afro-American Society. They then began issuing various demands: for separate, black-only living quarters; for an Afro-American Studies Program, again, for blacks only; finally, they demanded that the university create an autonomous degree-granting college-within-a-college for the exclusive use of black students, the aim of which was to "create the tools necessary for the formation of a black nation." One statement informed the world that "whites can make no contributions to Black Studies except in an advisory, non–decision making or financial capacity."

Of course, such separatist militancy was totally at odds with Perkins's liberal principles. He had brought these blacks to Cornell to integrate them into academic society, not to watch them reproduce a segregated environment. But liberal principles, at least in the hands of men like Perkins, turn out to be remarkably pliable. The demand for the autonomous college was presented to him as an ultimatum. After a certain amount of tergiversation, Perkins acceded, noting petulantly that he was "extremely reluctant to accept this idea of a college exclusive to one race, but [that he was] not finally opposed to it; it would involve a lot of rearranging of [his] own personality." In "The Assault on the Universities: Then and Now" (1997), the political philosopher Walter Berns, a professor at Cornell in the 1960s, noted that "in the event . . . [Perkins's] 'personality' needed no rearrangement." Temperamentally, he was predisposed to capitulate. As Perkins himself put it later, "there is nothing I have said or will say which will not be modified by changing circumstances." Events, which began to unfold rapidly, showed that he was not exaggerating.

In 1968, black students at Cornell charged a visiting professor of economics with racism because he had dared to judge African nations by a "Western" standard of development. The administration required an apology from the professor; he complied, but the students were not satisfied and took possession of the economics department, holding the chairman and his secretary prisoner for eighteen hours. The students were never punished. An investigating dean exonerated the professor but charged Cornell with "institutional racism." As Walter Berns noted, what began as an attack on "racism" "quickly became an assault on the integrity of the academic enterprise, an assault that was bound to succeed because it was met with only nominal resistance on the part of the faculty and none at all from the administration."

The following months saw an escalating pattern of "nonnegotiable demands," vandalism, and violence. Buildings were occupied, hostages taken, college property destroyed. In December 1968, a white reporter for the college newspaper was beaten up by a black student. When black students requested seventeen hundred dollars to buy bongo drums for Malcolm X Day, the administration compromised by offering them a thousand dollars and flying two students to New York City in the college plane to buy the drums. In February 1969, at a symposium on South Africa, Perkins was challenged to defend Cornell's investment policy, which included holding stock in banks that lent money to South Africa. During his talk, a black student leaped onto the stage, grabbed Perkins by the collar, and seized the microphone from him. When the head of Cornell's security force rushed to Perkins's aid, he was held at bay by another black student wielding a two-by-four. According to the college newspaper, blacks in the audience responded by beating on the bongo drums the university had so graciously bought for them while Perkins was heard to whisper, "You better let go of me, you better let go of me!"

Matters came to a crisis in the spring of 1969. On Saturday, April 19, during parents' weekend, some one hundred black students walked into Willard Straight Hall shortly before 6:00 A.M. and gave the occupants ten minutes to leave. Eleven doors were broken down with crowbars when occupants were slow in responding. Some thirty parents and forty college employees were forcibly ejected from the building. University officials then stood by passively while the black students armed themselves with knives, rifles, and ammunition. With militants from the Students for a Democratic Society (SDS) forming a protective guard outside, the blacks settled down for what turned out to be a thirty-five-hour occupation of the building. According to a broadcast on a student radio show, the protest had been undertaken because of Cornell's "racist attitudes" and because it "lacked a program relevant to the black students." When some white students broke into the building later in the day, a scuffle ensued that sent several students to the infirmary. One black shouted out the warning that "if any more whites come in . . . you're gonna die here." Allan Bloom, who was teaching at Cornell at the time, reflected on the significance of this episode later in an essay called "The Democratization of the University": "When black students carrying guns and thousands of white students supporting them insisted that the faculty abandon the university's judicial system, the minimal condition of civil community within the university, and backed up that insistence with threats, the faculty capitulated." At the time of the confrontation, Bloom told Homer Bigart, who did a masterly job reporting on the episode for *The New York Times*, that "the resemblance on all levels to the first stages of a totalitarian take-over are almost unbelievable."

"We want to be your friends"

Central to the demands issued by the occupiers was that disciplinary action against three black students involved in an earlier incident be dropped. Steven Muller, vice-president for public affairs at Cornell, promised to recommend to the faculty that they vote to nullify the reprimands. An agreement was worked out and signed, and the black students, in an image that made the front page of newspapers across the country, vacated the building victorious, clutching rifles and sporting ammunition belts, their clenched fists raised in defiance. (Asked by a reporter if he would characterize the agreement as a "complete capitulation," Muller responded that he would "characterize it as anything but." He neglected, however, to say why.)

On Monday, the deeply divided Cornell faculty, in perhaps the last show of spine by an academic body in the U.S., voted, by a margin of 726 to 281, not to dismiss the penalties. "The presence of arms and the seizure of Willard Straight Hall," the motion read, "make it impossible for the Faculty to agree at this meeting to dismiss the penalties imposed on the three students." In response, white and black radicals joined forces and occupied a faculty building. Soon they had attracted some twenty-five hundred students. Thomas W. (Tom) Jones, one of the gun-toting blacks involved in the Straight Hall takeover, informed them that the faculty had voted for a "showdown." The next day, speaking on a local radio station, Jones threatened that seven faculty members and administrators would be "dealt with." "If you believe in your principle sufficiently," he warned, "then be ready to die for it." In response, several professors moved their families to motels for the night. Jones, demanding that the faculty meet again and nullify the penalties, declared that "Cornell has three hours to live. . . . We are moving tonight."

In the event, Jones waited, with the two-thousand or more students occupying the building, until the faculty met the next day to reconsider the demand for nullification.

Not all of the professors were cowards. James J. John, for example, a professor of history, eloquently argued that

> if we had a good reason for not dismissing the charges on Monday, . . . we have a stronger reason for not doing so today. . . . This university, I believe, can survive the expulsion or departure of no matter what number of students and the destruction of buildings far better than it can survive the death of principle.

But apparently a vast majority of the faculty agreed with Max Black, the Sage Professor of Philosophy, who, declaring that "I don't need to be intimidated," assured students that "we want to be your friends." When a voice vote was taken, nullification passed by an estimated seven hundred to three hundred. The hand-wringing rationalizations of the Cornell faculty for this unconscionable collapse make for nauseating reading. They all said how badly they felt about changing their vote; they "resented" the pressure; it was a "bitter pill." *But, still, however*: it reminds one of nothing so much as Ralph Buchsbaum's classic zoological text, *Animals Without Backbones*. As Tom Jones observed when addressing a crowd of students after the vote: "That decision was made right here. They didn't make any decision; they were told from this room what to do."

There were other humiliations. That evening, when Perkins went to address the students, he was publicly mocked by a black student leader who ostentatiously kept him waiting to speak. A white student "picked his way across the crowded stage, grabbed a can of Pepsi-Cola that Perkins had been drinking from, and lifted it high for all to see. Then he drank from it and handed it back to the president." Perkins's response, when he was finally allowed to speak, was to salute the meeting as "one of the most positive forces ever set in motion in the history of Cornell."

And what was the upshot of this disgusting episode? Several of Cornell's most distinguished professors resigned, including Walter Berns, Allan Bloom, and Allan P. Sindler, chairman of the government department. There was some justice. Perkins resigned—or was forced to resign (accounts vary)—and went to a foundation job in New York (he died in 1998). But Steven Muller went on to become president of Johns Hopkins University. And Tom Jones, one of the most militant of the black radicals, eventually became the president of TIAA-CREF, the world's largest pension fund. In 1993, Jones was appointed to the Cornell board of trustees. And in 1995, in a final surreal twist, he made a large contribution to Cornell to endow the annual Perkins Prize "for the student, faculty, staff member or program that has done the most during the preceding year to promote interracial understanding and harmony on campus."*

The panther and the bulldog

These grotesque events were bad enough in themselves. But their real significance was as a prelude to similar depredations elsewhere. As Allan Bloom noted at the time, when the Cornell faculty caved in, students discovered that "pompous teachers who catechized them about academic freedom could, with a little shove, be made into dancing bears." While it would be a mistake to saddle Perkins with responsibility for all the horrors that have been visited upon

---

* Readers nervous at the thought of Jones at the helm of TIAA may rest easy: as of this writing he is chief executive officer of the Smith-Barney Asset Management division.

higher education since his tenure at Cornell, his capitulation to the totalitarian demands of the student radicals had ramifications far beyond Ithaca, New York. "By surrendering to students armed with guns," Walter Berns pointed out, Perkins had

> made it easier for those who came after him to surrender to students armed only with epithets ("racists," "sexists," "elitists," "homophobes"); by inaugurating a black studies program, Perkins paved the way for Latino studies programs, women's studies programs, and multicultural studies programs; by failing to support a professor's freedom to teach, he paved the way for speech codes and political correctness; and of course he pioneered the practice of affirmative action admissions and hiring.

In other words, by his capitulations, Perkins did a great deal to politicize the university and undermine its claims to intellectual independence. As Donald Alexander Downs noted, "the Cornell crisis was a watershed in terms of the tension between the pursuit of social justice and academic freedom, which in turn reflects the larger debate over the meaning of the university."

The pusillanimous collapse of Cornell's administration and faculty when faced with threats of violence was in some ways the most depressing spectacle of the whole student protest movement. But perhaps equally, if more subtly, significant for the future of higher education was the rally-cum-university-wide-strike that took place at Yale University in the Spring of 1970. By that time, the antics of student radicals not only had become a well-established, almost habitual, part of university life, but also had forged strong links with radical elements elsewhere in American culture. The dramatis personae were nearly always the same: On one side were a dithering administration and faculty only too willing to compromise on essential principles of academic integrity in the quest to be hip, liberal, "with it." On the other side was a student body increasingly inflamed by drugs, puerile political slogans, and the astonishing realization that their elders were prepared to countenance almost any outrage as long as it was suitably packaged as an expression of anguished idealistic passion. Indeed, as the decade unfolded, those elders went from tolerating or countenancing adolescent "idealism" to embracing it themselves. The maturation of the student protest movement turned out to be part of the infantilization of the American intelligentsia.

Like the Cornell debacle, the story of the New Haven rally and Yale strike forms a complex tale with many actors and subplots. The whole story is admirably laid out by John Taft, a student at Yale at the time, in *Mayday at Yale: A Case Study in Student Radicalism* (1976). Here it is enough to recount a few highlights. In the background was the murder trial in New Haven of Bobby Seale, chairman of the Black Panther Party, and eight other Panthers. Seale had been accused of ordering the torture and murder of Alex Rackley, a young black man suspected of being a police informer. In May 1969, Rackley's battered body—covered with bruises, burns from cigarettes and boiling water, and ice-pick wounds—had been fished out of the Coginchaug River, twenty-five miles north of New Haven. The Panthers, in collusion with radicals at and outside of Yale, began fomenting unrest in the Yale community and planning a rally to support Seale and his co-defendants.

Early on in the court proceedings, a judge charged two Panthers who were sitting in the visitors' section with contempt of court and jailed them. This galvanized radical elements in and around Yale, who began complaining loudly that the Black Panthers could not get a fair trial.* Fresh from his stint defending the Chicago Seven, William Kunstler—a classmate and old friend of Yale's patrician president Kingman Brewster—came to New Haven to speak at a Panther fund-raiser held at Yale's Woolsey Hall. Doug Miranda, area captain of the Black Panthers, began his remarks by asserting that Yale ("one of the biggest pig organizations") clearly had "something to do with the conspiracy" against the Panthers.

> Basically, what we are going to do is create conditions in which white folks are either going to have to kill pigs or defend themselves against black folks. . . . We're going to turn Yale into a police state. . . . You have to create peace by destroying the people who don't want peace.

Tensions grew quickly. At a meeting of campus radicals on April 15, 1970, various proposals to help the Panthers were floated, from kidnapping Kingman Brewster and shutting off New Haven's water supply to demanding an immediate moratorium on classes and requiring that the Yale Corporation donate half a million dollars to the Pan-

---

* Among those at Yale who vociferously supported the Panthers were Bill Lann Lee, now head of the Justice Department's Civil Rights Division, and Hillary Clinton (then Hillary Rodham). As David Brock noted in his book *The Seduction of Hillary Rodham* (a generally sympathetic account of its subject), "Hillary was not just one of the faceless thousands who appeared on the [New Haven] Green to show symbolic support. Rather than fire-bombing buildings, she was busy using the legal system to further the Panther cause." It was a strategy that worked. Ericka Huggins, who boiled the water with which Rackley was tortured, was later elected to a California school board. Warren Kimbro, who confessed to shooting Rackley in the head, won an affirmative-action scholarship to Harvard and became an assistant dean at Eastern Connecticut State College.

ther Defense Fund. A few days later, Miranda told a group of students that they had the "power to prevent a bloodbath at Yale." He proposed calling a student strike and having Yale demand that the Panthers be released. "There's no reason the Panther and the Bulldog [the Yale mascot] can't get together!" The slogans came fast and furious. "Shut it down, or burn!" "If Bobby dies, Yale fries!"

At Yale's twelve residential colleges, students congregated to discuss the Panthers' demands and to vote on whether to support a student strike. Robert Triffin, the Belgian-born master of Berkeley College, attempted to introduce a note of deliberation and sanity: "Do you know what you are doing? Do you realize what you are saying? Revolution is not a game. You do not play with revolution!" But his words, as Taft noted, had little effect. Typical was the attitude of a female undergraduate at Jonathan Edwards College: "Why don't we just vote to strike tonight, and we'll decide tomorrow what we're striking for!"

The two Yale officials who figured most prominently in this drama were the Rev. William Sloane Coffin, Jr., the university chaplain, and Kingman Brewster. Coffin—like the Berrigan brothers—was one of those self-infatuated radicals who poached on the authority of religion to bolster his sensation of righteousness. He was never happier than when organizing acts of civil disobedience. Accordingly, he proposed a nonviolent march to the New Haven Courthouse, where the demonstrators would then peacefully submit to arrest. The "white oppressors" of the Panther party, he said, should be treated as American colonials treated George III. Declaring that the trial was "legally right but morally wrong," he suggested that the Panthers should be set free.

For his part, Kingman Brewster was a model of cunning equivocation. With a symmetry that connoisseurs of hypocrisy will admire for decades to come, he showed himself capable of the ultimate pliability. His response to Coffin's support for the Panthers was to say that he regarded the university chaplain as worth "three full professors." On April 19, a few days before the faculty was to vote on whether or not to strike, Brewster solemnly affirmed Yale's official neutrality, noting that "it would not be proper to assume that justice cannot be dispensed by the courts in this state." On April 23, as a crowd of about a thousand students and Black Panthers gathered outside, the faculty met. With what might be deemed Perkinsian bravura, Brewster addressed the faculty: "I am skeptical," he said "of the ability of black revolutionaries to achieve a fair trial anywhere in the United States."

According to Taft, this declaration—which instantly gained nationwide notoriety was greeted by the faculty with "thunderous applause." Brewster then suggested various Orwellian changes in language: the black demand for a "suspension of normal academic function" would be altered to a "modification" of "normal expectations"; the proposal that faculty "should suspend their classes" would be changed to "should be free to suspend their classes." This was promptly adopted, voted on, and passed. But as one dissenting faculty member argued,

> A compromise was absurd. Either a university continues to operate as a university or it doesn't, and to say we shall stop being a university, but just for a while, compromises principles so much that it leaves no basis for existing.

The bottom line, as Taft comments, was that the faculty had "voted overwhelmingly to compromise the neutrality of the university. In response to intimidation, they had placed themselves in the hands of an administrator who, in the crunch, took a strictly pragmatic view of his duties as the head of an academic institution." The university-wide strike-cum-rally on the New Haven Green went ahead more or less as planned. Classes were temporarily suspended, and the Yale faculty voted to modify normal academic expectations for the term. A May Day demonstration drew some 15,000 people, including countercultural stars from Tom Hayden to Allen Ginsberg, Jerry Rubin, and Abbie Hoffman.

When authority falters

The liberal capitulation at Yale was perhaps not quite as ostentatiously fainthearted as the one at Cornell. But in some ways it may have been even more fateful. Yale is the more prominent institution. In 1970, the entire nation had its eyes fixed on events in New Haven, which, involving as they did a major criminal trial, implicated the legitimacy of our entire system of justice. An editorial in *The New York Times* called "Murdering Justice" observed,

> Those students and faculty members at Yale who are trying to stop a murder trial by calling a strike against the university have plunged the campus into new depths of irrationality. Some are so enamoured with the Black Panthers' revolutionary rhetoric that they reject the legitimacy of any court that might try Panther Chairman Bobby Seale.

Then, too, Kingman Brewster was a more commanding figure than James Perkins. Rich, handsome, articulate, he came to the Yale presidency with impeccable liberal credentials, above all in the area of civil rights. Had Kingman Brewster chosen to take a stand, the faculty might well have backed him up. The history not only of Yale's involvement in that sordid affair but also of American higher education in the decades that followed might well have been different. Like Perkins, Brewster aided in selling out the American university to forces that were inimical to its very essence. If colleges and universities continue to thrive today, they do so grievously compromised by political allegiances that stand in direct opposition to the ideals of academic independence and scholarly disinterestedness.

As for William Sloane Coffin's infatuation with law-breaking acts of civil disobedience, that, too, has cast a long and obfuscating shadow on American society. Coffin was prominent among those establishment liberals who taught their followers that contempt for the law was fine as long as one was certain of one's own higher virtue. It is an attitude that has taken hold throughout our society, and with disastrous results. As George Kennan observed in "Rebels Without a Program," one cannot purchase leave to break the law simply by being willing to pay the price:

> The violation of law is not . . . a privilege that lies offered for sale with a given price tag, like an object in a supermarket, available to anyone who has the price and is willing to pay for it. It is not like the privilege of breaking crockery in a tent at the county fair for a quarter a shot. Respect for the law is not an obligation which is exhausted or obliterated by willingness to accept the penalty for breaking it.

William Sloane Coffin and his like-minded peers did a great deal to delegitimize not only the laws and policies they disapproved of but also the very ideal of respect for law.

At the deepest level, the liberal capitulation signalled a crisis of confidence that was at the same time a crisis of values. It was not surprising that failures of authority were soon challenged by hostility. As the sociologist Edward

Shils noted in "Dreams of Plenitude, Nightmares of Scarcity" (1969), "Where authority abdicates through failures, ineptitude, and weakened self-confidence, it invites aggression against itself." A culture increasingly in thrall to politics is the fruit of that aggression.

Allan Bloom once observed that "the liberal university appears to be both the highest expression of liberal democracy and a condition of its perpetuation." The former, alas, has ceased to be true; and so anyone who cares about the future of this society must hope that the latter is untrue as well.

Chapter 5
The Politics of Delegitimation

We must recognize that justice is a higher social goal than law and order.
—William Sloane Coffin, Jr., 1972

To be radical is habitually *to do things which society at large despises.*
—Daniel Berrigan, S.J., 1968

We shall be told . . . that actions which bring damnation to the world-ling may be inculpable in the children of light. We must be prepared for strange alternations of rigorism and antinomianism as our history unfolds.
—Ronald Knox, *Enthusiasm*, 1950

The warm glow of self-satisfaction

In "Man's Second Disobedience" (1989), an essay about radicalism and the French Revolution, the English phi-losopher Roger Scruton observed that "the decisive feature of the revolutionary credo . . . is its provision of a criterion of legitimacy that no actual institution can ever pass." Note that there are two sides to this credo. One side—the smiling side—involves the seductive lullaby of perfectionism. Here we have a beguiling mixture of utopian dreams, elevating rhetoric, and ideals as simple (and often as simple-minded) as they are abstract. Proposing an impossible criterion of legitimacy, one is able to indulge in credulousness as a deliberate policy, undistracted by any contact with the less edifying realities of human nature. The other, more dour side of the revolutionary credo is the militant hangover from these intoxications: smug, righteous, peremptory, alternating wildly between the ecstasies of absolute self-regard and the implacable condemnation of the status quo.

In periods of brute political upheaval, this combination of toxins is deadly. The French Revolution, honing its guillotines with a rhetoric of virtue derived from Rousseau, dramatized this as surely as have the many grisly efforts to instantiate the tenets of Marxism, Fascism, and other utopian schemes in the course of this unhappy century. The philosopher Leszek Kolakowski summed it up neatly in his essay "The Death of Utopia Reconsidered" (1983): "Utopians, once they attempt to convert their visions into practical proposals, come up with the most malignant project ever devised: they want to institutionalize fraternity, which is the surest way to totalitarian despotism."

Of course, this utopian impulse expresses itself differently in a liberal democracy. When tumbrels and firing squads are unavailable, the upheaval tends to be primarily cultural or moral. But the element of fanaticism remains: a despotic subtext beneath the progressive rhetoric. The legal scholar Alexander Bickel was undoubtedly correct when he wrote, in 1970, that "to be a revolutionary in a society like ours, is to be a totalitarian, or not to know what one is doing." Or, he might have added, both. One of the most prominent features of the long march of America's cultural revolution was the sudden appearance in the mid-Sixties of utopian agitation where prudent affirmation and common sense once reigned.

The great catalyst for this development was without doubt the Vietnam conflict. Almost overnight, it seemed, the entire climate of elite opinion in the country underwent a startling metamorphosis. The ostensible issue was U.S. military involvement in Vietnam. But it soon became clear that Vietnam was merely the occasion for disruptions and demands that went far beyond any specific government policy. Vietnam became the banner under which the entire range of radical sentiment congregated. Michael Lind was right when he observed in *Vietnam: The Necessary War* that the conflict in Vietnam "uncovered, but did not create, deep divisions in the American body politic." Vietnam provided a rallying point, a crusade large enough to submerge all manner of ideological differences. Susan Sontag spoke for many left-wing intellectuals when she noted that "Vietnam offered the key to a systematic criticism of America." The Yippie leader Jerry Rubin put it even more bluntly: "If there had been no Vietnam war, we would have invented one. If the Vietnam war ends, we'll find another war." As Paul Hollander noted, Vietnam was "more a catalyst than a root cause of the rejection of American society in the 1960s." As the Sixties evolved, it became increasingly clear that what was at stake was not only the war. The real issue was our way of life: what used to be called without apology "the American way of life," with its social and political institutions, its moral assumptions, its unspoken confidences about what mattered.

One measure of the change wrought by this cultural offensive is the fact that even now, thirty or more years on, it is nearly impossible for anyone with a college education to speak of "the American way of life" without irony. To a large extent, that is because it is now practically taken for granted that going to college involves not so much the "questioning" as the repudiation of traditional moral and political values. (Or to put it another way: the academic "questioning" or "interrogation" of traditional values has only one right answer, "No.") The greater the exposure to higher education, the more thorough the repudiation is likely to be.* As Paul Hollander has shown in meticulous detail in his book on anti-Americanism, "institutions of higher education in America have since the 1960s become major resources or reservoirs of the adversary culture, the setting in which its values and beliefs are most frequently elaborated and displayed in the most unqualified form."

Not that such exhibitions of adversarial animus are confined to the academy. Far from it. They are part of the air we breathe: implicit as much in our degraded pop culture as they are in our assumptions about our responsibilities as citizens and moral agents. To put it somewhat paradoxically: one of the most profound effects of the long march of America's cultural revolution has been to institutionalize the assumption of institutional illegitimacy. It is less a matter of cynicism than a rejection of established authority: as if the very fact of being established undermined the legitimacy of an idea or institution.**

---

* The Australian philosopher David Stove spoke of "the frivolous elevation of 'the critical attitude' into a categorical imperative" in colleges and universities today. The principal result, Stove noted, has been "to fortify millions of ignorant graduates and undergraduates in the belief, to which they are already too firmly wedded by other causes, that the adversary posture is all, and that intellectual life consists in 'directionless quibble.'"

** One can trace this idea back at least to John Stuart Mill's attack on "the despotism of custom" and the "tyranny of [established] opinion" in *On Liberty*. For a criticism of Mill's position, see my essay "Mill, Stephen, and the Nature of Freedom" in *The Betrayal of Liberalism: How the Disciples of Freedom and Equality Helped Foster the Illiberal Politics of Coercion and Control*, edited by Hilton Kramer and Roger Kimball (Chicago: Ivan R. Dee, 1999), pages 43–69.

There are many facets to this phenomenon. One of the most curious concerns the role of certain religious figures who, in the mid-Sixties and early Seventies, brandished the phrase "civil disobedience" as a patent of moral rectitude and a license for lawlessness.

It was sanctioned by the civil rights movement, when various religious leaders participated in marches and demonstrations to end racial segregation. The nobility of that cause imbued the idea of civil disobedience with an aura of supreme moral urgency. Whether, even then, civil disobedience—i.e., illegal though (generally) nonviolent agitation—was justified was a question that could hardly be raised. The rightness of the cause made this question seem impertinent at best. Besides, there was the warm glow of self-satisfaction that attended participation in such activities. Increasingly, "civil disobedience" came to imply, at least to its advocates, obedience to a higher authority—the authority of one's conscience, first of all, but construed in such a way as to suggest the gratifying thought that the dictates of one's conscience were indistinguishable from the dictates of justice itself.

Those addicted to the pleasurable feeling of moral superiority found it an irresistible brew. By the time that Vietnam became an issue, civil disobedience had established itself as a prescription for moral intoxication, not to say anesthesia. Sanctioning illegality as an expression of higher virtue, the ethic of civil disobedience promised to transport its partisans to the ranks of a moral elect even as it undermined the authority of the law and its supporting institutions and beliefs. Never mind the contradictions that this situation bred: opportunities for moral megalomania were too precious to squander. Among the many individuals responsible for proselytizing the ethic of civil disobedience as a form of higher virtuousness, three deserve special mention: William Sloane Coffin, Jr., chaplain at Yale University during a crucial period in the Sixties and Seventies; and the Berrigan brothers, Daniel and Philip, Catholic priests whose names became synonymous with the antinomian uproar of Sixties radicalism.

Wrapping themselves in the mantle of a religious authority that, in one way or another, they repudiated by their actions, the Rev. Coffin and the Berrigan brothers made an enormous effort to legitimize the politics of delegitimation. Although they all seem like museum pieces today, in the late Sixties and early Seventies they epitomized one prominent side of America's cultural revolution. Members of the establishment, they nevertheless embraced a political program dedicated to the destruction of the establishment.

"The universal conscience of mankind"

Born in 1924 to a prominent New York WASP family, William Sloane Coffin, Jr., grew up in a privileged world of servants, penthouse apartments, summer houses, and expensive schools. He served in the army in World War II and matriculated at Yale after the war, "shamelessly bypass[ing] the Yale admissions office," he explains in his memoir, *Once to Every Man* (1977), "accepting the offer of Henri Peyre, the chairman of Yale's French department, that he accompany me on a visit to Dean De Vane." In the late 1940s, his fluency in Russian caught the notice of the newly formed Central Intelligence Agency. He had agreed to a two-year stint in the CIA when a lecture by Reinhold Niebuhr intervened and he decided instead to enroll in Union Theological Seminary, where he committed himself to "as much of God as I believed in." When the Korean War broke out in the summer of 1950, he left the seminary and joined the CIA, working as an operative in Germany until 1953. Looking back from the late 1970s, Coffin was clearly a bit embarrassed by his earlier, patriotic self. "National security," he comments, "is not a very important consideration in the Bible—not as compared to national righteousness and world security." Perhaps fortunately, he doesn't attempt to give chapter and verse for that conviction.

In the following years, Coffin completed his education at Yale Divinity School, worked as a chaplain at Andover and Williams College, and, in 1958, returned to Yale as chaplain. By the early 1960s, he was very active in the civil rights movement and was (as he puts it in a chapter title from his memoir) "Moving Toward Civil Disobedience"—toward a species of political activism he later described as "a form of moral jiu-jitsu." Gradually, he emerged as a national figure, lending the appearance of ecclesiastical gravitas to the Movement. And as he gained in prominence, he more and more cast himself in the self-dramatizing role of the man of conscience battling the world's injustices. "If we are to serve our country with our consciences," he wrote in a lecture delivered in 1972, "we must recognize that what is most important is not what the law requires but what justice demands."

As it turned out, Coffin was seldom in doubt about what justice demanded. When the Vietnam War got going, it demanded that he aid and abet young men in burning their draft cards, that he participate in marches on the Pentagon, and that he travel to Hanoi courtesy of the North Vietnamese government (where he promptly discovered "a very special feeling for the North Vietnamese, a feeling I attributed to the fact that we were friends because we had deliberately refused to become enemies"). As we have seen, in 1970, when Bobby Seale and eight other Black Panthers were on trial for murder in New Haven and it looked for a moment as if New Haven would erupt in a riot, justice demanded that William Sloane Coffin publicly declare in a sermon that the Panthers should go free because their trial was "legally right but morally wrong." Concluding that the situation was "prerevolutionary," he urged the Yale community to engage in nonviolent protests and acts of civil disobedience. "To those who say 'what if this were a Klansman on trial and his fellow Klansmen were threatening destruction?'" Coffin wrote, "I can only answer that, while releasing a Klansman would be increasing the power of the oppressor, the releasing of the defendants in this case would mean the sharing of power with the oppressed."

The New York Times, which was a very different sort of paper in 1970 from what it has since become, editorialized that, by delivering this sermon, Coffin had done

> his best to guarantee moral confusion among his student followers. Mr. Coffin said that even if Mr. Seale were to be found guilty as charged, the entire nation stands accused of bringing him to the state of mind in which the alleged crime might have been committed. This is a legally and morally wrong and dangerous concept, even when supposedly elevated to the level of theological doctrine.

The truth is that by the early 1970s, Coffin was dazzled by his sense of himself as a representative of what he described in one lecture as "the universal conscience of mankind." Acts of civil disobedience that dramatized the conflict between Coffin's own morality and the requirements of the law were his preferred means of exhibiting the workings of that conscience.

For Coffin and those who emulated him, it was the work of a moment to distinguish between what was "legally right but morally wrong." But as Morris I. Liebman noted in a debate with Coffin about civil disobedience, "in democratic societies any violation of the law is an uncivil act. This is true notwithstanding the motives of the violator." Indeed, there is a sense, Liebman remarked, in which "civil disobedience" is a misnomer, since its activities, by breaking the law, are by definition uncivil. Like most advocates of civil disobedience, Coffin was quick to cite the example of Henry David Thoreau. But Liebman is right to point out that Thoreau, who was essentially an anarchist, not a democrat, provides an unedifying precedent. Everyone remembers Thoreau's remark: "That government is best which governs least." It is less often recalled that he went on to say that "'that government is best which governs not at all;' and when men are prepared for it, that will be the kind of government they will have." As Liebman observed dryly, "the day that men are so prepared will be the day that men are angels."

Similarly, Coffin's appeal to the "rule of conscience" turns out to be a rule whose content is determined by William Sloane Coffin and his like-minded friends. "The advocates of civil disobedience," Liebman points out, "insist upon license which they would not permit to their opponents. The police, it seems, are to arrest members of the Ku Klux Klan, but not members of the Weathermen. Laws may be violated if, and only if, one is a member of the elite."

Purified by persecution

Coffin was hardly alone in seeing himself as part of a moral vanguard whose prerogatives included breaking the law when "the rule of conscience" said it was OK. Indeed, this form of self-infatuation was a defining characteristic of the new generation of radicals that populated America's cultural revolution. For example, the left-wing historian Howard Zinn once blithely informed his readers that civil disobedience should be allowed for programs of "liberal" but not "reactionary" reform. And who was to decide what counted as suitably "liberal"? Why, Mr. Zinn, of course. (The Marxist philosopher Herbert Marcuse, in a statement we shall return to in the next chapter, put this extraordinary idea in perhaps its baldest form: "Liberating tolerance," Marcuse wrote, "would mean intolerance against movements from the Right, and toleration of movements from the Left.")

William Sloane Coffin, acting from his position as a civil rights leader, chaplain of Yale University, and member in good standing of the American WASP aristocracy, did a great deal to legitimize this form of illegitimacy and illegality. His example helped to convince a generation that the law was dispensable when it conflicted with duly ratified liberal sentiments. That these sentiments should seem to be invested with the authority of religion made them all the more appealing to anyone seeking to enhance his sense of moral election. Of course, Coffin was not the only cleric to avail himself of this opportunity for self-aggrandizement. In fact, he was outflanked on the Left by a pair of Catholic priests who would remain important activists long after Coffin lapsed into irrelevance. Indeed, when it came to the sentimental blending of religious rhetoric and radical activism, Daniel and Philip Berrigan had few equals.

In background, the Berrigans could not have been more different from Coffin. He hailed from the genteel ranks of New York society; the Berrigans came from a poor Irish Catholic family that settled, finally, in Syracuse. Their father was a scrappy, depressive railroad man and farmer: a fount of bitter labor-union sentiment, bad poetry, and temper tantrums. Their mother was a devout and long-suffering woman who held the family of six boys together. Philip, the youngest, was born in 1923. Like four of his five elder brothers, he was bluff, athletic, and robust. Daniel, born in 1921, was delicate, with weak eyes and weak ankles—"a species of house boy," as his father contemptuously put it.

Daniel entered a Jesuit seminary near Poughkeepsie in 1939 when he was eighteen and was ordained in 1952. Philip, who fought with distinction in France and Germany during the war (an achievement he later disdained), entered a seminary of the Society of Saint Joseph—an order founded in the nineteenth century to help blacks—in 1950. (A third Berrigan son, Jerry, also entered the seminary but left before being ordained.) Although both of the younger Berrigans have written books, Daniel is by far the more literary. Like his father, he has produced prodigious quantities of bad poetry; unlike his father, he has managed to get reams of it published and even praised. (In *Disarmed and Dangerous*, a joint hagiography of Daniel and Philip by Murray Polner and Jim O'Grady that appeared in 1997, we are told that Daniel "had become a holy man, perhaps even a prophet, . . . to be admired, read, and reread fifty and one hundred years from now.")

Daniel's radicalization began on two trips to France and Eastern Europe in the mid-Fifties after his ordination. He affected the dress and hauteur of French worker-priests and came to regard persecution as a prerequisite of seriousness. In 1964, recalling with relish the hardships faced by religion in the Marxist countries he visited, he wrote that the churches there

> are small but purified by persecution. . . . The Christians under Marxism have returned to their pre-Constantinian

situation of being poor, pure, and persecuted, and they are leading the life which I believe God has decreed for the Church . . . what a great feeling, to be in a country where there's no head of state going to church every Sunday and corrupting it!

For Philip, political awakening came mostly from witnessing racial discrimination in the South. He was consumed by the injustices he saw around him. About both brothers there was a strong current of what Francine du Plessix Gray, in an admiring profile published in 1970, rightly called "moral fundamentalism"—an evil thing in conservatives, of course, but laudable indeed in political radicals eager to engage in histrionic gestures to declare their solidarity. Daniel summed up the attitude frankly in 1968: "one had to go to jail. It was an irreplaceable need, a gift not to be refused."

It was a gift they have both been treated to frequently, especially Philip. The Berrigans' great moment was in the 1960s and early 1970s. For them, as for so many others, the Vietnam conflict sharpened their radicalism and provided an overarching cause that seemed to explain all manner of evil in American society. In 1971, Daniel wrote that

> I have a great fear of American violence, not merely out there in the military and the diplomacy, in economics, in industry and advertising, but also in here, in me, up close among us.
>
> On the other hand, I must say, I have very little fear, from first-hand experience, of the Vietcong or the Panthers . . . for their acts come from the proximate threat of extinction.

Or again, in the preface to *Night Flight to Hanoi* (1968):

"the American ghetto and the Hanoi 'operation' were a single enterprise—a total war in both cases." Yes, Daniel, too, went to Hanoi—accompanied by Howard Zinn—courtesy of the North Vietnamese government. From about 1965 to the early Seventies, Hanoi was a prized pilgrimage spot for starry-eyed American radicals, from Tom Hayden and Jane Fonda to Mary McCarthy and Susan Sontag: they all felt, as Hayden put it, that "here we begin to understand the possibilities for a socialism of the heart."

The Berrigans' favorite pastime was to raid draft boards and destroy the files of young men declared to be A1 by pouring blood on the files or setting them afire after dousing them with homemade napalm. In October 1967, Philip led a raid on the draft board offices at the Baltimore Customs House. In May 1968, he, Daniel, and seven others made their most notorious raid, on the draft board at Cantonsville, Maryland. They snatched hundreds of files from the hands of startled clerks, spirited them out to the parking lot, and burned them while singing the Lord's Prayer for the benefit of the news media that had been carefully tipped off about the event beforehand.

Such conjunctions of illegality and smug parodies of religion were a Berrigan speciality. Writing about the Cantonsville raid in *Night Flight to Hanoi*, Daniel offered this rationale, half mocking, half maudlin, and entirely self-righteous:

> Our apologies, good friend, for the fracture of good order, the burning of paper instead of children, the angering of orderlies in the front parlor of the charnel house. We could not, so help us God, do otherwise. For we are sick at heart, our hearts give us no rest for thinking of the Land of the Burning Children. And for thinking of that other Child, of whom the poet Luke speaks.

(The *poet* Luke? Well, this *was* 1968.) Asked later whether he had given any consideration to the feelings of the draft board clerks, Daniel snapped that "anyone who works for the draft board deserves no more consideration than the guards at Belsen and Dachau."

The Berrigans were eventually sentenced to jail. Daniel first became a fugitive from justice for several months, an action that greatly enhanced his status as a countercultural hero. While on the lam, he wrote a letter to *The New York Review of Books* complaining that

> the time has arrived on the national scene, as well as the prison scene, when priests and [Black] Panthers are to be given the same treatment. . . . We are the objects of a search-and-destroy mission, borrowing its tactics from the military treatment of the Vietnamese.

This was signed melodramatically "Daniel Berrigan, S.J., Underground in America." When he was finally apprehended and put in jail, we are told that he was able to catch up on the latest volumes of Che Guevara, Herbert Marcuse, Régis Debray, and other similarly edifying revolutionary authors.

Casual antinomianism

It is difficult to say what is more repulsive about the Berrigans: their sanctimoniousness or their naïveté. Both qualities are on prominent view in *Night Flight to Hanoi*. The book has two main themes: the unspeakable evil of the United States and the great nobility of the North Vietnamese. The two are woven together with an unbreakable thread of self-satisfaction. Early on in the book, Daniel acquaints us with his idea of "the biography of the white Westerner. He requires (1) someone to kill for him and (2) someone to die for him. His power is such that he can arrange both requirements, that of vicarious executioner and of vicarious corpse." Meeting some U.S. embassy officials in Laos, he and his sidekick Howard Zinn "see what 'foreign service' does to human faces. Dead souls. They fix their gaze on the middle distance and announce the utter impossibility of all suggestions." But getting to the prelapsarian city of Hanoi—for Sixties' radicals the Eternal City—was worth any number of cantankerous civil servants, even American ones. "It was," Berrigan tells us, "like stepping out upon the threshold of a new planet, and then reporting back to those whose lives and history and future had wedded them to earth. . . . It was as though . . . a new creation was in its first stages. History being woven by a people who refused to die."

The purpose of the trip was to receive, as a gesture of goodwill from the Hanoi government, three captured American pilots (whom Berrigan later described as having been brainwashed . . . by the American military). It is when the pilots are herded before him by their captors that the pap really starts flowing. "I was struck," Berrigan writes, "by the thought, How well they look, how ruddy, how clean cut, how unkillably American."

They seemed eager and nervy and somewhat overanxious to please. They declared without prompting that they were well fed and cared for and grateful to the North Vietnamese military for the kindness with which they had been treated. . . . They said they had been given news of the war regularly, that they had visited Hanoi during Christmastime, that they had had a Christmas celebration "with a tree in that corner there," that their Christmas dinner had consisted of turkey and rice, that they had even received a kind of gift package at that time.

(And one recalls that George Bernard Shaw, visiting the Soviet Union in 1931, boisterously announced that he could find no trace of famine anywhere.) It is extraordinary that the pilots should have consented to leave such a paradise.

Both Berrigans, as of this writing, are still with us. Although he continues to protest against the United States whenever the opportunity occurs, Daniel has faded almost entirely from public notice. Philip, who secretly married a nun in 1969 and was defrocked in 1973 when he publicly announced the marriage, continues to intrude periodically through his group Plowshares. Although the Vietnam conflict is long over, Plowshares carries on, traveling around the country breaking into military installations and beating with hammers on submarines, missiles, and jet fighters. *Disarmed and Dangerous* describes a typical episode from the 1980s:

> Six of them entered a building . . . and proceeded to shatter part of two Mark 12A casings (the damage was estimated at $28,000) and then dumped blood . . . onto blueprints, work orders, and assorted equipment. Then they knelt in a circle, held hands, and sang hymns.

This, we are told, was "a small but stubborn challenge to ascendant Reaganism."

Even more than for William Sloane Coffin, the Berrigan brothers are men for whom calculated illegality became a patent of moral seriousness. Dazzled by the thought of their own virtue, they exempted themselves from the claims of established authority to pursue the calling of a "higher" morality. Poaching on the prestige they commanded by virtue of their status as clerics, they helped to undermine respect not only for the Church's authority but also for the authority of the various laws they broke with such regularity and insouciance. And by their example, they helped to license the spirit of casual antinomianism that has had such destructive effects on American life and culture.

Howard Zinn, in a preface he contributed to *Night Flight to Hanoi*, blithely observed that "of course [Daniel Berrigan] violated the law. But he was right. And it is the mark of enlightened citizens in a democracy that they know the difference between law and justice, between what is legal and what is right." But who is to decide what counts as enlightenment? Howard Zinn? As Montesquieu noted, "in a society where there are laws, . . . liberty is the right to do everything the laws permit; and if one citizen could do what they forbid, he would no longer have liberty because the others would likewise have this same power."

Many Sixties radicals regarded civil disobedience as a form of no-fault political theater. One broke the law in as noisy a way as possible, and then one was hauled off to jail, generally for a token sentence. The willingness to endure jail (which radical activists rarely did for more than a few hours before their lawyers arrived to bail them out) was supposed to legitimize the illegality. In the last chapter, I quoted from George Kennan's essay "Rebels Without a Program" (1968). It is worth repeating Kennan's reflections about civil disobedience and lawlessness. "The violation of law," Kennan wrote, "is not . . . a privilege that lies offered for sale with a given price tag, like an object in a supermarket, available to anyone who has the price and is willing to pay for it."

Kennan is an especially noteworthy critic in this context because he, too, was deeply opposed to U.S. involvement in Vietnam. But he understood, as the Coffins and Berrigans of the world do not, that in a democracy illegality is not a justifiable brand of political opposition. And he also understood that, even when one disagrees with specific policies, one's country continues to exercise a legitimate claim on one's allegiance, a claim that cannot be disposed of in a fit of self-righteous bravado. "It seems to me," Kennan writes,

> that the citizen who lives under a system that assures him not only voting rights but extensive guarantees for the inviolability of his person and property, and who accepts the protection of the state in the enjoyment of these rights, owes to the state at least a high measure of respect and forbearance in those instances where he may not find himself in agreement with its policies.

The alternative, as William Sloane Coffin and the Berrigans illustrated so graphically, is not a higher morality but the delegitimation of the institutions and attitudes that guarantee freedom. Edmund Burke once observed that

> men are qualified for civil liberty in exact proportion to their disposition to put moral chains upon their own appetites. . . . Society cannot exist unless a controlling power upon will and appetite be placed somewhere, and the less of it there is within, the more there is without. It is ordained in the eternal constitution of things that men of intemperate minds cannot be free.

Figures like William Sloane Coffin and the Berrigan brothers illustrate one way in which civil liberty can be compromised by exorbitance. Wilhelm Reich, Herbert Marcuse, and other prophets of sexual license demonstrated other ways in which intemperate minds enslaved themselves—and many others —through fantasies of absolute freedom.

Chapter 6
The Marriage of Marx & Freud

It is impossible to overlook the extent to which civilization is built up upon a renunciation of instinct.
—Sigmund Freud, *Civilization and Its Discontents*, 1930

I will not give up on Paradise.
—Paul Goodman, *Five Years*, 1966

Lust strives to become intellectualized, the concrete operations of the flesh are blended with decorous abstractions, human loves tend toward the impossibilities of angelic embraces. Magic and pseudo-mysticism . . . become so many spices which are used to give a new taste to the well-known feast of the senses.
—Mario Praz, *The Romantic Agony*, 1933

The promise of sexual utopia

"Make love, not war." The imperative now seems as antique as Timothy Leary's "Tune In, Turn On, Drop Out." And yet one of the most conspicuous features of the cultural revolution that swept through America and Western Europe in the 1960s was just such a demand for politically inspired "sexual liberation." In some respects, of course, this demand was not new. The revolt against traditional sexual mores had been an important ingredient of "advanced" thinking at least since the 1920s. Freud was the most important intellectual authority underlying the new obsession with sex. The culture of psychoanalysis not only encouraged people to sexualize everything: it also encouraged them to talk about sex endlessly. The notorious Kinsey Report of 1948 also did an extraordinary amount to help popularize the possibilities of sexual utopianism. Its pretense to clinical exactitude—its effort, in Lionel Trilling's words, "to make the anatomical and physiological description the 'source' of the emotional and then to consider it as the more real of the two"—did not so much demystify sex as transform it into a branch of erotic calisthenics.

Kinsey presented himself as a man of science, come to spread enlightenment and relieve us of the burden of superstition. In fact, as Joseph Epstein has observed, he was "a moral revolutionary in scientist's clothing."

> The science was bad, even bogus; the man himself may now be forgotten; but the revolution came to stay, with a vengeance. Kinsey's message—fornicate early, fornicate often, fornicate in every possible way—became the mantra of a sex-ridden age, our age, now desperate for a reformation of its own.

What was novel about Kinsey was not the message but the widespread acceptance of his missionary zeal about sex. The increasing penetration of Freudian ideas into the general culture made Kinsey possible; his expert deployment of social-scientific jargon made him palatable; what made him inevitable was the union of these elements with the atmosphere of liberation—sexual, social, political—that was becoming an ever more prominent part of American life. Kinsey was a Fifties phenomenon; but (like Hugh Hefner's

Playboy, which began publication in 1953) his gospel of sex did not really come into its own until the Sixties. The idea of sexual utopia can be traced back at least to the early nineteenth century and the Romantic cult of feeling and spontaneity. Even the union of sexual liberation and radical politics—a hallmark of the 1960s—had important antecedents going back to such disparate apostles of liberation as Rousseau, Fourier, Blake, Godwin, and Shelley. As Irving Kristol has noted,

> "Sexual liberation" is always near the top of a countercultural agenda—though just what form the liberation takes can and does vary, sometimes quite wildly. Women's liberation, likewise, is another consistent feature of all countercultural movements—liberation from husbands, liberation from children, liberation from family. Indeed, the real object of these various sexual heterodoxies is to disestablish the family as the central institution of human society, the citadel of orthodoxy.

Nevertheless, whatever its antecedents, the Sixties introduced novel elements into this perennial countercultural dispensation. First of all, there was the matter of numbers. In the past, movements for sexual liberation had been sporadic and confined largely to a bohemian elite. In the 1960s sexual liberation suddenly became an everyday fact of middle-class life. This was due partly to the perfection of the birth control pill and other reliable forms of contraception, partly to greater affluence and mobility. What had been a fringe phenomenon became an established fashion; by the late Sixties, it had become a social norm.

David Allyn's new book, *Make Love, Not War: The Sexual Revolution: An Unfettered History*, provides a detailed overview of the progress of the sexual revolution in the 1960s and 1970s. Weaving together interviews and documentary history, Allyn provides a casebook of libertinage—a litany of excess—though his detached, almost clinical tone makes for an odd contrast between style and content. Born in 1969, Allyn is too young to have participated in the 1960s, something he clearly regrets. He begins his book by noting that he grew up "with the vague sense of having missed something magical and mysterious."

> For all its faults and limitations, the sexual revolution had contributed to an era of openness, self-examination, and questioning of the status quo. It was a time of popular inquiry into important philosophical questions. For twenty-some years, a significant segment of the population had publicly explored the possibility of a rational approach to personal behavior and social organization. . . . [I]t had been an era of devotion to the idea of freedom in all its forms. It had been an era of erotic possibility. Now that era was over.

A sense of nostalgia informs Allyn's entire discussion. It leads him to underestimate the tremendous moral damage that the sexual revolution inflicted. It also leads him to underestimate the manifold ways in which the sexual revolution continues to make itself felt today in the age of so-called "safe sex." According to Allyn, the sexual revolution ended "in the late seventies, when opponents on both sides of the political spectrum waged a largely successful campaign against sexual permissiveness." All it takes is a look at the highly eroticized advertisements festooning billboards, or the sorts of graphic sexual fare available even on network television today, to show how little any "campaign against permissiveness" has succeeded.

Make Love, Not War is useful mostly as a pathologist's scrapbook. Allyn has assembled a vivid collage of examples and anecdotes: he samples everything from Masters and Johnson's books about human sexuality to memoirs extolling the pleasures of gay bathhouses in the years before AIDS. He cites academic experts who praise pornography for "defining new possibilities in arbitrary sexual relationships, breaking down the stereotypes as to what is male, what is female," and describes various episodes of group sex and other efforts to "smash monogamy" (in the phrase of Bernadine Dohrn, a leader of the violent Weather Underground). Like many observers, Allyn exaggerates the depth of sexual ignorance and restrictiveness before the watershed decade of the 1960s. (One thinks of Philip Larkin's observation that "Sexual intercourse began/ In nineteen sixty-three/ . . . Between the end of the *Chatterley* ban/ and the Beatles' first LP.") He also grossly exaggerates the positive aspects of the sexual revolution itself. "For all its faults," he concludes, "the sexual revolution taught us how to speak about sex more directly, more clearly, and, most important, more authentically than we ever knew how to before."

In fact, the sexual revolution merely encouraged everyone to speak more graphically—that is, more pornographically—about sex than ever before. That habit is not more "authentic," merely more brazen. What the critic Rochelle Gurstein (adopting a phrase from Agnes Repplier) called "the repeal of reticence" has led not to greater openness but to greater vulgarity. Gurstein notes that "the price of too frequently and too regularly crossing the ever-shifting border between desire and taboo, curiosity and injunction, is desensitization: what was once shocking becomes commonplace and trivial, what was once obscene becomes banal and dull."

What began earlier in this century as a plea for greater candor about sexual matters resulted in the abolition of genuine intimacy. "The more people became obsessed with achieving 'successful sex' *and* talking openly and endlessly about it," Gurstein observes, "the more intimacy was to be stripped of privacy and meaning." Consider the mainstream "lifestyle" magazines available at every grocery store checkout counter and newsstand. Cover stories in the December 1999 issue of *Complete Woman* (available in the "Family" section of my local newsstand) promised "New Sex Positions: Rock His World In Ways He's Only Dreamed About ('Til Now!)," "Would You Have Sex on the Very First Date? Readers Confess," "Naughty Money: Fully-Clothed Ways These Women Earn $$$ From Sex!," and so on. The December 1999 *Redbook* tells its readers about "The Hot New Sex Potion: Can It Change Your Life?," while *Marie Claire* offers "Orgasm: Secrets You're Entitled to Know" and *Cosmopolitan* leads off with the "Cosmo Sex School: Study Up On Seduction, Learn New Tricks with Your Lips, Now Go to the Head of *His* Class," etc. ("Start by manually or orally tantalizing his member . . ."). Magazines like *Maxim* provide identical quasi-pornographic pabulum for young middle-class men. These publications are nothing if not "direct." They represent the triumph of the Kinsey view of sex filtered through the ethic of *Playboy* and recast in the consumerist idiom of magazines like *Vanity Fair*. They are also models of inauthenticity.*

Allyn is wrong: The sexual revolution is not over. It is still very much in progress, even if AIDS and other sexually transmitted diseases have focused attention more on the

---

* By way of contrast, in 1960 *Redbook* was featuring such stories as "Christmas and Santa Claus: A Revelation" (December) and "Queen Elizabeth's New Baby: Fascinating Preview by a Veteran Royal Observer" (January). In 1960 no one would have assumed that "revelations" about Christmas and Santa Claus contained anything untoward; today, a story with that title would be the occasion of ribald jokes.

proper use of condoms than on group sex, wife swapping, and one-night stands. What is different now from the Sixties and Seventies is the temperature of the rhetoric and the amount of philosophical baggage. Demands for sexual liberation were a regular, though not invariable, concomitant of revolutionary politics in the past (with the conspicuous exception of the Bolshevik revolution). But seldom had sexual emancipation been invested with a more forbidding panoply of political mystification and high-flown verbiage than it was in the 1960s and 1970s. Plenty of revolutionary movements have made sexual emancipation one of their political causes; rarely has sexual gratification so thoroughly defined the *content* of revolutionary politics. The Yippie leader Jerry Rubin, with his inimitable logic, epitomized the radical attitude: "How," he asked, "can you separate politics from sex? It's all the same thing."

> Puritanism leads us to Vietnam. Sexual insecurity results in a supermasculinity trip called imperialism. American foreign policy, especially in Vietnam, makes no sense except sexually. . . .
>
> The revolution declares war on Original Sin, the dictatorship of parents over their kids, Christian morality, capitalism and supermasculinity trips. . . .
>
> Our tactic is to send niggers and longhair scum invading white middle-class homes, fucking on the living room floor, crashing on the chandeliers, spewing sperm on the Jesus pictures, breaking the furniture and smashing Sunday school napalm-blood Amerika forever.

Today most people who remember Rubin (who died in 1994 at 56) think of him as having occupied the lunatic, histrionic fringe of the counterculture before retiring from street theater to Wall Street. But in fact, Rubin represented the epicenter of the Sixties' counterculture. It is worth recalling that if Rubin's attitudes, pronouncements, and behavior were indeed far out, he was nonetheless an emblematic figure of the times. And it is also worth recalling how many of the ideas and attitudes Rubin espoused have, in suitably repackaged form, survived into contemporary society.

Wilhelm Reich and the function of the orgasm

Of course, Rubin did not emerge from nowhere. His ideas about the inseparability of sex and politics have a long lineage. A large part of the credit for the sexual revolution and its mixture of hedonism and politics must go to Wilhelm Reich (1897–1957), the Austrian-born psychiatrist, demobbed Communist, renegade Freudian, militant atheist, and all-around celebrant of sexual orgasm. As the journalist Hal Cohen noted in a recent article on Reich in *Lingua Franca*, "his work seems to be a hidden thread running through the proto-counterculture of the 1950s."

At the center of Reich's teachings were two convictions: that "the sexual question must be politicized," as he put it in *The Mass Psychology of Fascism* (1933), and that establishing "a satisfactory genital sex life" was the key not only to individual but also to societal liberation and happiness, as he put it in *The Function of the Orgasm* (1942) and in practically everything else he wrote. As one critic acknowledged, "Reich, in truth, did feel that sex was everything."

Reich was always obsessed with sex. As Hal Cohen reports, at the age of twelve "he watched his tutor seduce his mother."

He was also twelve when he revealed this fact to his father

—a jealous and brutish man who regularly referred to his wife as "whore" anyway—resulting soon after in his mother's suicide. A year later, young Wilhelm bedded a household servant. In his university days, he was an insatiable womanizer; by most accounts, he never gave up the habit. Nor was it separated from his work: He met his first wife, Annie, . . . when she came to him for therapy; he was known to have seduced several of his other patients; and he had an affair with the wife of his assistant Myron Sharaf.

G. K. Chesterton once observed that when someone abandons belief in God, what he will then believe is not nothing but *anything*. Reich was one of many modern figures who would seem to confirm this observation. In 1939, after shuttling around Europe for several years— Reich attracted official opprobrium wherever he went—he got a faculty appointment at New York's New School for Social Research. It was around this time that he began publishing his theories about "cosmic orgone energy" and "orgastic potency." Orgone (which Reich named after the sexual orgasm) is supposedly the animating energy of the universe. "Its color," Reich said, "is *blue*." It is omnipresent (*"orgone radiation is indeed present everywhere"*) and of inestimable therapeutic value: *"it charges living tissue and brings about an expansion of the plasmatic system."* (Reich was very fond of italics.) He built "Orgone Energy Accumulators" —empty wood and metal boxes to the rest of us—which he sold to patients so that they might mobilize their "plasmatic currents" and thereby overcome sexual repression and, incidentally, ameliorate if not cure everything from cancer to schizophrenia.

Our orgone therapy experiments with cancer patients consist in having them sit in an orgone accumulator. The orgone energy "accumulated" in the interior of this enclosure penetrates the naked body and, moreover, is breathed in. . . . *The effect of the orgone energy radiation is vagatonic.* In other words, it acts as a counter-force resisting the general sympatheticotonic shrinking of the organism. . . . This "plasmatic expansion" is accompanied by a reduction of the typical cancer pain.

It is perhaps worth noting that orgone accumulators come in a variety of shapes and sizes. "Boxes ranged from full-body models about the size of a phone booth to smaller models designed to accommodate specific body parts in need of treatment. Sometimes they included attachments that intensified and sprayed orgone like a removable showerhead. There were also orgone blankets that could be folded up for easy traveling."* The Beat writer William Burroughs showed how versatile these devices could be. Having built his own mini–orgone accumulator out of a gas can, Burroughs explained to a correspondent, "one day I got into the big accumulator and held the little one over my joint and came right off."

It is difficult to convey the distinctive loopiness of Reich's theories, a combination of pseudoscientific argot and sexual exhortation. Reich's "experiments" with orgone went far beyond therapy. They also included such things as "cosmic orgone engineering," in which Reich gives instructions on "DOR removal and cloud-busting" ("DOR" is Reich's acronym for "deadly orgone"): "It has become possible," Reich noted in the *Orgone Energy Bulletin* in 1952, "to apply the principle of the orgonomic potential to the dissolution and formation of clouds." Poor Reich believed that

---

* Orgone accumulators are still easily available. See, for example, the web page at http://www.orgone.org/orgonaccoo.htm.

masses of negative energy had been accumulating over his research laboratory in Organon (Reich's name for Rangeley), Maine. He provides little sketches showing how long, hollow pipes can be constructed to draw off the bad kind of orgone energy from clouds and redirect it *"not into the ground but into water,* preferably into the *flowing* water of brooks, lakes, and rivers." It was all nonsense, of course, and fraudulent nonsense at that. Reich spent the last years of his life in a Federal penitentiary, courtesy of the Food and Drug Administration, for transporting orgone accumulators across state lines.

Although by the end he was almost certainly mad, Reich was also immensely influential. Norman Mailer professed a great admiration for Reich. ("If I were ever to look for a therapist," he wrote, "I would be inclined to get me to a Reichian.") So did William Burroughs and Allen Ginsberg. So even did more sober figures like Irving Howe and Saul Bellow, who under the influence of Isaac Rosenfeld subjected himself to Reichian therapy. In "The Strange Case of Wilhelm Reich," a hostile article about Reich published in *The New Republic* in 1947, Mildred Edie Brady noted that Reich's theories had received enthusiastic praise in Leftist magazines from *Politics* and *The Nation* to *Science and Society.* One scientific journal characterized his writings as "a surrealistic creation," but many others accorded Reich and his theories great respect. He was duly listed in *American Men of Science* and, Brady observed, his books "have been assigned in university seminars for serious consideration." (Characteristically, Reich responded to Brady's article with the contention that "Brady believes that I am the only man who could help her achieve an orgasm, which she so desperately needs.") Even today there are plenty of Reichian analysts. There is even a *Journal of Orgonomy,* staffed by Reich's latter-day disciples, who are eager to tell you all about the dangers of "character armor" (another of Reich's fantasies) and about the orgasm as "the ultimate regulator of the individual's energy economy."

Early on in his career, Reich declared himself a "Freudo-Marxist." He helped to pioneer that strange amalgam of radical politics and emancipatory sex that fueled the sexual revolution of the 1960s. And while Reich later abandoned Marxism—he declared Stalin to be "anti-sex" and Russia itself to be "sex-reactionary—he preserved the radical utopianism. Today, the familiarity of this union between Freud and Marx tends to obscure its oddness. Harvey Mansfield pointed out that the sexual revolution depended on "an illicit, forced union between Freud and Marx in which Mr. Marx was compelled to yield his principle that economics, not sex, is the focus of liberation, and Mr. Freud was required to forsake his insistence that liberation from human nature is impossible."

As is so often the case, contradiction proved no bar to credulity. For Reich and his disciples and spiritual heirs, sex was the primary focus of political activism, and human nature was a harsh but dispensable fiction. Reich came too soon and was too much of a quack to see his ideas triumph in their original form. But by the early 1960s, variations on his core theories about sex and politics were everywhere. Norman Mailer's "The White Negro" (1957), for example, with its adolescent radicalism and hymns to the "apocalyptic orgasm," is Reichian boilerplate refitted with Mailerean bombast.

Mailer had a part to play in popularizing Reich. But the three men who really popularized the Reichian gospel were the anarchist poet-psychologist Paul Goodman, the classicist turned neo-Freudian guru Norman O. Brown, and the Frankfurt School Marxist philosopher Herbert Marcuse. None would have described himself as a follower of

Reich, but all read and commented on his work and drew upon his theories. Whatever their particular disagreements with Reich or with one another, all absorbed the essential Reichian tenets about politicizing sex and investing it with a kind of redemptive significance. As Richard King noted in *The Party of Eros: Radical Social Thought and the Realm of Freedom*, all three "sought to combine a concern for instinctual and erotic liberation with political and social radicalism, cultural with political concerns."

It would be difficult to overestimate their influence. The critic Morris Dickstein was quite right to insist, in *Gates of Eden: American Culture in the Sixties* (1977), that Goodman, Brown, and Marcuse were prime catalysts in "the rise of a new sensibility," the thinkers "whose work had the greatest impact on the new culture of the sixties." At the same time, it is worth stressing that the importance of Goodman, Brown, and Marcuse was not so much intellectual as emotional and affective. Despite the elaborate scholarly machinery they employed in their books, their chief appeal was not to people's minds but to their hearts—and to other, lower, organs. They came bearing arguments, but, as the Sixties wore on, they were increasingly acclaimed as prophets. Their ideas were embraced less as reasoned proposals than as talismans of personal and political transformation. As Dickstein put it, the trio of Goodman, Brown, and Marcuse spoke with such urgency to his generation because "we knew that at bottom their gospel was a sexual one, that sex was their wedge for reorienting all human relations."

Paul Goodman and the gonad theory of life

Of the three, Paul Goodman (1911–1972) is the one whose reputation has faded most completely. Having graduated from City College in 1931 with a degree in philosophy, Goodman early on determined to be a writer. Today, most people familiar with Goodman's work would probably describe him as a kind of social psychologist. But in fact his literary interests—like his sexual interests, as it turned out —were extremely promiscuous. He contributed to all manner of left-wing publications, including *Partisan Review*, *Politics*, *Commentary*, *Dissent*, and *The New York Review of Books*. He wrote literary criticism (and even took a Ph.D. in literature from the University of Chicago) as well as poems, short stories, and novels; in 1951, he collaborated on a book about Gestalt psychology. He wrote essays on everything from city planning and decentralization to education, youth work camps, pornography (he was for it), Wilhelm Reich, and making antiwar films.

During World War II, Goodman's draft-dodging and anarchist views made him *persona non grata* at some of his usual outlets, and he receded somewhat from the scene. But in 1960 his big break came. Norman Podhoretz had just taken over the editorship of *Commentary*. As a declaration of editorial intention, he decided to publish three large segments of Goodman's *Growing Up Absurd*, the manuscript of which had just been turned down by over a dozen publishers. In his memoir *Making It*, Podhoretz recalled that *Growing Up Absurd* represented "the very incarnation of the new spirit" that he wanted both for *Commentary* and for the world at large.

Looking back from the mid-1970s, Morris Dickstein described the book as a "masterwork in social criticism . . . that did much to inform the whole frame of mind of thinking people in the sixties." By the mid-1960s, Goodman had achieved enormous celebrity. He was an invariable participant at rallies, sit-ins, protest marches, and other events sure to attract large numbers of young men. "Like Allen

Ginsberg," Dickstein noted, "Goodman was more than a writer in the sixties: he was a pervasive and inescapable *presence* . . . the most tireless and incandescent Socratic figure of the age."

Today, it is hard to understand the excitement. For one thing, Goodman's prose is atrocious. "Encountering Goodman's style," Norman Mailer once observed, "was not unrelated to the journeys one undertook in the company of a laundry bag." The critic Kingsley Widmer in *Paul Goodman*, a monograph designed to outline Goodman's achievement, regularly comments on his subject's deficiencies as a writer. Of his literary works generally Widmer observes that, "pathetically, they are often quite literally incompetent—marked by trite and mangled language, bumblingly inconsistent manners and tones, garbled syntax and forms, embarrassing pretentiousness and self-lugubriousness, and pervasive awkward writing."

In a curious way, however, some of Goodman's failings as a stylist actually contributed to his effectiveness. Goodman had a knack for reformulating current anxieties and clichés in the astringent language of the social sciences. This had the double advantage of imbuing his sociological writings with an aura of authority while reinforcing his readers' settled prejudices—a tactic sure to inspire gratitude. He managed the neat trick of balancing pathos and jargon in such a way that—for those susceptible to his spell—the underlying banality of his thinking momentarily disappeared.

By the time that *Growing Up Absurd* was published, Goodman's main point was wearisomely familiar: postwar America was said to be a conformist wasteland that stifled anything beginning with the letter S—spirit, spontaneity, self-expression, and of course sexuality. Goodman said virtually nothing new in *Growing Up Absurd*. But somehow, his method of recycling received opinions about the problems of youth culture in what he liked to call the "Organized System" struck a chord. His success was due partly to the way he combined the radical clichés of the moment with a traditional language of virtue. "My purpose is a simple one," Goodman wrote in his first chapter: "to show how it is desperately hard these days for an average child to grow up to be a man, for our present organized system of society does not want men." (Girls and women do not figure much in Goodman's scheme of things.)

In other words, Goodman cannily blended rhetoric appropriate to a Marine recruitment poster with portentous fantasies about America being an "unnatural system" that warps young souls. Given current conditions in America, Goodman wonders, "Is it possible, being a human being, to exist? Is it possible, having a human nature, to grow up?" But the pertinent question is whether it really *was* "desperately hard" for the average child to grow up in the United States in the 1950s—an era, it is worth remembering, of tremendous prosperity, excellent public education, and potent national self-confidence. Was it true, as Goodman insisted, that "the young men who conform to the dominant society become for the most part apathetic, disappointed, cynical, and wasted"?

Part of Goodman's purpose was to sympathize with and exonerate those elements of youth culture that had chosen *not* to conform to "the dominant society"—the Beats and other fringe groups who believed that "a man is a fool to work to pay installments on a useless refrigerator for his wife." (Not so useless if one wishes to keep food from spoiling, of course, but Goodman never acknowledges that side of things.) He praises the Beats for being "pacific, artistic, and rather easy-going sexually." Indeed, as one reads through *Growing Up Absurd*, it becomes increasingly clear that being "easy-going" when it comes to sex is one of his chief criteria of psychological health. "My impression is," he writes in one gnomic passage, "that—leaving out their artists, who have the kind of sex that artists have—Beat sexuality in general is pretty good, unlike delinquent sexuality, which seems, on the evidence, to be wretched."

Richard King observed that Goodman's works "reveal a man obsessed with two things—sex and general ideas." Although he had two common-law wives and fathered three children, Goodman was aggressively bisexual, which meant —as his diary, *Five Years* (1966), makes clear—predominantly homosexual. His sexual behavior was so flagrant that he managed to get himself dismissed from teaching positions at a progressive boarding school and even at that bohemian outpost of the South, Black Mountain College. He seems to have been obtuse as well as importunate. "I distrust women clothed," he wrote in his diary. "Naked, they are attractive to me like any other animal. Male dress passes —but I have to reach for their penises, to make sure. This has damaged my reputation." Imagine that! *Five Years* records a steady stream of one-night stands, rough trade, and hasty pick-ups in bars. "There have been few days going back to my 11th year," Goodman noted, "when I have not had an orgasm one way or another."

C. Wright Mills and P. J. Salter described one of Goodman's articles from the 1940s as putting forward "the gonad theory of revolution." In truth, Goodman propounded the gonad theory of life. Joseph Epstein summed it up aptly in 1978: "the good society, for Goodman, started at the groin." Responding to Epstein's criticism, a Goodman enthusiast quoted from a letter that Goodman had written some years before: "My own view . . . is that no sexual practices whatever, unless they are malicious or extremely guilt-ridden, do any harm to anybody, including children"—a statement that not only epitomizes Goodman's philosophy, but also helps to explain why he became such an idolized figure for the counterculture of the 1960s.

Norman O. Brown and the Dionysian ego

To move from the work of Paul Goodman to the work of Norman O. Brown is to move from the grubby and prosaic to the cerebral and fantastic. Born in 1913, Brown was educated at Oxford, the University of Chicago, and the University of Wisconsin. A classicist by training, he labored in obscurity at Wesleyan University through the 1950s. His discovery of Freud was (to use a term he might like) a metanoia: a conversion experience that changed his life. In 1959, he published *Life Against Death: The Psychoanalytic Meaning of History*, a dense, learned academic tract that blends Freud, Marx, idealist philosophy, and mysticism, East and West, in a preposterous but intoxicating brew. Brown's premise, in *Life Against Death* and in his other main book, an aphoristic mélange called *Love's Body* (1966), is that there is an "intrinsic connection between social organization and neurosis." His goal is to break that connection by abolishing "repression," thus curing "the disease called man." This, you see, is the way to affirm the "life instinct," which "demands a union with others and the world around us based not on anxiety and aggression but on narcissism and erotic exuberance."

Naturally, this sort of thing was a tremendous hit on American campuses, where the homeless radicalism of irresponsible affluence made all manner of utopian schemes seem attractive. Morris Dickstein doubtless spoke for many when he wrote, in *Gates of Eden*, that "I can recall no public event more inspiring and electrifying at that time than Brown's vatic, impassioned Phi Beta Kappa oration at

Columbia in 1960." Vatic, indeed. That oration, called "Apocalypse: The Place of Mystery in the Life of the Mind," published the following year in *Harper's*, is a piece of obscurantist nonsense. But what seductive nonsense it was! Brown began by declaring a state of emergency: the mind was "at the end of its tether," just as H. G. Wells had said it was. Civilization, ruined by rationality, had to be "renewed by the discovery of new mysteries" and "magic." What was needed, Brown told the newly elected key-holders, was "the blessed madness of the maenad and the bacchant." He himself came seeking "supernatural powers."

Brown's great gift was infusing mystic pronouncements with a radical, antibourgeois animus and a febrile erotic charge. How nice to learn, for example, that time was simply the product of "neurosis." Or that "all sublimations are desexualizations." Or that the roots of "alienated consciousness lay in "the compulsion to work" and that this compulsion was exacerbated by "capitalism," which "has made us so stupid and one-sided that objects exist for us only if we can possess them or if they have utility." How exciting to discover that "all thinking is nothing but a detour" and that the chief task now facing the spiritual vanguard was "the construction of a Dionysian ego" that would free us from the tyranny of "genital organization." "The work of constructing a Dionysian ego is immense," Brown acknowledges, as if he were talking about building the Hoover Dam, "but there are signs that it is already under way."

Paradise now

Brown offered his readers a little of everything: the rhetoric of Christian eschatology *and* neo-Marxist radicalism *and* polymorphous sexuality. Was his vision of "body mysticism" littered with contradictions? No problem! Faced with evidence of contradiction one could always resort to Walt Whitman: "Do I contradict myself? / Very well then I contradict myself, / (I am large, I contain multitudes)." Or one could quote Brown himself: "We may therefore entertain the hypothesis that formal logic and the law of contradiction are the rules whereby the mind submits to operate under general conditions of repression." In other words, genuine liberation for Brown entails liberation from rationality, i.e., from sanity.

Brown claimed to be plumbing "the psychoanalytic meaning of history." But, as he more or less admits, he adopts Freudian rhetoric while totally inverting Freud's fundamental understanding of civilization and human nature. (The one thing that Brown took from Freud without distortion was Freud's extraordinary overestimation of sex as the most important thing—almost the only important thing—in human life.) The writer John Passmore, in "Paradise Now," a long article about Brown published in *Encounter* in 1970, summed it up well: "Freud presented a dilemma: either civilization, which rests on repression, or unrepressed enjoyment. When it came to the point he preferred civilization, if with some misgivings. Brown, in typical mystical fashion, chooses the other horn of the dilemma." In fact, the choice is not even between civilization and "unrepressed enjoyment" but rather between the ordered enjoyments that civilization makes possible and the carnage and savagery of Dionysian—i.e., barbaric—chaos.

Brown everywhere talks about "abolishing" repression. In *Love's Body*, for example he waxes prophetic about it: "The unconscious to be made conscious; a secret disclosed; a veil to be rent, a seal to be broke open; the seal which Freud called repression." You might have thought that art in its best sense is a sign and ornament of civilization. He tells us on the contrary that art, if it is to fulfill its redemptive function, must be "subversive of civilization." In other words, like all Romantics, Brown pretends that the alternative to civilization, with its tedious checks and balances, is paradise; in fact, as every real breakdown of civilization in history reminds us, the alternative to civilization is much closer to hell on earth.

Brown's popularity rested on two points: his promise of an ecstatic world- and self-transforming sexuality and his attack on rationality. The two go together. Sex, in the world according to Brown, has little or nothing to do with the family or children; in the end it has little to do with sex as ordinarily understood. It is more a mystical than a carnal or emotional reality. Sex for Brown is a synecdoche for spiritual redemption, though his musings about polymorphous perversity and the abolition of repression inspired a great deal of distinctly mundane activity among his acolytes. Likewise Brown's attack on rationality. He asked his followers to dispense with "quantifying rationality" and "morbid" science, whose aims were to gain "possession or mastery over objects."

> What would a nonmorbid science look like? It would presumably be erotic rather than (anal) sadistic in aim. Its aim would not be mastery over but union with nature. And its means would not be economizing but erotic exuberance. And finally, it would be based on the whole body and not just a part; that is to say, it would be based on the polymorphously perverse body.

That is to say, it would be based on a groundless fantasy about what constituted knowledge, a grotesque misunderstanding of nature, and a narcissistic worship of the body. Brown pretended that the alternative to rational thought ("formal logic," "the law of contradiction") was a "higher" knowledge. In fact, it was a lower form of ignorance: a word-besotted mysticism incapable of distinguishing verbal legerdemain from the claims of reality. It is easy to dismiss Brown as a "gnostic curiosity," as one critic did. The problem is that his gnostic fantasies seduced some of the most influential and articulate thinkers of the 1960s, and, through them, the hearts and minds of an entire generation. Take, for example, Susan Sontag's famous conclusion to "Against Interpretation: "In place of a hermeneutics we need an erotics of art." This bit of avant-garde word play is totally nonsensical; but it is exactly the sort of nonsense that is inconceivable without the example of Brown's polysyllabic eroticism.

Herbert Marcuse and the abolition of repression

With the work of Herbert Marcuse (1898–1979), we descend a little closer to earth, but not much. Born in Berlin and educated at the University of Berlin and the University of Freiburg, Marcuse began his academic career as a radical interpreter of Hegel. He was later associated with the so-called "Frankfurt School" of Marxist intellectuals. When the Nazis came to power, Marcuse fled first to Geneva, where he taught for a year, and then to the United States, where he remained for the rest of his life, teaching at Columbia, Harvard, Brandeis, and the University of California at San Diego. Marcuse's two most influential books, *Eros and Civilization: A Philosophical Inquiry into Freud* (1955) and *One-Dimensional Man: Studies in the Ideology of Advanced Industrial Society* (1964), lay out a position that, in essentials, anticipates and parallels Brown's. Like Brown, Marcuse blends Marx and Freud to produce an emancipatory vision based on polymorphous, narcissistic sexuality, antibourgeois animus, and quasi-mystical theories about art, redemption, and the abolition of repression.

The chief difference between Brown and Marcuse is one of tone. Brown poses as a visionary: William Blake with a Ph.D. and an extensive bibliography. For him, the revolution is primarily a cataclysm in consciousness. Marcuse makes more of an effort to keep his Marxist credentials in good order. Where Brown might quote the mystic Jacob Boehme, Marcuse will add a "Political Preface" to the second edition of *Eros and Civilization* in order to announce "the gradual undermining of capitalistic enterprise in the course of automation." Where Brown described himself frankly as a seeker after "magic" and "supernatural powers," Marcuse became the mentor of the radical Communist black-power spokeswoman Angela Davis, whom he extolled as the best student he ever taught.* In 1972, in *Counter-Revolution and Revolt*, Marcuse accused the "Western world" (i.e., the United States) of practicing "the horrors of the Nazi regime" and looked forward to "the fall of the capitalist superpower," an event that he believed would allow the Chinese and Cuban revolutions "to go their own ways—freed from the suffocating blockade and the equally

---

* Davis's career provides a splendid example of Marcuse's political thought in action. Indicted in 1970 for supplying guns to aid in an attempted courtroom escape that ended in four deaths, she became a fugitive for two months. Arrested, she was tried for murder, conspiracy, and kidnapping, but was acquitted by a sympathetic jury. Davis subsequently toured several Communist regimes, receiving various honors while denouncing American society for its racism and injustice. In 1994, she was appointed to the Presidential Chair in African American and Feminist Studies at the University of California, where she is still employed.

suffocating necessity of maintaining an ever more costly defensive machine." Brown might agree, but one can hardly imagine him acknowledging the existence of Cuba without first quoting Paracelsus. In other words, both men were political utopians, but Marcuse was more likely to insist on the real-world implications of his thought.

In a famous review of *Love's Body* published in *Commentary* in February 1967, Marcuse accused Brown of systematically "mystifying" love, politics, and human nature. He was quite right, but the charge applies equally to Marcuse. Both men were fantasists. Their world view proceeds from the assumption that human nature can be repealed. In *Eros and Civilization*—a book that became a bible of the counterculture—Marcuse spins a fairy tale about the fate of man in industrial society. Like Brown, he conjures up the image of a "non-repressive reality principle" in which "the body in its entirety would become . . . an instrument of pleasure." What this really amounts to is a form of infantilization. Marcuse speaks glowingly of "a resurgence of pregenital polymorphous sexuality" that "protests against the repressive order of procreative sexuality." He recommends returning to a state of "primary narcissism" in which one will find "the redemption of pleasure, the halt of time, the absorption of death; silence, sleep, night, paradise—the Nirvana principle not as death but as life." In other words, he looks forward to a community of solipsists.

Marcuse is much more explicit than Brown about the social implications of his experiment in narcissism. "This change in the value and scope of libidinal relations," he writes, "would lead to a disintegration of the institutions in which the private interpersonal relations have been organized, particularly the monogamic and patriarchal family." That is to say, ultimate liberation is indistinguishable from ultimate self-absorption. Of course, there are one or two impediments to fulfilling this dream. Mortality, for example. "The brute fact of death," Marcuse admits, "denies once and for all the reality of a non-repressive existence." But not to worry. A couple of pages after acknowledging the inconvenient reality of death, Marcuse assures us that the emancipation of eros means that "the instinctual value of death would have changed." He goes on to explain that

> the necessity of death does not refute the possibility of final liberation. Like other necessities, it can be made rational— painless. Men can die without anxiety if they know that what they love is protected from misery and oblivion. After a fulfilled life, they may take it upon themselves to die—at a moment of their own choosing.

It is sad, really, that a man so extensively educated should be so naïve.

The philosopher Arthur Schopenhauer once observed that no one should read Hegel before the age of forty: the dangers of intellectual corruption were just too great. Marcuse is a case in point. He was so intoxicated by Hegel's dialectic that he could no longer register the most commonplace realities. His Marxist view of the world mandated that capitalism led to oppression, ergo capitalist societies were monuments of misery and unfreedom: Q.E.D. Never mind that the United States has developed into the most tolerant and prosperous society in history: the theory says that it can't happen, therefore what looks like freedom and prosperity *must* be an illusion. Marcuse's boldness in this direction is breathtaking. The fundamental point of *One-Dimensional Man* is that the better things appear to get, the worse they really are. "Under the rule of a repressive whole," he writes, "liberty can be made into a powerful instrument of domination." And again, "a rising standard of living is the almost unavoidable by-product of the politically manipulated society."

Repressive tolerance

Marcuse came up with several names for the idea that freedom is a form of tyranny. The most famous was "repressive tolerance," which was also the title of an essay he wrote on the subject in 1965. He even offered a simple formula for distinguishing between, on the one hand, the "repressive tolerance" that expresses itself in such phenomena as freedom of assembly and free speech and, on the other, the "liberating tolerance" he recommends. "Liberating tolerance," he wrote, "would mean intolerance against movements from the Right, and toleration of movements from the Left." In other words, "liberating tolerance" means acceptance of the ideas you agree with and rejection of those you disagree with. The usual name for this sort of attitude, of course, is intolerance, but no doubt it would be terribly intolerant to insist on such a repressive if elementary point.

What Marcuse wanted is "not 'equal' but *more* representation of the Left," and he blithely sanctioned "extralegal means if the legal ones have proved to be inadequate." Marcuse admitted that "extreme suspension of the right of free speech and free assembly is indeed justified only if the whole of society is in extreme danger," but he went on to note that "I maintain that our society is in such an emergency situation."

> Different opinions and "philosophies" can no longer compete peacefully for adherence and persuasion on rational grounds: the "marketplace of ideas" is organized and

delimited by those who determine the national and the individual interest. In this society, for which the ideologists have proclaimed the "end of ideology," the false consciousness has become the general consciousness—from the government down to its last objects.

No wonder Leszek Kolakowski concluded that Marcuse's philosophy advocated "Marxism as a Totalitarian Utopia." In the end, Kolakowski points out, Marcuse's entire system "depends on replacing the tyranny of logic by a police tyranny. . . . The Marcusian union of Eros and Logos can only be realized in the form of a totalitarian state, established and governed by force; the freedom he advocates is non-freedom."

The ideas put forward by people like Paul Goodman, Norman O. Brown, and Herbert Marcuse—to say nothing of Wilhelm Reich—are so extravagant that one is tempted to dismiss them as ridiculous figments of a diseased understanding. The problem is that these figments, deceptive though they undoubtedly are, have been extolled as liberating wisdom by an entire generation. If they are no longer declared with the same proselytizing fervor that they were in the 1960s, that is because they have become part of the established intellectual and moral climate we live with. We are no longer pioneers in the sexual revolution but settled inhabitants of the territory it claimed. Missionary zeal is pointless when practically everyone is already a tithe-paying member of the congregation.

The unlikely marriage of Marx and Freud is, as Harvey Mansfield has pointed out, based on a basic misreading of both authors. It is a marriage contracted out of fantasy and consummated in contradiction. It joins the revolutionary fervor of Marxism with Freud's apotheosis of sex but ignores Marx's premise that economics determines culture

171

even as it neglects Freud's insistence that civilization requires the repression of instinct. Among other things, this unlikely union shows that it is a great mistake to believe that ideas, because untrue or even preposterous, cannot therefore do great harm. As Irving Kristol observed in "Utopianism, Ancient and Modern," "the truth is that ideas are *all*-important. The massive and seemingly solid institutions of any society . . . are always at the mercy of the ideas in the heads of the people who populate these institutions." Goodman, Brown, and Marcuse promised boundless liberation. What they delivered was mystification and immorality. Their ideas seduced a generation, sowing emotional sterility and shamelessness: what Roger Scruton rightly described as "the dissipation of the self in loveless fantasy."

Chapter 7
The Greening of America

It is characteristic of this kind of movement that its aims and premises are boundless. A social struggle is seen not as a struggle for specific, limited objectives, but as an event of unique importance, different in kind from all other struggles known to history, a cataclysm from which the world is to emerge totally transformed and redeemed.
—Norman Cohn, *The Pursuit of the Millennium*, 1957

. . . the consciousness of the liberals had proved inadequate to the task.
—Charles Reich, *The Greening of America*, 1970

Woodstock generation

The unlikely marriage of Marx and Freud helped put into circulation a new demand for absolute freedom together with the promise of absolute ecstasy. This impossible union helped fuel America's cultural revolution. It was one of the primary realities that gave the long march its staying power—its "legs." What began in the 1950s with the gassy theorizing of figures like Herbert Marcuse, Wilhelm Reich, and Norman O. Brown came to fruition in the 1960s in the demand for "free love" and a life unencumbered by the impediments of everyday obligations and responsibilities. No event epitomized that mood more graphically than the Woodstock Festival in the summer of 1969.

It seems so long ago now: the sea of dancing, mud-caked, blissed-out teenagers, swaying in rain-soaked fields to the amplified beat of Jimi Hendrix and other pop icons of the day. But Woodstock is an illusion that will not go away. The reprise of the festival in 1994 and again in 1999 brought forth a flood of nostalgia for the original "summer of love." Of course, spoil-sports poked fun at the later festivals. Following the 1994 event, for example, one cartoon depicted a man on stage gazing out over an enormous crowd punctuated with tents advertising espresso and other yuppie comestibles: "People," he warned, "there is some bad Chardonnay going around." Although there were plenty of drug overdoses at Woodstock '94, there was something ridiculous about a commemoration of the counterculture that featured cash machines, ads for Pepsi and American Express, and a security force of twelve hundred.

The usual gloss on the event was that it represented the unfortunate "commercialization" of the original Woodstock: a beautiful idea besmirched by contact with the still-pervasive ethos of the greedy 1980s—that unenlightened time presided over by Ronald Reagan and his minions. One thing that this canard fails to acknowledge is that the promoters—who were the same for all the events—tried just as hard to clean up on the original Woodstock as they did on its successors. Only inexperience and bad planning prevented them from making the original celebration of peace and love a commercial triumph. Back in '69, they hadn't even thought of marketing Woodstock T-shirts. The reign of Häagen-Dazs ice cream and bottled water was yet a twinkle in the entrepreneurial eye.

It was not only a matter of hypocrisy. There was also a large dollop of self-delusion: about the extent to which communal hedonism was the path to enlightenment, for example, as well as the extent to which narcissistic self-gratification was tantamount to existential daring. As the critic Midge Decter observed in writing about Woodstock '99 in *The Wall Street Journal*,

> the fact that many of the young people there found themselves not only hungry but in dire need of medical attention, for dehydration, or drug overdose, or just general hysteria, was a subject that quickly became unmentionable in polite society. For in those muddy fields in 1969 what had been demonstrated to the extreme satisfaction of the liberal culture was that it had spawned a truly superior new generation, a generation, said the press and the clergy and the professoriate, whose idealistic like had never before been seen in a country so dismally in thrall, as ours supposedly was, to mere getting and spending.

As Decter concludes, "the culture's infatuation with the first Woodstock generation was as nothing compared with that generation's infatuation with itself."

And yet the champions of the "myth" of Woodstock were right about one thing. The festival really did epitomize the longings—the moral temperature as it were—of a generation. There were the drugs and music and clothes, of course—the LSD, rock, and denim—but there were also the blasé, pre-AIDS promiscuity, the grandiose political posturing, the extraordinary combination of naïveté and self-righteousness.

Above all, perhaps, there was the arrogant sense of entitlement that presupposed the very affluence and bourgeois economic largess that it pretended to reject. These were the defining elements of the original Woodstock. Its partisans were right in thinking that they added up to a cultural revolution, a "new sensibility" that would radically transform personal and institutional life.

The liberated lifestyle

It was this sensibility—the sensibility of the Sixties—that Woodstocks '94 and '99 were meant to commemorate in their orgies of nostalgia and regression to adolescence. And their success, both in themselves and as media events—as catnip for the public imagination—suggests the extent to which that sensibility has triumphed in our culture. In this sense, the later Woodstocks were not so much an elegy for past glories as a reminder of how deeply the basic imperatives of that new sensibility have penetrated. If they no longer seem revolutionary, it is because they have been thoroughly assimilated and are now simply taken for granted: they are part of the air we breathe.

No single figure or theme captures the totality of that revolution. But few figures better embody the ethos of Woodstock and the new sensibility it incarnated than the sometime tenured Yale law professor turned guru of higher consciousness, Charles Reich (no relation, except spiritual, to Wilhelm). His book *The Greening of America*, published in 1970 when he was forty-two, was both a blueprint for America's cultural revolution and a paean to its supposedly glorious results.

The Greening of America long ago took its place beside incense, love beads, and bellbottoms as part of the stale, slightly comic cultural paraphernalia of the Sixties. Reading the book's nearly four hundred pages today, it is difficult to appreciate the enormous sensation the book created when it first appeared. Did the country suddenly go mad? Quoth Reich:

In the world that now exists, a life of surfing *is* possible. *

Even businessmen, once liberated, would like to roll in the grass.

All choices are the 'right' choice.

Rationality does not like to blow its mind.

An examination or test is a form of violence.

Finally, speaking of the "ultimate sign of reverence, vulnerability, and innocence" of the liberated youth consciousness that he celebrates, Reich says: "'Oh wow!'"

"'Oh wow!'" Do not think that Reich sounds silly because he is quoted "out of context." As Thomas Mallon observed in a look back at *The Greening of America* in *The American Spectator* a few years ago, Charles Reich is one author who actually *benefits* by being quoted out of context. The more context you give him, the more preposterous he sounds. And yet the late William Shawn, then the editor of *The New Yorker*, thought the book important enough to excerpt in his magazine, thus reminding us that his publication of Jonathan Schell's hysterically alarmist book *The Fate of the Earth* in *The New Yorker* some years later was not simply a loopy aberration. Whatever his virtues as an editor, William Shawn had a large soft spot for unhinged left-wing drivel.

---

* Perhaps Reich was correct about surfing. In March 1999, newswires carried a story about Plymouth University in England, where students can now obtain a degree in surfing. Emphasizing the academic rigor of "Surf Science and Technology," Dr. Colin Williams, identified as the "head of surfing," said applicants would need A-levels as well as surf boards. The university's course catalog explains that "the three year (or four year with placement) course offers a broad perspective on the marine sciences and the technology underpinning the surf industry and the surf culture itself." Matthew Arnold, where art thou?

"Unhinged left-wing drivel"? Does that sound too severe, too judgmental, too hard? Read on.

The New Yorker was still an intellectually respectable magazine in 1970, and the appearance of The Greening of America in its pages in September 1970 gave the book tremendous advance publicity and cultural cachet. It also shows what tremendous inroads the long march of America's cultural revolution had already made. When The Greening of America was published by Random House in October, it instantly became a best-seller: more, it became a national preoccupation. The New York Times had just started its Op-Ed page in September 1970, under the editorship of Harrison Salisbury. That fall, Reich appeared not once but three times on the Op-Ed page with restatements of his argument. In short order, John Kenneth Galbraith, George F. Kennan, Herbert Marcuse, and Marya Mannes weighed in there with commentary on the book. This is in addition to the reviews and feature articles that the Times ran about Reich and his publishing phenomenon. Everywhere one turned, The Greening of America was being discussed, praised, criticized, often in the most solemn terms.

It was an intoxicating draught for many commentators. Writing in The New Republic, Peter Caws suggested with a straight face that "the genuine strengths of the book are two: its history and its economics." Just so we have our bearings, here are a couple of brief examples of Reich's thinking about economics:

Since machines can produce enough food and shelter for all, why should not man end the antagonism derived from scarcity and base his society on love for his fellow man?

The wisdom of the new generation is simply this: buy bread at the store when you want to spend your time in some other way than baking; bake your own bread when you feel the need to get back to basic things like dough and yeast.

Not that the responses to *The Greening of America* were uniformly admiring. Many, maybe most, serious responses were critical. Roger Starr wrote a long and politely devastating anatomy of the book in *Commentary* (a piece that we can only hope Caws read, since it patiently makes mincemeat of Reich's historical claims). The poet L. E. Sissman wrote an even more polite criticism of the book in *The Atlantic Monthly*. Sissman remarked on the curiosity that the first-person singular pronoun never appeared in a book that asserted that "the individual self is the only true reality." Who or what is the "we" that Reich decorously employs throughout his book? It is, Sissman concludes, "the communal we of 'all the people of the dining hall' whose help Reich acknowledges in a postscript, of all the confused and alienated young admirers Reich has become in his thoughts." (Reich confides in that postscript that much of his book "was written in the Stiles-Morse dining halls at Yale.") Perhaps the pithiest critical summary of the book was provided by Stewart Alsop, in *Newsweek*, who called the book "a bag of scary mush."

Stewart Alsop was right. But it didn't matter. None of the criticism mattered. One needn't be a Hegelian or a follower of Oswald Spengler to recognize the existence, at times, of something like a *Zeitgeist*. Reich began work on what became *The Greening of America* in 1960 when he left his job at a high-powered Washington law firm to go to Yale. His career hitherto—beginning with his editorship of the *Yale Law Review* and clerkship for Justice Hugo Black— made him seem an unlikely candidate for the post of cheerleader for the cultural revolution. But by the time the book appeared a decade later, he had shed whatever lawyerly sobriety he once possessed and had become a veritable weather vane for the *Zeitgeist*, breathless-with-starry-eyes department. In an extraordinary passage at the beginning of *The Greening of America*, he furnishes us with prediction, manifesto, and credo all rolled into one. "There is a revolution coming," Reich tells us.

> It will not be like revolutions of the past. It will originate with the individual and with culture, and it will change the political structure only as its final act. It will not require violence to succeed, and it cannot be successfully resisted by violence. It is now spreading with amazing rapidity, and already our laws, institutions, and social structure are changing in consequence. It promises a higher reason, a more human community, and a new and liberated individual. Its ultimate creation will be a new and enduring wholeness and beauty—a renewed relationship of man to himself, to other men, to society, to nature, and to the land.
>
> This is the revolution of the new generation. Their protest and rebellion, their culture, clothes, music, drugs, ways of thought, and liberated life-style are not a passing fad or a form of dissent and refusal, nor are they in any sense irrational. The whole emerging pattern, from ideals to campus demonstrations to beads and bell bottoms to the Woodstock Festival, makes sense and is part of a consistent philosophy. It is both necessary and inevitable, and in time it will include not only youth, but all people in America.

It is difficult to say what is more remarkable about this testimonial: its fatuousness or its accuracy. Whether or not the revolution Reich describes was "necessary and inevitable," it certainly did occur, and largely along the lines he delineates. His only mistake was in misconstruing the results: for whatever America's cultural revolution promised, it delivered not a "new and enduring wholeness and beauty" but a cultural and moral catastrophe whose consequences we are still reckoning.

Con games

As the manufacturers of successful patent medicines and miracle cures know, what matters is not the efficacy of the potion but the scope and vividness of the claims made on its behalf. The spiritual nostrum that Reich formulated consists essentially of two parts: 1. an attack on contemporary life in America; and 2. a utopian rhapsody about the emergence of a new, liberated consciousness. Neither part is distinguished by subtlety.

"America," Reich tells us, "is one vast terrifying anti-community." The source of the problem is the American Corporate State (upper case, please!), that "vast apparatus, working unceasingly to create a false consciousness in people." Consequently,

> work and living have become more pointless and empty. There is no lack of meaningful projects that cry out to be done, but . . . our working days are used up in work that lacks meaning: making useless or harmful products, or serving the bureaucratic structures. For most Americans, work is mindless, exhausting, boring, servile, and hateful.

More succinctly, "the majority of adults in the country *hate their work.*" In Reich's view, this is not really so surprising, since "beginning with school, if not before, an individual is systematically stripped of his imagination, his creativity, his heritage, his dreams, and his personal uniqueness, in order to style him into a productive unit for a mass, technological society. Instinct, feeling, and spontaneity are repressed by overwhelming forces." Which presumably means that the instinctive, spontaneous revulsion one feels for writing such as this is merely an illusion.

In chapters called "The Failure of Reform" and "Anatomy of the Corporate State," Reich makes some stabs at explaining how we came to be in such dreadful spiritual torpor. He speaks of the failure of the New Deal, the rise of multinational corporations, the insidious influence of advertising and the media, war, both the Cold and Vietnam varieties. There was nothing new in his diagnosis: scores of left-wing pundits had been decrying these and kindred evils at least since the end of World War II. But *The Greening of America* did stand out. This is partly because of the extremity of Reich's indictment: "America is one vast terrifying anti-community," etc. It is also because of his quasi-evolutionary model of "three general types of consciousness" that supposedly "predominate in America today." In fact, although his discussion is laughably crude, it was with his typology of "Consciousness I," "Consciousness II," and "Consciousness III" that Reich made his most indelible impression upon readers. Some went into ecstasies over it; others ridiculed it, twisting Reich's talk of "Con III people" into "Con-game," "Con-manship," and the like. Everybody remembered it.

According to Reich, Consciousness I originated in the nineteenth century. Its hallmarks are the rugged independence and pragmatism of laissez-faire capitalism. Its proponents believe "that success is determined by character, morality, and hard work, and self-denial." Once upon a time, such homely virtues had their uses. No more, though. Today, Reich explains, "Consciousness I types" include "farmers, owners of small businesses . . . AMA-type doctors . . . gangsters, Republicans, and 'just plain folks.'" (Gangsters, Republicans: you see what a master of subtlety Reich is.) But just as other Sixties radicals abominated the mainstream liberal establishment more than they hated any conservative orthodoxy, so Reich saves his bitterest words for the liberals who embody Consciousness II.

Consciousness I he regarded as a crude anachronism, no longer much of a threat to the emergence of paradise. Consciousness II, however, defines the *prevailing* reality—"the inhuman structure in which we now live," *viz* the ACS—the American Corporate State. Although Consciousness II began in the (for Reich) laudable reforms of the New Deal, its progressive force spent itself long ago. Now it is typified in the mindset of "aircraft employees, old leftists, young doctors, Kennedy men, suburban housewives." (Reich did have a talent for making lists.) With its "ethic of control, of technology, of the rational intellect," Consciousness II was the real enemy of liberation. It was the rational intellect, especially, that bothered him, because "when experience is classified or analyzed it is also reduced." Never mind that some such "reduction" is required if experience is to be articulate, coherent, or publicly communicable: Reich wants his experience raw and unedited. Consciousness II, he explains, "has been persuaded that the richness, the satisfactions, the joy of life are to be found in power, success, status, acceptance, popularity, achievements, rewards, excellence, and the rational competent mind."

Well, that's a start, you may say. But the problem is that Consciousness II "wants nothing to do with dread, awe, wonder, mystery, accidents, failure, helplessness, magic."

"I'm glad I'm me"

Like many radicals, Reich was both terrified and obsessed by power: "It is not the misuse of power that is the evil," he assured us; "the very *existence* of power is an evil." Don't bother raising objections: objections, arguments, qualifications, evidence: all the paraphernalia of rationality belongs to the unenlightened domain of Consciousness II. Reich has no time for any of that. He is interested in the supposedly higher Con, Consciousness III. Introducing Consciousness III, Reich sounds at first like an epidemiologist. It began with "a few individuals" in the mid-1960s; it "sprouted up, astonishingly and miraculously, out of the stony soil of the American Corporate State"; no one foresaw its appearance, but it soon "spread, here and abroad, by means invisible." Though it spread like the measles, Consciousness III is difficult to describe because, as Reich notes, the very attempt to say what it is draws on intellectual habits that Consciousness III rejects: "Authority, schedules, time, accepted customs, are all forms which must be questioned. Accepted patterns of thought must be broken; what is considered 'rational thought' must be opposed by 'nonrational thought'—drug-thought, mysticism, impulses."

Not entirely, though. Reich does allow that the "foundation" of Consciousness III is "liberation." He adds that "the meaning of liberation is that the individual is free to build his own philosophy and values, his own life-style, and his own culture from a new beginning." More generally, Consciousness III comes into being when an individual frees himself from the "false consciousness" that society imposes. People infused with the spirit of Consciousness III do "not believe in the antagonistic or competitive doctrine of life," they "do not compete 'in real life.' . . . People are brothers, the world is ample for all. . . . No one judges anyone else." Also, everyone rather likes himself: "Consciousness III says, 'I'm glad I'm me.'"

If you are looking for a concrete example of what Reich

had in mind when he praised this higher consciousness, think back to the American campus in 1970. "One of the few places to observe man partially free of the competition and antagonism that are the norms of our social system is in a college dining hall where many of the students are Consciousness III people." Be that as it may, Reich was certainly correct to see the American university as one of the chief breeding grounds for the revolution he envisions. He speaks in this context of the "conversions" that are "constantly seen on campuses today": "a freshman arrives, his political views are hometown–Consciousness I, and suddenly he is radicalized." Reich is correct about this. "In a brief span of months, a student, seemingly conventional in every way, changes his haircut, his clothes, his habits, his interests, his political attitudes, his way of relating to other people, in short, his whole way of life." Indeed.

One might have thought that the author of these millenarian sentiments must himself be a happy Consciousness III type, full of confidence, optimism, and sassy derring-do. Not a bit of it. In *The Sorcerer of Bolinas Reef*, an autobiography that he published in 1976, Reich reveals himself to have been a pathetic soul, paralyzed with nameless fears and unsatisfied longings. The ordinary tasks of daily life filled him with dread; normal human relations were completely beyond him. "The most constant presence in my life was fear and anxiety," he wrote.

> I would wake up in the morning and feel the need to clench my fists and clamp my teeth and squeeze my toes together, which sent tension all through my body as waves of fear and worry came over me. The particular things I worried about changed from day to day or hour to hour or week to week but that terrible feeling of dread remained with me almost all the time. I hated that feeling. It made me afraid

of living. It made me not want to wake up, not want to go out, not want to come home, not want to go to sleep.

I worried about getting to work on time. I worried about my clothes and my appearance. A tiny slip in a brief I wrote might cause inconceivable disaster. I feared criticism or pressure from the senior partners. A business trip by plane filled me with worry about reservations and hotels and connections. And yet work was the least of my worries. It was in the rest of my life that I was most overwhelmed. I think I feared most the discovery and exposure of my secrets. All of my sexual feelings were repressed into an intense fantasy world that filled me with unsatisfied desire.

The Greening of America is in part a paean to sexual liberation and polymorphous sensuality, an obvious heir to the thought of countercultural gurus like Herbert Marcuse, the other Reich—Wilhelm—and Norman O. Brown. "What the new generation has already achieved is a way of being with other people that is closer, warmer, more open, more sensitive, more capable of sharing, than prior generations have known." But in *The Sorcerer of Bolinas Reef*, Reich tells us that in December, 1971, he left Yale for a six-month leave of absence and went to San Francisco. There he responded to an ad placed by a male model and for $35 the prophet of Consciousness III and "closer, warmer, more open, more sensitive" relationships had his first sexual experience at the age of forty-three.

Revolutionary bellbottoms

Charles Reich's sad and tawdry autobiographical revelations tell us something important about the psychological origins of his profound dissatisfaction with America and his fantasies of inhabiting a "higher," trouble-free consciousness. What they don't explain is why this personal diatribe against the world should have struck such a sympathetic chord. Perhaps many other people felt similar frustrations, though Reich surely presents an extreme case. From the perspective of the 1990s and beyond, what is most extraordinary about *The Greening of America* is the extent to which its complaints, its modes of thought, and its ideals summarized the radical agenda of America's cultural revolution. Reich's insistence that utopia was to be won through "a higher, transcendent reason," not politics per se, distinguishes his project from the violent activist crusades of the Weathermen, the Black Panthers, and other such groups, which were achieving critical mass just as his work was published. (At one point he writes that "the hard questions—if by that is meant political and economic organization—are insignificant, even irrelevant.") But apart from this, *The Greening of America* offered an impressive inventory of radical concerns and shibboleths, most of which are still very much in circulation.

At the center of Reich's gospel is an indictment of rationality coupled with a profound craving for extra-rational modes of experience. His celebration of drugs —which he described as "one of the most important means for restoring dulled consciousness"—has to be understood in this context, as do his hosannas to polymorphous sexuality and rock music. According to Reich, rock music possesses "a complexity unknown to classical music"; it offers "the mystical transcendence of ordinary experience." In comparison to rock, he said, "Beethoven seems like a series of parallel lines." Without drugs and rock music, Woodstock and the sensibility it celebrated—the sensibility that Reich eulogizes in *The Greening of America*—would have been impossible. Allan Bloom was quite right when he observed, in *The Closing of the American Mind*, that "Nothing is more singular about this generation than its addiction to music."

> Rock music provides premature ecstasy and, in this respect, is like the drugs with which it is allied. It artificially produces the exaltation naturally attached to the completion of the greatest endeavors—victory in a just war, consummated love, artistic creation, religious devotion, and discovery of the truth.

What rock offers is a prefabricated Dionysian ecstasy, blatantly sexual, conspicuously nonrational.

The rejection of rationality has many advantages. For one thing, it relieves Reich of the burden of producing evidence for his pronunciamentos—e.g., the claim that "the majority of adults in the country *hate their work.*" Reasons, evidence, arguments: what are they but stodgy appurtenances of the rational intellect? Transcending rationality also allows one to stop worrying about details like contradiction and consistency. Reich's classification of people as belonging to one of three types of consciousness is the crudest, most patronizing sort of stereotyping imaginable. And yet in the midst of excoriating "farmers, owners of small businesses, . . . AMA-type doctors . . . gangsters, Republicans, and 'just plain folks'" he tells us that Consciousness III refuses "to evaluate people by general standards, it refuses to classify people, or analyze them." Of course, it is not that Reich wishes to stop classifying or evaluating people; by no means; he wishes only to classify and evaluate them according to the essentially subjective standard of "lifestyle." We see something similar in his rejection of "the whole concept of excellence and comparative merit." Reich goes pretty far, far enough to suggest that he might have a bright future in a politically correct college administration or, indeed, in a Washington administration. "Someone may be a brilliant thinker," he says, "but he is not 'better' at thinking than anyone else, he simply possesses his own excellence. A person who thinks very poorly is still excellent in his own way." And yet here, too, it is clear that Reich is "non-judgmental" in a very selective fashion. To take just one example: reflecting on traditional morality, Reich assures us that "to observe duties toward others, after the feelings are gone, is no virtue and may even be a crime." "Crime" is a troubling word, surely, especially when used by a lawyer who believes that "there is no situation in which one is entitled to act impersonally . . . with another human being."

Reich did make a few gestures toward common sense. But they were only gestures. Early on he acknowledges that his categories of Cons I, II & III "are highly impressionistic and arbitrary." And yet he proceeds to build his entire argument around them. Again, he tells us that the "basic stance" of Consciousness III is "openness to any and all experience." Only later did it occur to him that this might have unpleasant implications. So he hastened to assure us that a "Consciousness III person" will not "engage in actions that violate his basic values; he will never kill or rape to try the experience." One is glad to know that, of course; but why not? If one's "basic stance" is openness to "any and all experience," who's to say that rape and murder are not among one's "basic values," especially as values are something Reich insisted each individual must "create" for himself?

With the passage of time, the mushiness of Reich's diagnosis has become painfully obvious. Sometimes, it is downright funny, as when Reich tells us that bellbottoms and other certified articles of countercultural apparel "deny the importance of hierarchy, status, authority, position, and they reject competition"—unless, that is, they come from a New York designer: "Bell bottoms fashioned by New York stylists do not have the revolutionary potential of Consciousness III culture." What makes the mush scary, as Stewart Alsop discerned, is Reich's moralistic pretension to special virtue and a knowledge that transcends "mere" facts. It is here that he is in perfect continuity with today's champions of political correctness. (One inevitably thinks of that other graduate of the Yale Law School, Hillary Clinton, who became a champion of the "politics of meaning" in the mid-1990s.) Again and again we have seen how the demand for total freedom has paradoxically resulted in greater and greater restrictions on freedom. What began in license ends in regulation. "Consciousness III people," Reich tells us, "see effortlessly what is phony or dishonest in politics, or what is ugly or meretricious in architecture and city planning, whereas an older person has to go through years of education [or perhaps we should say 're-education'] to make himself equally aware." Simply by virtue of having the right attitude, of adopting the correct "life-style," Reich's apostle of Consciousness III is vouchsafed a "new knowledge": "He does not 'know' the facts, but he still 'knows' the truth that seems hidden from others."

The hubris of such claims is a familiar ingredient of millenarian enthusiasms. The historian Norman Cohn noted that "at the core" of certain medieval millenarian sects was the adept's belief that "he had attained a perfection so absolute that he was incapable of sin. . . . Every impulse was experienced as a divine command." Cohn also noted that, translated into political terms, the presumption of such "new knowledge" is a recipe for totalitarian arrogance. Hannah Arendt observed in *The Origins of Totalitarianism* that the claim to special insight is closely related to "totalitarian movements' spurious claims to have abolished the separation between public and private life and to have restored a mysterious wholeness in man." (One recalls Susan Sontag's contention that the North Vietnamese "are 'whole' human beings, not 'split' as we are.")

Charles Reich assured us that "the consciousness of the liberals had proved inadequate to the task" of restoring the lost wholeness he sought. Nevertheless, the liberal establishment was delighted to conspire in its own disparagement along the lines Reich suggested. The path to enlightenment that Reich extolled was a path to nowhere —to "utopia" in its etymological sense. That did not prevent it from becoming a major highway for the long march through American life. The unhappy example of Charles Reich—his silly book, his fifteen minutes of celebrity—should not distract us from the malevolence of the message he helped promulgate. He himself was rather like the unfortunate Seth, emperor of Azania, whom Evelyn Waugh described in his novel *Black Mischief*:

> The earnest and rather puzzled young man became suddenly capricious and volatile; ideas bubbled up within him, bearing to the surface a confused sediment of phrase and theory, scraps of learning half understood and fantastically translated.

Although Reich managed pretty well to destroy his own life, he was too fuzzy-headed and inept to find many real disciples. In this respect, he was more a symptom than a cause. In the hands of people like Timothy Leary, however, the nonsense that made up Reich's pseudomystical "philosophy" damaged countless lives and insinuated itself into the inner fabric of American life.

Chapter 8
The Project of Rejuvenilization

*The adepts of the Free Spirit did not form a single church but rather a
number of likeminded groups, each with its own particular practices,
rites, and articles of beliefs; and the links between the various groups
were often tenuous. But these people did keep in touch with one another;
and the Free Spirit was at all times recognizable as a quasi-religion
with a single basic corpus of doctrine. . . . They divided humanity into
two groups—the majority, the "crude in spirit," who failed to develop
their divine sensibilities, and themselves, who were the "subtle in spirit."
. . . The heart of the heresy was in fact not a philosophical idea at all
but an aspiration; it was a passionate desire of certain human beings
to surpass the condition of humanity and to become God.*
—Norman Cohn, *The Pursuit of the Millennium*, 1957

*For us the planet was without Original Sin, designed for our
sacramental pleasure.*
—Timothy Leary, *Flashbacks: An Autobiography*, 1983

Becoming mystics on the spot

No account of the long march of America's cultural
revolution can omit the career of Timothy Leary,
"promoter, apologist, and high priest of psychedelia non-
pareil," as Theodore Roszak put it in his book *The Making of*

a Counterculture (1969). Dr. Timothy Leary, Ph.D., had his first experience of LSD in the spring of 1962, when he was forty-two and teaching in the psychology department at Harvard University. In the summer of 1963, Leary and his colleague Richard Alpert—who would later turn himself into a guru and take the Hindu name Baba Ram Dass— would be expelled from the Harvard faculty for disseminating drugs to students. If Charles Reich could assure his readers that psychoactive drugs were "one of the most important means for restoring dulled consciousness" and get away with it, it was largely because the ground for such credulousness had been prepared beforehand by apostles of the drug culture like Leary and Alpert. In the early 1960s, both men were sedulous in "researching" the effects of these drugs. They eagerly "experimented"—to use the preferred euphemism—on themselves and on hundreds of others with various hallucinogenic drugs, especially psilocybin.

But LSD was something new and much more powerful. First synthesized in 1938, it had, Leary knew, been secretly tested by the CIA* in the late 1950s for possible use in inter-

---

* Leary later claimed that the whole psychedelic movement had been "planned and scripted by the Central Intelligence [Agency]." *Acid Dreams: The Complete Social History of LSD* by Martin Lee and Bruce Shlain offers an extensively documented exploration of that thesis. Written from a hard left-wing perspective—it is endorsed, *inter alios*, by William S. Burroughs and Allen Ginsberg—*Acid Dreams* is part paean to psychedelics, part paranoid anti-American diatribe. The authors repeatedly assure us that people will continue to take LSD "to satisfy a deep rooted need for wholeness and meaning," etc., even as they excoriate the CIA for its experiments with the drug on various unwitting individuals. The book needs to be taken with a grain of salt—it will appeal, as Andrei Codrescu says in his introduction to the 1992 edition, to "believers in capital C Conspiracy." Nevertheless, it provides disturbing and credible evidence of abuses by the CIA and other agencies of the United States government.

rogations and unconventional warfare. Its mind-altering effects were prodigious. In the words of an official intelligence document, LSD was "capable of rendering whole groups of people, including military forces, indifferent to their surroundings and situations, interfering with planning and judgment, and even creating apprehension, uncontrollable confusion and terror."

Leary's introduction to the drug came through an English academic named Michael Hollingshead. "On the basis of his claim to have ingested more LSD than anyone in the world," Leary recalled in *Flashbacks*, the autobiography he published in 1983 (new edition, 1990), "I invited him to stay at our house and act as a project consultant." A short while before, Hollingshead had inadvertently taken a large dose of LSD with a colleague. "They became," Leary wrote, "mystics on the spot."

Like so many apostles of mind-altering drugs, Timothy Leary was very big on the idea of becoming a mystic on the spot. He did it hundreds, indeed thousands, of times. Leary first sampled hallucinogenic drugs in Mexico in 1960 (more "research" for his new job at Harvard). Describing the experience years later, he wrote that

> I gave way to delight, as mystics have for centuries when they peek through the curtains and discovered that this world—so manifestly real—was actually a tiny stage set constructed by the mind. . . .
>
> Starting back to the terrace. Hello, my walk had changed to a rubber-leg slither. The room was apparently filled with invisible liquid. I undulated over to Poet Betty. Her classic face unfolded like a sunflower. She was in some sort of bliss. . . .
>
> Next came a trip through evolution, guaranteed to everyone who signs up to this Brain Tour. Slipping down

the recapitulation tube to those ancient mid-brain projection rooms: snake-time, fish-time, down-through-giant-jungle-palm-tree-time, green lacy fern leaf–time. . . . Hello, I am the first living thing.

The journey lasted a little over four hours. Like almost everyone who has had the veil drawn, I came back a changed man.

Among other things, he discovered that "the world was divided into those who had had the experience (or were eager to have it) and those who had not (and shuddered at the possibility)."

Such pronouncements are a wearying staple of Leary's many books and pamphlets about the beneficent "mind-expanding" properties of hallucinogens. *The Psychedelic Experience* (1964), *Psychedelic Prayers from the Tao Te Ching* (1967), *How to Start Your Own Religion* (1967), *The Politics of Ecstasy* (1968), *High Priest* (1968), and on and on. They all revolve around Leary's reports of the life-changing enlightenment that he enjoyed thanks to drugs. When he was finally introduced to LSD, he found it "the most shattering experience of my life."

I have never recovered from that ontological confrontation. I have never been able to take myself, my mind, or the social world quite so seriously. Since that time, I have been acutely aware that everything I perceive, everything within and around me, is a creation of my own consciousness. And that everyone lives in a neural cocoon of private reality. From that day I have never lost the sense that I am an actor, surrounded by characters, props, and sets for the comic drama being written in my brain.

Untangling everything that is incoherent and prepos-

196

terous about such reports would require many pages. Just
for starters, one might ask why, if everyone is trapped in the
cocoon of a private reality, anyone bothers to write books
advertising the fact. Who could read them? And if Leary's
amateur solipsism were right, how could such a thing as a
book even exist? Think about how much solid social reality
there must be before books could be written, printed, cir-
culated, read. And on the question of mystical illumination,
what depths of credulity must be plumbed before someone
could mistake a deliberate pharmacological assault on the
nervous system for an experience of divine truth, a chemical
emergency for an "ontological confrontation"? Among
other things, such credulity reminds one of how elaborate
are the excuses one can generate and embrace for the sake
of a hedonistic evasion of reality. Leary's perception that he
had become an actor in a "comic drama" of his own making
has a little more to be said for it, though it would be more
accurate to describe the situation he created as a tragedy
with distinctly farcical elements. In any event, histrionics,
not to say melodrama—not to say outright hucksterism—
played a prominent part in Leary's activities from the
beginning.

"Turn on, tune in, drop out"

Long before his death in 1996 at the age of seventy-six,
Timothy Leary had become an absurd and pitiable figure.
The absurdity and the pathos culminated in the gruesome
theater of his death. In his autobiography, Leary had
speculated that "it may become possible to postpone dying
indefinitely while advances in molecular reconstruction
eliminate involuntary irreversible death. Fewer subjects," he
added, "are of greater personal interest to me at this mo-

ment." Accordingly, Leary directed that when he died his brain be cryogenically preserved "with the expectation of reanimation and brain-transplant to a healthy body in the future." ("It seems to me," he explained, "that the person who dies a 'natural' death is a deluded victim of state-managed suicide.") His final moments and the surgical removal of his head were captured on video tape for the edification of his acolytes.*

Leary's preposterousness did not make his influence any less widespread or any less malign. His life was in many respects a cautionary tale—not least as an example of the extent to which it had become possible to be ridiculous and profoundly destructive at the same time. This was an amalgam that the Sixties rather specialized in. Like many of his peers, Leary illustrated the fact that being an object of pity does not necessarily exempt someone from being also an object of censure.

His advocacy of hallucinogens was, as Theodore Roszak put it, the advocacy of a "counterfeit infinity." Roszak was himself an apologist for many aspects of the counterculture. But like many politically committed Leftists, he understood that Leary's obsession with drugs was not aiding the cause of political revolution. Leary's assurance that "the LSD trip is a religious pilgrimage" was a gross, psychically maiming deception—of himself, possibly; certainly of the thousands

---

* That is according to some sources. According to the Timothy Leary website (http://www.leary.com), the film in question "was a simulation created by profiteering filmmakers." The authors of the website explain that although "Leary was excited by the possibility of freezing his body in cryonic suspension," he discovered that the company with which he contracted to perform the procedure planned "to defame Leary and exploit the situation" for its own benefit. Instead, Leary's ashes, together with those of Gene Roddenberry, the creator of "Star Trek," and others were blasted 300 miles into space.

upon thousands whom he seduced with his gospel of instant ecstasy. Leary produced an endless stream of books,
pamphlets, and manifestos (his annotated bibliography
runs to 305 pages). But his teaching—if "teaching" is the
mot juste—is accurately epitomized in his most famous
slogan: "Turn on, tune in, drop out," a pithy formula he
came up with in 1966 after Marshall McLuhan (himself a
false prophet of considerable influence) advised him that
"your advertising must stress the religious."

Three decades on, it is difficult to recapture the peculiar
intensity of Leary's presence in the 1960s and early 1970s. A
popular rock band, The Moody Blues, wrote a hit song
about him; he fraternized with the super-chic from New
York to Hollywood and San Francisco; in 1970, when he
planned to run for Governor of California, John Lennon of
The Beatles wrote a campaign song for him; President
Nixon described him as "the most dangerous man in
America." For a brief period in the mid- to late Sixties,
Leary was ubiquitous: a beaming, gurulike presence at the
first Love-Ins and Be-Ins, barefoot and ponytailed, dressed
in white duck trousers and a flowing white silk shirt,
spouting such nostrums as "laws are made by old people
who don't want young people to do exactly those things
young people were meant to do—to make love, turn on,
and have a good time."

A bit earlier, it was Leary the clean-cut Harvard special-
ist who first introduced Allen Ginsberg—another self-
described "student of altered states"—to psilocybin. (It was
Leary also who first gave the drug to Arthur Koestler,
Robert Lowell, Maynard Ferguson, and Jack Kerouac. He
even traveled to Tangier to introduce it to William S. Burroughs.) Reflecting later on his experience of psilocybin
with Ginsberg and two friends, he announced that "the
four of us had reached a place where we were momentarily

beyond social roles, beyond normal strivings. We had apparently tapped some meditative overview circuit of our brains that allowed us to share a moment of philosophic understanding." This, he concluded, "suggested exciting social applications."

Different though their backgrounds were, Leary and Ginsberg exerted a similar influence on the counterculture. By the mid-Sixties, both had emerged as iconic figures. For both men, drugs were a central part of their gospel of liberation. But drugs were not the only part; promiscuous sex was also crucial. Leary was not quite in Ginsberg's league here, but he did his best. He appropriately titles one chapter of *Flashbacks* "The Ultimate Aphrodisiac," referring to LSD. Again and again in his autobiography Leary doses himself and some friends with hallucinogens and then treats his readers to passages like this: "My eyes connected with hers. We rose as one and walked to the sun porch. She turned, came to me, entwined her arms around my neck. . . ." Or this, about his honeymoon in the Far East with his second wife:

> Ever since my Easter Sunday session at the Millbrook Meditation House I had been convinced that the linkage of opposites was the key to personal evolution. Nanette shared this belief that a man and a woman who learned how to shift realities in unison, moving from one level of consciousness to another together, were a powerful creative force. . . . Nanette and I had one more LSD session in the Himalayas to see if we could get fused again.

(They didn't, alas, and the marriage soon ended.)

Then there was rock music. Ginsberg and Leary both wholeheartedly embraced its Dionysian promise. Leary dedicates *High Priest* to a dozen rock groups—The Beatles,

The Byrds, The Rolling Stones, etc.—as the "authentic priests, the real prophets" of "the psychedelic revolution." Finally, there was the bogus embrace of Eastern religion: the chanting, the incense, the pilgrimages to India and Tibet, the *I Ching*, *The Tibetan Book of the Dead*, assorted Hindu and Buddhist scriptures—a nauseating goulash of pseudospirituality. It was, as Philip Beidler noted, a "new age gospel" drawn from "various hip oracles and spare parts of the world's major religions." There was Allen Ginsberg with his finger-cymbals chanting Hare Krishna and antiwar slogans, and Leary filling his books with snippets from the *I Ching* and dismissing "the Judeo-Christian commitment to one God, one religion, one reality that has cursed Europe for centuries and America since our founding days." It was all window-dressing, really, for at bottom Leary's attitude toward religion was summed up in another chapter title in his autobiography: "Drugs Are the Origin of Religion and Philosophy." His own "church," incorporated in New York in 1966, was called the League for Spiritual Discovery—LSD for short—"an orthodox, psychedelic religion" whose "sacraments" "are psychedelic chemicals which at every turning point in human history have been provided by God for man's illumination and liberation."

The chief difference between Ginsberg and Leary was what we might call the *direction* of their influence. Ginsberg brought the existential sanction of bohemia: here he was, a poet, a denizen of New York's East Village, taking on the stuffy middle-class morality of white-collar America. Leary *was* white-collar America. Even if his childhood and college years were far from placid, he radiated patrician confidence and good looks. From his perch at Harvard, the young, handsome, charismatic psychologist brought the authority of the Ivy League to the ingestion of mind-altering drugs and the hedonism of the counterculture.

He also brought the authority of science—or more accurately the appearance of that authority. Looking back on his writings now, one sees that one of their most peculiar features is the oscillation between the vocabulary of science and the grammar of intoxication. Leary met few drugs he did not like. He has some mildly disapproving things to say about heroin in his autobiography: he found it a "euphoric downer" of "no appeal" but noted that his "experiments" with it were "useful in the context of my work as a drug researcher." The word "research" covered a multitude of sins. Leary was always on hand with "research projects," "content analyses," and plans to "develop a scientific classification model of the levels or circuits of the nervous system." Of course what he was really talking about was mind-shattering inebriation caused by the most powerful psychoactive agents known to man:

> Training centers like ours, we believed, could be set up in any medical school, in any divinity school, in the psychology, philosophy, anthropology, sociology departments of every college in the land. In another year or two anyone with philosophic ambitions and a thoughtful desire to increase intelligence could learn how to use drugs effectively. Freshman courses in college curricula could train students to activate their own nervous systems according to instructions of the manufacturers.

It is hard to know what is best about this typical paragraph: the invocation of "training centers" or the casual reference to "anyone with philosophic ambitions." In any event, it is worth noting that Leary the "researcher" was never content simply to dispense drugs to others and record their reactions; right from the beginning, he was a participant, eagerly seizing every opportunity for intoxication, even when he experimented with psilocybin on prisoners in the Concord State Prison. ("The bowl of pills was placed in the center of the table. To establish trust I was the first to ingest.") It should be noted, too, that Leary got his wish: it really was only a year or two before college students became quite expert at "activating their own nervous systems" with drugs. There was nothing to it, really. The manufacturers didn't need to supply elaborate "instructions."

If Leary brought the authority of Harvard and the Ivy League to the counterculture, he brought it as a chastened, a dethroned authority. That is part of what made him so seductive. Leary was a Harvard professor who had seen through the "superficialities" and conventions of the hidebound academic establishment:

> I was at that time a successful robot—respected at Harvard, clean-cut, witty, and, in that inert culture, unusually creative. Though I had attained the highest ambition of the young American intellectual, I was totally cut off from body and senses. My clothes had been obediently selected to fit the young professional image. Even after one hundred drug sessions I routinely listened to pop music, drank martinis, ate what was put before me.

Leave aside the sillinesses in this passage. (Why shouldn't he eat what was put before him? What else was he supposed to do with a martini?) The important thing is that Leary had discovered how to have the best of both worlds. He could enjoy the prestige of being a Harvard professor *and* the delicious frisson of rejecting it all at the same time. His expulsion from Harvard further burnished his image: now he was a martyr as well as a witness for a truth too dangerous for "the establishment" to accommodate.

A nationally recognized symbol of change

In fact, despite attaining an appointment at Harvard, Leary had always been at odds with the world. An only child, he was born in Springfield, Massachusetts, in 1920. He describes his mother's family as dour Irish Catholic, his father's as "urban, urbane, well-to-do." (Leary's paternal grandfather was thought to be the richest Irish Catholic in Western Massachusetts.) The expected inheritance had all but evaporated by the time Leary's grandfather died, however, and this disappointment sent Leary's father—a drunken, part-time dentist—around the bend and away from the family. Still, Leary seems to have harbored warm feelings about his irresponsible father. "During the thirteen years we lived together," Leary wrote, "he never stunted me with expectations."

With such a patrimony, Leary did not find the discipline required by school and college easy. Nevertheless, he was voraciously curious and often excelled in his studies. After a year at Holy Cross College in Worcester, Massachusetts, he transferred to West Point. Within a year he found himself in punitive isolation and soon agreed to leave. He then enrolled at the University of Alabama, but was expelled for spending the night in the girls' dormitory. Drafted, he worked at an army hospital where he met his first wife, Marianne. He finished his B.A. in the army, took an M.A. at Washington State University and his Ph.D. at the University of California at Berkeley. On his thirty-fifth birthday, he woke up to find that Marianne had committed suicide by shutting herself in the garage and starting the car. Leary suggests that the suicide was the result of postpartum depression—they had two children, then six and eight (a lengthy case of baby blues, that)—although he does acknowledge that Marianne was less than happy about his long-term affair with the wife of a friend. ("For two years Delsey and I met three or four times a week. . . . We really liked each other.")

Leary worked for several years as a psychologist at the Kaiser Foundation Hospital in Oakland, California. In 1959, disillusioned with the profession, he quit his job and moved to Florence. It was there that he met the director of Harvard's Center for Personality Research, impressed him with words like "existential" and "transaction," and landed himself a job. The name of Harvard naturally provided Leary's activities with a patina of respectability. It also ensured that his exaltation of drugs would cause a major scandal when it finally became apparent that this young researcher was passing out powerful mind-altering substances to almost anyone who asked for them. It is difficult to say exactly which of Leary's outrages sealed his fate with the Harvard authorities. Maybe it was his collusion in the "medically supervised, double-blind pre- and post-tested" experiment of dosing thirty students with psychedelics at a Good Friday church service while thirty received placebos. (The placebos were a waste of time, Leary tells us: "After thirty minutes everyone knew who had taken the pill.") Or perhaps it was his letter, written with Richard Alpert, to the Harvard *Crimson* in the Spring of 1963 outlining plans to establish a nationwide drug research project called the International Foundation for Internal Freedom (IFIF for short: Leary was always coming up with sly acronyms). "The national headquarters would publish a scholarly journal, . . . help locals to obtain good quality drugs, and coordinate summer workshops in Mexico."

Whatever the back-breaking straw, Leary and Alpert found themselves expelled from the Harvard faculty in the summer of 1963. The news came when Leary was "coordinating a workshop" in Mexico. Far from impeding him, though, the widely reported firing added luster to his reputation as a psychedelic guru. Leary managed to get himself deported from Mexico and the Caribbean island of Dominica that summer; but by September things were looking up. Two rich Americans lent Leary and Alpert a huge estate in Millbrook, New York, and gave them money to establish a new foundation and pursue their "studies." Millbrook, as Leary notes, soon became a preferred retreat for "jet-setters, celebrities, curious aristocrats. A weekend at Millbrook was the chic thing for the hip young rich of New York. At the same time we entertained biologists from Yale, Oxford psychologists, Hindu holy men." Soon, he was catapulted from notoriety to real celebrity. By the mid-Sixties, Leary boasted, "I had become a nationally recognized symbol of change."

Leary was also becoming a nationally recognized concern of the police. At the end of 1965, he was arrested with Rosemary, his new girlfriend, and his two children in Laredo, Texas, for possession of a small amount of marijuana. (It was actually in the possession of his daughter, but he gallantly claimed responsibility.) He was initially sentenced to thirty years in prison and a twenty thousand dollar fine.

Back in Dutchess County, New York, Leary's neighbors were exceedingly displeased by the sordid goings-on at the Millbrook estate. That winter, the estate was raided by a team from the Dutchess County sheriff's office led by G. Gordon Liddy, later of Watergate fame. In 1967, Leary moved to Los Angeles. One of his first acts was to marry Rosemary (number three of four wives). The service took place on a mountaintop in the Joshua Tree National Monument. A Plains Indian medicine man presided. "We partied until midnight," Leary recalled, and then the assembled company, "numbering fifty, dropped large doses of acid and reclined on soft ledges to talk things over with the stars."

Leary's campaign to be governor of California two years later was interrupted by another arrest for possession of marijuana. This time, he was not only found guilty but also remanded to jail immediately. Leary's career now rapidly devolved into melodramatic farce. In September 1970, he managed a daring escape from his minimum-security prison in San Luis Obispo. By prearrangement, he was picked up by members of the Weather Underground, one of the most violent of American radical groups. Leary himself repudiated his earlier pacifism and came to think of himself as "a psychedelic revolutionary." In a manifesto called "Shoot to Live," he advocated sabotage and other "acts of resistance," explaining that "to shoot a genocidal robot policeman in defense of life is a sacred act." In a postscript, he warned that "I am armed and should be considered dangerous to anyone who threatens my life and freedom."

Leary was disguised, given a new passport and new identity ("Mr. William McNellis"), and was soon bundled out of the country to Algeria, where he and Rosemary enjoyed the hospitality of the Black Panther Eldridge Cleaver, who was presiding there over an American "government in exile." After a brief period of enthusiasm, Leary's relationship with the Panthers degenerated "into a battle of egos." Cleaver soon had Leary and Rosemary under house arrest. Only when he announced that a large money order had arrived at his bank did Leary and Rosemary manage to escape from the "protective custody" of the Panthers and flee to Geneva. Pressure from the U.S. government then forced them to leave Switzerland for Afghanistan. In 1973, Leary was arrested at the Kabul air terminal and returned to the United States, where he was shuttled among various prisons and did a brief spell with the notorious LSD-crazed murderer Charles Manson.

Forgetting his brief and largely rhetorical career as a violent revolutionary, Leary tended to present himself as an impish, benignly antiestablishment figure, freed by his drug-induced excursions from the petty material concerns that bind lesser mortals. ("I was," Leary wrote, "precisely, intelligently re-created to play a role necessary for the evolution of our human gene pool.") Nevertheless, according to a recent report in *The New York Times*, Leary "quietly cooperated with the Federal Bureau of Investigation in 1974 and informed on a radical leftist group in hopes of winning his freedom from jail." He even "reportedly identified his collaborators in a 1970 escape from prison." In 1976, when Edmund ("Jerry") Brown became governor of California, Leary was granted early parole for "good behavior." After that, he became an early devotee of computers and "cyber reality" as well as a fixture on the lecture circuit, where he frequently appeared debating G. Gordon Liddy, also lately released from prison.

Forms of rejuvenilization

It is easy to dismiss Timothy Leary as a crank, a period figure whose relevance disappeared with bellbottoms and love beads. This would be a mistake. Leary was undoubtedly a crank, and he was assuredly profoundly misguided. But his example was immensely influential. His importance extends far beyond the thousands of lives he blighted with drugs. As Andrei Codrescu noted in his introduction to the 1992 edition of *Acid Dreams*, the mystique of hallucinogens "now permeate[s] almost every aspect of high and low American culture." As much as anyone, Leary helped to change the moral temper of the times. Long after taking psychedelics ceased to be a preferred recreational pastime, the rationale that Leary provided for indulging in such drugs retained a large measure of credibility: they "increased sensitivity," even "increased intelligence," they freed one from "conventions" and produced "mystical" feelings of unbounded ecstasy. "With the aid of these drugs," Leary wrote, "I was exposing myself to the most intense emotions available to the human nervous system." In fact, he was exposing himself to a seductive counterfeit of emotion: a spiritual, soul-withering lie in capsule form.

In "The Legacy of the Late Sixties," the philosopher Harvey Mansfield observes that the phrase "mind-expanding" as applied to drugs is intended to mean "something grander than merely opening a mind previously closed by prejudice or superstition."

> It means actually expanding what the mind can grasp and conveys the excitement . . . [of] freeing oneself not only from conventions but even from one's nature. Man is an animal that naturally lives by conventions, so denying his conventions is denying his nature and replacing it with the desire to go beyond whatever has been fixed, crossing all boundaries, breaking all rules. The appeal of drugs is that of infinite power together with infinite desire. No doubt there is in human nature a yearning to rise above conventions, on occasion to get high. Previously this was thought necessary to control; now it was let loose among the young of the elite and invested with the moral superiority that comes from knowing that the system was corrupt.

Leary and his fellow champions of chemical emancipation helped to acclimatize our entire culture to a demand for blind emotional transport: a feeling of illumination vouchsafed by darkness. In 1979, Leary remarked that "the American people today are quantum jumps more sophisticated" than they had been when he began proselytizing for LSD. "Pleasure," he candidly noted, "is now the number one industry in this country. Recreational travel, entertainment, sensory indulgence. There's no question about that being Number One. Now *that* was my goal." Drugs opened up one road to this goal; rock music, as Leary understood, opened up another. Writing in the mid-1980s, Leary reported that some 80 percent of the American public was "currently involved in personal fulfillment projects, most of which involve some form of re-juvenilization." No doubt he was right. And that, finally, is what Timothy Leary was all about: rejuvenilization. What he offered was not greater intelligence, feeling, and sophistication, but a permanent holiday from those virtues for the sake of a delusion as toxic as it is widely embraced.

Chapter 9
Eldridge Cleaver's Serial Extremism

Through reading I was amazed to discover how confused people were.
—Eldridge Cleaver, *Soul on Ice*, 1968

Minds like Cleaver's are sorely needed, minds that can fashion a literature which does not flaunt its culture but creates it.
—Jack Richardson, *The New York Review of Books*, 1968

A pathology of credulousness

In 1970, when Timothy Leary broke out of jail and he and his girlfriend arrived in Algiers, there was a brief moment of euphoria. They were guests of the Black Panthers and that seemed splendid at first. "Panthers are the hope of the world," Leary wrote to Allen Ginsberg. "Socialism works here. . . . Eldridge is a genial genius. Brilliant! Turned on too!"

It couldn't last, and it didn't. "They intimidated us for money," Leary reported in his autobiography,

> spied on us, intercepted our mail, turned away friends and journalists who came to see us, quartered Eldridge's sullen mistress in our apartment as a resident informer. When I

protested, they kidnapped us at gunpoint, held us in "jail" in various apartments around town, issued press releases announcing our "arrest" for lack of discipline, and searched our apartment vainly for documents proving we were CIA operatives.

And then, in the cruelest cut of all, the Panthers even confiscated their drugs, "a small amount of LSD and hashish."

If it is difficult to work up much sympathy for Leary, it is also worth noting that he was lucky to escape so easily from the Panthers' clutches. Founded in Oakland, California, in 1966 by Bobby Seale and Huey P. Newton, the Black Panthers, in direct repudiation of the moderate spirit of the civil-rights movement of the late Fifties, sought to achieve black liberation in America by means of revolutionary violence. David Horowitz, who was deeply involved with the Panthers in the days when he still considered himself a radical, wrote recently that "the Panthers had killed more than a dozen people in the course of conducting extortion, prostitution, and drug rackets in the Oakland ghetto." There have been many books about the Panthers, critical as well as adulatory. But the liberal establishment that embraced the Panthers as an exciting new form of political theater has still never really faced up to their criminality. The radical sociologist Todd Gitlin, a former president of Students for a Democratic Society, was right when he noted that "nothing made the idea of revolution more vivid to the white Left than the Black Panther Party. *Image:* Eldridge Cleaver writing in *Ramparts* how he fell for the Panthers when he saw Huey P. Newton hold a shotgun on a San Francisco cop in front of the *Ramparts* office, and face him down."

In *Radical Chic*, his classic account of the society-gathering-cum-fund-raiser for the Panthers at Leonard Bernstein's

Park Avenue duplex in 1968, Tom Wolfe caught the politically correct liberal temper exactly:

> Shoot-outs, revolutions, pictures in *Life* magazine of policemen grabbing Black Panthers like they were Vietcong —somehow it all runs together in the head. . . .
> The black movement itself, of course, had taken on a much more electric and romantic cast. What a relief it was —socially—in New York—when the leaders seemed to shift from middle class to . . . *funky!* From A. Philip Randolph, Dr. Martin Luther King, and James Farmer . . . to Stokely, Rap, LeRoi, and Eldridge! This meant that the tricky business of the fashionable new politics could now be integrated with a tried and true social motif: *nostalgie de la boue.* The upshot was Radical Chic.

The continuing appeal of Radical Chic is doubtless one reason that the liberal establishment has never acknowledged the folly of its love affair with the Black Panthers and other criminally inclined elements of the counterculture. Another reason is the reluctance of the liberal establishment to admit that it was wrong about the radicalism it so freely embraced—wrong not just "tactically," but wrong in its ideals, its aspirations, its vaunted ethos of "commitment." As David Horowitz pointed out,

> the fact remains that to this day not a single organization of the mainstream press has ever investigated the Panther murders, even though the story is one that touches the lives and political careers of the entire liberal establishment, including the first lady and the deputy attorney general in charge of civil rights for the Clinton administration. Both Hillary Rodham Clinton and Bill Lann Lee began their political careers as law students at Yale by organizing

demonstrations in 1970 to shut down the university and stop the trial of Panther leaders who had tortured and then executed a black youth named Alex Rackley.

Bobby Seale and Huey Newton certainly deserved the notoriety they elicited from their various clashes with the law, which included charges of murder for both. But it was Eldridge Cleaver—the histrionic author of *Soul on Ice*, one-time presidential candidate for the Peace and Freedom Party, and Minister of Information for the Panthers from 1967 to 1971—who embodied the Panther ideology most vividly. He also became a widely admired symbol for countercultural revolt. As Jerry Rubin put it in *Do It!* (1970)— the once-famous bible of loopy anarchism to which Cleaver contributed an introduction—"We are all Eldridge Cleaver."

Cleaver was only sixty-two when he died in May 1998. Nearly all the obituaries—and they were plentiful and long—noted that Cleaver's family refused to disclose the cause of death; his periodic addiction to crack cocaine leads one to suspect the worst. (In 1994, the Berkeley police found him staggering about with a severe head wound and crack in his pocket.) By the time he died, Cleaver had been almost totally forgotten. Like many other Sixties radicals (Abbie Hoffman, Jerry Rubin), Cleaver descended into a kind of buffoonery in the later years of his life. An obituary in *The New York Times* sardonically noted that, in the last decades of his life, Cleaver "metamorphosed into variously a born-again Christian, a follower of the Rev. Sun Myung Moon, a Mormon, a crack cocaine addict, a designer of men's trousers featuring a codpiece, and even, finally, a Republican."

"Even, finally, a Republican": well, Cleaver clearly came to a bad end, at least from the *Times*'s point of view. The *Times*, like the rest of the liberal establishment, saw something ludicrous in Cleaver's having become a Republican. No one on the Left saw anything ludicrous in his being a poet of rape and an apologist for "picking up the gun." In fact, Cleaver's career is a good illustration of the important but easily forgotten truth that buffoonery is no enemy of violence or savagery. Mussolini was a buffoon; so was Idi Amin. Cleaver was not quite in their league, but our Paper of Record honored the former Black Panther with a long obituary because he had once been a nationally recognized hero of the counterculture, a figure who was as feared by the establishment as he was lionized by the radical Left. When Cleaver began teaching an experimental course at the University of California at Berkeley in the fall of 1968, then-Governor Ronald Reagan was outraged: "If Eldridge Cleaver is allowed to teach our children, they may come home one night and slit our throats." The *Times* quotes Mr. Reagan's warning almost in jest, as if to say, "You see how silly Reagan was, worrying about Eldridge Cleaver! Why, in 1982, he was booed by Yale's Afro-American student society for supporting Reagan."

Yes, but that was in 1982. Fifteen years earlier it was a different story.

Born in Arkansas in 1935, Cleaver grew up in the Watts section of Los Angeles. His father was a dining-car waiter, his mother worked as a janitor. His childhood was marked by a string of petty crimes and convictions. He was first sent to prison in 1954, when he was eighteen, for possession of marijuana. Released in 1957, he was soon arrested again, this time for rape and attempted murder. It was while serving a two-to-fourteen-year sentence for these crimes that Cleaver immersed himself in the writings of various revolutionary authors (Marx, Tom Paine, Lenin, Bakunin, et al.), black American writing (Richard Wright, James Baldwin, W. E. B. Du Bois), and the gritty beginnings of countercultural bombast (Norman Mailer, Allen Ginsberg, William S. Burroughs). Starting to write himself, Cleaver, through his lawyer, came to the notice of various literary figures, including Norman Mailer, who petitioned the authorities to have Cleaver paroled.*

Rape as an insurrectionary act

Cleaver was catapulted to fame in 1968 with the publication of his book *Soul on Ice*. Written almost entirely while he was in Folsom Prison, the book is a loosely knit series of letters and essays about race relations in America, prison life, one or two black literary figures, and, above all, Cleaver's sexual obsessions, especially his obsession with white women. ("Desire for the white woman," he wrote, "is like a cancer eating my heart out.") Most of the book had first appeared in *Ramparts* magazine, the incendiary, radical-Left monthly on whose masthead Cleaver later appeared as an editor. The book is remarkable partly for its rage, partly for its embarrassing sentimentality. On the one hand, Cleaver concludes an essay on Malcolm X with the warning that "we shall have our manhood. We shall have it or the earth will be leveled by our attempts to gain it." On the other, his concluding piece, "To All Black Women, From All Black Men," is full of hortatory appeals such as this: "let me drink from the river of your love at its source, let the lines of force of your love seize my soul by its core and heal the wound of

---

* Helping to get scribbling violent criminals—especially ones who professed admiration for his work—out of jail became something of a habit with Norman Mailer. As noted above in Chapter 2, in the early 1980s Mailer helped get the murderer Jack Abbott released from prison. Abbott promptly stabbed and killed a waiter in New York and was then placed beyond even Mailer's intercession.

my Castration, let my convex exile end its haunted Odyssey in your concave essence, . . ." etc.

Soul on Ice is not a good book. Indeed, it is barely a book at all: more a collection of manifestos and imprecations. But in its day it had an enormous influence and reputation. It was widely assigned in schools and colleges (I first came across it in high school), and it is still in print, thirty years later, in a mass-market edition. The introduction, by the critic Maxwell Geismar, established the tenor of the book's reception: "Cleaver is simply one of the best cultural critics now writing. . . . He rakes our favorite prejudices with the savage claws of his prose until our wounds are bare, our psyche is exposed, and we must either fight back or laugh with him for the service he has done us."

Here, from the book's title essay, is a sample of what "one of the best cultural critics" then writing sounds like:

> I'd like to leap the whole last mile and grow a beard and don whatever threads the local nationalism might require and comrade with Che Guevara, and share his fate, blazing a new pathfinder's trail through the stymied upbeat brain of the New Left, or how I'd just love to be in Berkeley right now, to roll in that mud, frolic in that sty of funky revolution, to breathe in its heady fumes, and look with roving eyes for a new John Brown, Eugene Debs, a blacker-meaner-keener Malcolm X, a Robert Franklin Williams with less rabbit in his hot blood, an American Lenin, Fidel, a Mao-Mao, A MAO MAO, A MAO MAO, A MAO MAO, A MAO MAO, A MAO MAO, A MAO MAO. . . . All of which is true [ellipsis in original].

Actually, that's only part of what Cleaver sounds like. Another critic noted that the book is also full of that "grand, old-fashioned Lawrentian and Maileresque myth-making" (this was meant as praise):

Each half of the human equation, the male and female hemispheres of the Primeval Sphere, must prepare themselves for the fusion by achieving a Unitary Sexual Image. . . . The quest for the Apocalyptic Fusion will find optimal conditions only in a Classless Society, the absence of classes being the *sine qua non* for the existence of a Unitary Society in which the Unitary Sexual Image can be achieved.

If it seems difficult to understand why such babbling should earn widespread respect, remember that Norman Mailer had wowed critical opinion a decade earlier with equally profound observations, *viz*: "the drama of the psychopath is that he seeks love. Not love as the search for a mate, but love as the search for an orgasm more apocalyptic than the one which preceded it."

By itself, Cleaver's Mailerian rhetoric would have earned him kudos, but not adoration. For that, he needed the added spice of racially infused criminality. Here is the passage that, perhaps more than any other, won Cleaver his converts:

I became a rapist. To refine my technique and *modus operandi*, I started out by practicing on black girls in the ghetto—in the black ghetto where dark and vicious deeds appear not as aberrations or deviations from the norm, but as part of the sufficiency of the Evil of the day—and when I considered myself smooth enough, I crossed the tracks and sought out white prey. I did this consciously, deliberately, willfully, methodically—though looking back I see that I was in a frantic, wild, and completely abandoned frame of mind.

Rape was an insurrectionary act. It delighted me that I was defying and trampling upon the white man's law, upon his system of values, and that I was defiling his women

—and this point, I believe, was the most satisfying to me because I was very resentful over the historical fact of how the white man has used the black woman. I felt I was getting revenge.

Had he been left at liberty, he notes, he undoubtedly would have "slit some white throats."

Of course, Cleaver includes a few words of contrition; he was, he admits, "wrong"; in the end, he "could not approve of rape." But what made his reputation—as much among whites as among blacks—was the militancy: his infamous image of "rape as an insurrectionary act," not his qualifying remarks; his slogan "If you are not part of the solution, you are part of the problem," not his later concessions. (Since he was "an extremist by nature," Cleaver reasoned, "it is only right that I should be extremely sick.")

There were a few dissenting notices. David Evanier writing in *The New Leader* was perhaps most accurate when he noted that "the style throughout . . . is pop Leftism, a mixture of sex and revolution characteristic of the New Left." But such demurrals were vastly overshadowed by the praise. "Original and disturbing" (*The Saturday Review*); full of "revolutionary zeal" (*The New York Times Book Review*); "a collection of essays straight out of Dante's *Inferno*" (*The Progressive*); "beautifully written. . . . A brilliant book" (*The Nation*), etc. Writing for *The New York Review of Books*, Jack Richardson tells us that *Soul on Ice* "has a rare honesty, . . . a dramatic temper that makes it a point gently to remind us of who is speaking and from where." *Gently?* Well, for Richardson, "minds like Cleaver's are sorely needed, minds that can fashion a literature which does not flaunt its culture but creates it." So it was hardly any wonder that *The New York Times* declared *Soul on Ice* one of the ten best books of the year.

"White Standards and Negro Writing"

Perhaps the most egregious act of critical adulation came from the Yale professor Richard Gilman. In a long review called "White Standards and Negro Writing" in *The New Republic*, Gilman trotted out all the usual adjectives: *Soul on Ice* was "unsparing," "tough," "lyrical," admittedly "foolish at times" but "extraordinarily convincing in the energy and hard morale of its thinking."

What made Gilman's essay notable, however, was not its praise but its effort to place Cleaver outside not only "white standards" of literary achievement but also "white standards" of legality. According to Gilman, writing by blacks like Cleaver "remains in some sense unassimilable for those of us who aren't black" because "the Negro doesn't feel the way whites do, nor does he think like whites." In contemporary America, "moral and intellectual 'truths' have not the same reality for Negroes and whites." (Note the scare quotes: does Gilman doubt there are such things as intellectual and moral truths?) Because "Negro suffering is not of the same kind as ours," he does not, as a white critic, have the "right" to compare Cleaver's thinking with "other 'classic' ways of grappling with sexual experience" or "to subject his findings to the scrutiny of the tradition." In short, "white criteria" are out of place in judging works by black writers.

Had Gilman been a conservative, or had he ventured to offer any substantial criticism of Cleaver's paean justifying black rage, his essay would have quickly been attacked for what it is: a piece of racist claptrap, justifying inferior work—and criminality—on the spurious grounds of racial difference. In the event, however, "White Standards and Negro Writing" was part of the radical propaganda of the day. When a respected critic and professor at Yale University tells his readers that "the Negro doesn't feel the way whites do, nor does he think like whites," is it any wonder that the Black Panthers should include in their "ten-point program" the demand that all black men be exempt from military service? Or the demand that all black prisoners be released from jail "because," as Cleaver explained in an interview, "they haven't had fair trials; they've been tried by all white juries, and that's like being a Jew tried in Nazi Germany"? Asked whether the Panthers were serious about having all black prisoners released, Cleaver replied: "We don't feel that there's any black man or any white man in any prison in this country who could be compared in terms of criminality with Lyndon Johnson."

Gilman was among those establishment critics who helped articulate a rationale for the blatant criminality of the Panthers. When Cleaver was involved in a gun battle with the Oakland police in 1968—an encounter that left a young Panther dead and Cleaver and a police officer wounded—his parole was revoked and he was returned to prison. Two months later, he was released when a judge ruled that he was being held as a political prisoner. A higher court overturned that ruling, however, and Cleaver was facing a long prison term on charges of assault and attempted murder. In New York, dependable radicals like Susan Sontag and the actor Gary Merrill demonstrated on his behalf; the filmmaker Jean-Luc Godard urged his audiences to donate to the Cleaver defense fund. Cleaver himself managed to flee the country, stopping first in Cuba before setting up his American "government in exile" in Algiers. In his frequent travels, he was given a warm welcome in the Soviet Union (as it then was), Vietnam, and (the most peculiar radical resort of all) Kim Il Sung's Korea.

Gradually, Cleaver grew disenchanted with his radical political beliefs; he broke with the Panthers in 1971 and moved to Paris, where he inaugurated his codpiece pants (called "Cleavers"). In the early 1970s, as he recounts in *Soul on Fire* (1979), he had a mystical vision in which the faces of Marx, Engels, Mao, Castro, and others appeared in the moon, followed by the face of Christ ("I fell to my knees"). Cutting a deal with the authorities, Cleaver returned to the United States in 1975; the attempted murder charge was dropped and he was sentenced to twelve hundred hours of community service.

Eldridge Cleaver was a serial extremist. The content of his beliefs was negotiable; only his fanaticism was constant. This ultimately made him something of a preposterous, indeed a pathetic, figure. But, again, preposterousness is by no means incompatible with malignity. And if Eldridge Cleaver became in his later years a kind of joke, this should not mislead us into thinking that his influence was not, after all, so bad. Like so much about the ethos of the counterculture, the influence of figures like Eldridge Cleaver has been as much in their afterlife as in their life. That is to say, the destructiveness of their ideas and example may be most severe not when they first appear and—whether they be championed or castigated—are regarded by one and all as outrageous. On the contrary, the really toxic effects of a cultural revolution begin to be felt only latterly, when the revolution is agreed to be "over." By then, its characteristic attitudes have been so widely incorporated into the mainstream of life that they are taken for granted: unnoticed because ubiquitous. Only then do the precepts of the counterculture find their way into the realm of habit, taste, and feeling, becoming along the way not only ideas that are espoused but also a way of life.

The critic Myron Magnet touched on this point in *The Dream and the Nightmare* (1993), his astute study of how the misguided "idealism" of the counterculture contributed to the plight of America's underclass:

Just as you didn't have to frequent singles bars to be affected by the sexual revolution, you didn't have to live in a commune and eat mushrooms to be affected by the counterculture's quest for personal liberation. The new adversary stance toward conventional beliefs and ideals, breathlessly reported by the press and diffused almost instantly among the young, quickly put traditional values on the defensive, making them newly problematic even for those who continued to hold them.

And because the counterculture belonged to the young, its influence has persisted into the present, as the original Aquarians have matured into middle age and assumed positions of influence. That's what accounts for the dreams of so many Silicon Valley entrepreneurs that they'll drop out before long, or for the widespread use of cocaine in Hollywood and on Wall Street until recently. What you believe at twenty, as one historian has remarked, has a way of leaving its stamp on your world view for life.

Indeed, a good index of the success of a cultural revolution is the extent to which it has managed to render the ideas and values it set out to subvert not merely "problematic" but inert. A counterculture has really triumphed when it ceases to encounter significant resistance, when its values seem not merely victorious but inevitable.

The long march of America's cultural revolution is partly the story of the social and moral malaise brought about by a pathology of credulousness. Euphoric hedonism exists on the smiling side of that pathology; on the dour side are clustered many other countercultural phenomena, not least the juvenile political activism and noisy readiness for violence that were such conspicuous features of the age. In the late 1960s and early 1970s, hundreds of bombs were detonated as various radical groups carried out their campaign against

"Amerika." According to a story in the *Los Angeles Times*, "in California alone, 20 explosions a week rocked the state during the summer of 1970." Fatalities from these insurrectionary acts were comparatively few. Nevertheless, as David Horowitz noted in his autobiography,

> far from being peripheral, a criminal-intellectual outlook was central to the vision of Sixties radicalism, articulated in the writings of its most-read authors (Sartre, Debray, and Fanon), and in the speeches of Malcolm X. It was, in fact, a core tradition of the radicalism that went back through Sorel, Bakunin, and Lenin to the Jacobins, the "conspiracy of equals," and Gracchus Babeuf—in short, to the very origins of the modern Left.

In America, no group better epitomized this militant radicalism than the Black Panthers, and among the Panthers Eldridge Cleaver was—as Susan Sontag might have put it—an *exemplary* figure. (What Sontag actually said was that *Soul on Ice* was "perhaps the most eloquent document," proclaiming that "in a culture judged as inorganic, dead, coercive, authoritarian, it becomes a revolutionary gesture to be alive.") Also exemplary was the liberal response to Cleaver, his book, and the cult of the Black Panthers. Sontag would scorn the name "liberal." But her celebration of Cleaver's paean to criminal violence was part of the liberal intelligentsia's collapse into the arms of Radical Chic sentimentality. The extent of that collapse even—indeed, especially—among intellectuals whose entire training should have inoculated them against such mendacities is a critical part of the long march that transformed so much of American life in the 1960s and 1970s.

Chapter 10
A Nostalgia for Molotovs

From the beginning it was pointless to argue about the sincerity of Radical Chic. Unquestionably the basic impulse, "red diaper" or otherwise, was sincere. But, as in most human endeavors focused upon an ideal, there seemed to be some double-track thinking going on.
—Tom Wolfe, *Radical Chic*, 1970

He oscillated . . . between identification with the Communists and violent hostility towards them. . . . At every stage, however, he endeavored to preserve his own reputation as a "Leftist," and even to represent himself and his philosophy as the embodiment of "Leftism" par excellence. *Consequently, even when attacking the Communists and reviled by them he made a point of directing far more vehement attacks against the forces of reaction, the bourgeoisie, or the United States Government.*
—Leszek Kolakowski, on Jean-Paul Sartre, 1978

Barbecuing pork

On December 4, 1969, *The New York Review of Books* published "The Trial of Bobby Seale." This special supplement contained a partial transcript of the 1969 trial of the infamous Black Panther leader who—along with Tom Hayden, Jerry Rubin, Abbie Hoffman, and other members of the "Chicago Seven"—was on trial in Chicago for conspiracy to incite a riot. (Seale was also facing a first-degree murder charge in New Haven.) The trial riveted the nation's attention. The disturbances instigated by Hayden (who said he expected twenty-five people to die in the melee) and others on the occasion of the Democratic National Convention in Chicago in 1968 had already emerged as an iconic moment in the mythology of the counterculture. The episode was as significant in its way as the Woodstock music festival or college anti-war demonstrations.

The transcript published in *The New York Review* covers the proceedings of one afternoon in which a mistrial was declared and Seale was cited for contempt of court. (At one point, his conduct had been so obstreperous that the court ordered him bound and gagged.) The transcript was prefaced with an essay by Jason Epstein, a co-founder of *The New York Review*. It is a remarkable document. Epstein, like most leftists at the time, was clearly sympathetic to Seale. He was also clearly contemptuous of Judge Julius Hoffman, the presiding magistrate. Epstein assured his readers that the source of Judge Hoffman's authority was "not in his juridical wisdom" (which, he claimed, was "hardly remarkable") but "in an unmistakable theatrical gift." The transcript was supposed to corroborate these contentions.

It was also supposed to garner support for Seale. Epstein assured his readers that the evidence against him "was sparse." The charges against the other defendants, too, Epstein suggested, were "metaphysically conceived." Seale himself, Epstein explained, "had been invited to come [to Chicago] only at the last minute as a substitute for Eldridge Cleaver." How then could he have been involved in a conspiracy? In Seale's case, according to Epstein, the evidence consisted of the allegation by an "undercover policeman" (read: an untrustworthy witness) that Seale, at a rally organized by Hayden and others, had urged his audience to "barbecue some pork." Over the objection of the defense, Judge Hoffman construed this to mean "burn some pigs," that is, policemen. Epstein did not offer his own interpretation of the phrase. Instead he launched into an exposition of the convoluted law governing conspiracy. It does not take any special hermeneutical gifts, however, to understand what Bobby Seale intended in his speech. What he said was, "If a pig comes up to us and starts swinging a billy club, and you check around and you got your piece, you got to down that pig in defense of yourself! We're gonna barbecue some pork!" After Seale's performance, Tom Hayden told the crowd to "make sure that if blood is going to flow, it will flow all over the city."

"The Trial of Bobby Seale" was typical of the political reporting one could expect to find in *The New York Review* in the late Sixties. It was the kind of piece that gave the paper its special place in the annals of America's cultural revolution. Plenty of other publications—*Ramparts*, for example, and *Rolling Stone*, *The Village Voice*, even old-Left stalwarts like *The Nation*—played important roles in defining the counterculture and propagating its spirit and its ideas.* Some of these publications were explicitly devoted

---

* The advertisements that ran in such publications in the late 1960s also give one a good sense of the radical atmosphere of the times. Among the ads one finds accompanying "The Trial of Bobby Seale," for example, is one for "the first-run campus premiere" of *Fidel*, a film brought to the world by "Review Presentations," an offshoot of *The New York Review of Books*. This "startling new film on Fidel and Cuba today" is described as "an extraordinary in-depth report on Fidel and the continuing revolution. Beautifully photographed in color, it shows Fidel among his people, listening, arguing, philosophizing, laughing, cajoling, reminiscing" and includes "a very moving section on Che called 'The Ballad of Che Guevara.'"

to promoting the drug culture, rock music, and sexual "liberation"; some were openly Marxist, frankly admiring of Castro, Ho Chi Minh, and other totalitarian leaders; all were infused with some version of political radicalism. And as the Sixties wore on, all were "against the war" in Vietnam—that is, against U.S. intervention in Vietnam—and adamantly opposed to the use of American military power. But none commanded anything like the intellectual cachet that *The New York Review* enjoyed and, to a lesser extent, continues to enjoy among the left-liberal intelligentsia. And none was, at that critical moment in the Sixties, quite so effective—or quite so pernicious—in helping to institutionalize the gospel of political radicalism among America's intellectual elite.

It is a curious story. *The New York Review* was the brainchild largely of Jason Epstein, the publishing wunderkind who created the distinguished paperback lines of Anchor Books at Doubleday and Vintage Books at Random House. By the late 1950s, the need for a serious, general-interest review was patent. The novelist and essayist Elizabeth Hardwick, who was then married to Robert Lowell and who went on to become advisory editor at *The New York Review*, summed up the received feeling in "The Decline of Book Reviewing," which *Harper's* published in 1959:

> Sweet, bland commendations fall everywhere upon the scene; a universal, if somewhat lobotomized, accommodation reigns. A book is born into a puddle of treacle; the brine of hostile criticism is only a memory. Everyone is found to have "filled a need," and is to be "thanked" for something and to be excused for "minor faults in an otherwise excellent work."

As Philip Nobile put it in *Intellectual Skywriting*, his intermittently hagiographic history of the first ten years of *The New York Review*, "everybody talked about a new book review, but nobody did anything about it."

The necessary spur came during the 114-day printers' strike in 1962–63. The strike shut down all the major New York newspapers, including *The New York Times* and the *Herald Tribune*, whose book pages, along with those of *The Saturday Review*, constituted the main sources of book reviews and, not incidentally, the chief venues for book advertising. (Looking back on the reviewing scene in *The New York Review*'s second issue in the summer of 1963, Edmund Wilson remarked that "the disappearance of the *Times* Sunday book section at the time of the printers' strike only made us realize it had never existed.") Although Epstein's association with Random House precluded his being the editor of the contemplated new book review, his energy, connections, and organizational acumen brought *The New York Review* into being. It was a fateful stroke that led him to appoint the precocious Robert B. Silvers as editor. (Epstein's wife, Barbara, has been co-editor from the beginning, but it was always Silvers who imparted to the *Review* much of its intellectual and nearly all of its ideological sheen.)

Filling a need

Then in his early thirties, Silvers had been working as an editor at *Harper's* since 1959. Something of a child prodigy, Silvers had matriculated at the University of Chicago in 1945 at the tender age of sixteen. He was graduated two and a half years later after, Nobile reports, "having numerous requirements waived." Silvers was briefly press secretary for Connecticut Governor Chester Bowles, Jr., in 1950, after which he went to the Yale Law School for a few semesters. He then joined the U.S. Army, which posted him to Paris. In the mid-Fifties, Paris was still Sartre's Paris: a Paris in which—among intellectuals, anyway—anti-Americanism was as *de rigueur* as were brittle intellectual snobbery and left-wing politics. Silvers seems to have found it an intoxicating combination. He lingered in Paris for some six years, absorbing the atmosphere and graduating from the Ecole des Sciences Politiques (where he met Raymond Aron) in 1956. He also worked part of the time for George Plimpton's newly launched *Paris Review* (to which he contributed an interview with the novelist Françoise Sagan in 1956). His energy and editorial flair were apparent from the beginning. John P. C. Train, then managing editor of the *Paris Review*, recalls a "shy but formidable" figure who "made the *Paris Review* what it was."

When the Algerian conflict escalated, the Front de Libération Nationale (FLN) embarked on a program of atrocities explicitly "designed to provoke the French army into savage reprisals." The policy succeeded. Torture had been officially abolished in France in 1789, but within a few years the French army had been provoked into authorizing the torture of Algerian prisoners to extract information about terrorist plans. The result, as the historian Paul Johnson noted, was "a competition of terror." The cause of Algerian independence was taken up by all right-thinking (that is, left-leaning) intellectuals. (Of course, the practice of torture by the French army was roundly condemned across the ideological spectrum.) Declaring that colonials had replaced the proletariat in the hierarchy of the oppressed, Sartre called upon French workers to "support Algerian fighters" in their efforts "to break the fetters of colonization." Numerous first-hand accounts of atrocities perpetrated by the French army were published, much to the consternation of the French authorities. Sartre himself contributed a preface to one such contraband pamphlet, Henri Alleg's *La Question*, thus conferring unimpeachable prestige on this mode of political activism. Alleg's pamphlet provoked moral outrage throughout France. At the request of John Fischer, the editor of *Harper's*, Silvers translated a chapter of another such report, *La Gangrène*, a grisly account by four Algerians of their torture in Paris at the hands of the French police.*

I mention these details because the intellectual and political posture—indeed, even the social posture—of *The New York Review* clearly owes a great deal to Silvers's extended holiday in Paris. By all accounts, Silvers is as shy of personal publicity as Sartre was addicted to it; and where Sartre was a graphomaniac who wrote and published millions of words, Silvers seems early on to have decided against writing. According to Philip Nobile, Silvers's only published writing, apart from the two items mentioned above, is "A Letter to a Young Man About to Enter Publishing," which ran, anonymously, in a supplement to *Harper's* about "Writing in America" in 1959. (He also published an interview with "David Burg," the pen name of a young Soviet defector, in *Harper's* in May 1961.) Silvers has disputed the influence of Sartre, claiming that his own views were more informed by the example of Sartre's great critic Raymond Aron. But he brought to his editorship of *The New York Review*—especially in the 1960s and early 1970s—an *engagé* attitude very similar to that perfected by Jean-Paul Sartre in the 1950s and 1960s: relentlessly haughty, cerebral, cliquish, at once socially ambitious and

---

* This chapter, with an introduction by Joseph Kraft, was published without identifying the translator in the March 1960 number of *Harper's*. Silvers subsequently translated the rest of the book, which was published in English as *The Gangrene* (New York: Lyle Stuart, 1960).

THE LONG MARCH

disdainful of society, ever in search of approved *gauchiste* "causes," instinctively anti-American.

The trick was knowing how and when to mix these qualities—which to emphasize, which to downplay—and at this task Silvers quickly proved himself a master. In the beginning, highbrow elements, leavened by celebrity, predominated. The first, trial issue of *The New York Review* was cobbled together on short notice in the winter of 1963. The very bulk of the issue was a testament that its time had come. It contained forty-odd pieces, including F. W. Dupee on James Baldwin's *The Fire Next Time*, Dwight Macdonald on Arthur Schlesinger, Jr.'s *The Politics of Hope*, Philip Rahv (a founding editor of *Partisan Review*) on Solzhenitsyn's *One Day in the Life of Ivan Denisovich*, Mary McCarthy on William Burroughs's *Naked Lunch*, and W. H. Auden on David Jones's *Anathemata*; there were also reviews by Norman Mailer, Lionel Abel, Steven Marcus, Susan Sontag, Gore Vidal, and Alfred Kazin; Robert Penn Warren contributed a poem, Irving Howe wrote about *The Partisan Review Anthology*. William Phillips, another founding editor of *Partisan Review*, reviewed Elias Canetti's huge book *Crowds and Power*. Richard Poirier wrote about Frank Kermode, William Styron wrote about Frank Tannenbaum, Midge Decter wrote about recent novels, and Robert Jay Lifton wrote about Arata Ossada's *Children of the A-Bomb*. Elizabeth Hardwick contributed two pieces, as did Robert Lowell (an obituary of Robert Frost, who had just died, and a poem) and John Berryman (a review of Auden's *The Dyer's Hand* and three "Dream Songs").

By any measure, this was an extraordinary performance. It met, deservedly, with instant and widespread acclaim, generating more than a thousand letters. A second large issue was duly published in the summer, with only a modest falling off of celebrity. In addition to Wilson's in-

232

terview with himself, the issue included pieces by (among others) Allen Tate, Arthur Schlesinger, Jr., Lionel Abel, Stephen Spender, F. W. Dupee. J. F. Powers, Alfred Kazin, Richard Wilbur, Robert Brustein, Joseph Frank, H. Stuart Hughes, Steven Marcus, and Kenneth Burke. Again, an extraordinary line-up. *The New York Review* began regular fortnightly publication in the fall of 1963. Printed on newsprint (and described by some as "*Partisan Review* on butcher paper"), it instantly established itself as an indispensable journal of academic left-liberal orthodoxy. At first, Silvers's main innovation was the inclusion of ever greater numbers of English writers, especially titled writers; indeed, a pronounced Anglophilia became a comically defining characteristic of the journal.

The assassination of President Kennedy in November 1963 marked an early turning point. *The New York Review* commemorated the event with a special issue in December 1963 "largely devoted to comments . . . about the present crisis in America." One contributor to that issue noted that, "as might be expected, the assassination stimulated a good deal of cant." Indeed. And that issue of *The New York Review* provided a home for a goodly amount of cant, although what turned out to be most significant was the tone of emergency that the journal adopted in "The Fate of the Union: Kennedy and After." Of course the mood of the nation following President Kennedy's assassination did a great deal to encourage grim rhetorical histrionics. But as one looks back over the evolution of *The New York Review* from the mid-1960s and early 1970s, it is difficult to escape feeling that its editors regarded the assassination more as an existential tonic than as a tragedy; or perhaps it would be more accurate to say that they regarded it as a tragedy that was itself an existential tonic. In any event, with that issue a new element of radical left-wing political hectoring made its appearance in the journal's pages. The cover story of *The New York Review*'s inaugural issue was F. W. Dupee's acerb review of Baldwin's *The Fire Next Time*. Describing Baldwin as a "Negro *in extremis*, a virtuoso of ethnic suffering," Dupee concluded by wondering "how *The Fire Next Time*, in its madder moments, could do anything except inflame" anti-black extremists and "confuse" blacks. By 1967 we find Tom Hayden declaring happily that "Middle-class Negro intellectuals and Negros of the ghetto have joined forces. . . . They assume that disobedience, disorder, and even violence must be risked as the only alternative to continuing slavery." Such exhortations became almost deafening as the Sixties wore on; it subsequently diminished, but that was only after elite opinion in this country had migrated markedly to the Left—partly under the influence of twice-monthly manifestos emanating from the *The New York Review*.

A platform of the radical Left

If Kennedy's assassination initiated a movement toward political fulmination, the Vietnam conflict precipitated a stampede. It was then, for example, that Noam Chomsky began contributing his lugubrious diatribes against American foreign policy, replete with such delicacies as his description of the Pentagon (in a piece called "On Resistance") as "the most hideous institution on earth." It was then, too, that Mary McCarthy filed her three-part report on the socialist paradise being prepared in North Vietnam and that I. F. Stone began bludgeoning readers with his interminable essays on the American military establishment (sample title: "The War Machine Under Nixon"). Stone's pieces read like neo-Stalinist equivalents of those multipart articles on staple crops with which *The New Yorker* used to anesthetize its readers.

The New York Review never lost its taste for upper-class English dons. But in the mid-Sixties the dons were joined by a more demotic element. Suddenly, political firebrands like Jerry Rubin, Stokely Carmichael, and Tom Hayden began appearing in the paper along with radical fellow-traveler Andrew Kopkind, a refugee from *Newsweek*. Of the ten pieces that Kopkind wrote for Silvers, the most notorious came in the issue of August 24, 1967. Headlined "Violence and the Negro," the cover announced in outsize type Kopkind's piece on Martin Luther King and Black Power and Hayden's report on the riots—what he called "The Occupation"—of Newark. Underneath was a large diagram instructing readers on the exact composition of a Molotov cocktail.* According to Todd Gitlin, a Berkeley commune that habitually trashed neighborhood stores believed that "massive retaliation might be imminent, . . . and for that contingency they kept a Molotov cocktail in the basement, designed to the specifications of *The New York Review of Books* cover of 1967."

It was about this time that even some of *The New York Review*'s ideological allies began having doubts about the direction that the journal was taking. Irving Howe, himself a socialist and founding editor of *Dissent*, noted scathingly in 1968 that the *Review* had managed to achieve "a link between campus 'leftism' and East Side stylishness, the worlds of Tom Hayden and George Plimpton." Howe continued:

---

* To his credit, the *Review*'s resident caricaturist, David Levine, refused to provide a drawing of the incendiary device. Though himself a self-described "radical-socialist" who cheerfully supplied malevolently grotesque send-ups of President Nixon and other political figures, Levine rightly regarded this seeming endorsement of violence as beyond the pale.

Opposition to communist politics and ideology is frequently presented in the pages of the *New York Review* as if it were an obsolete, indeed a pathetic, hangover from a discredited past or worse yet, a dark sign of the CIA. A snappish and crude anti-Americanism has swept over much of its political writing. . . . And in the hands of writers like Andrew Kopkind . . . liberal values and norms are treated with something very close to contempt.

Howe was not the only former contributor to express alarm. The sociologist Dennis Wrong, who had appeared in *The New York Review*'s inaugural issue, wrote a lengthy and thoughtful piece on the journal for the November 1970 issue of *Commentary*. Noting, with basic approval, *The New York Review*'s early campaign against the Vietnam War, Wrong pointed out that

> by 1966 and 1967 a new tone of extravagant, querulous, self-righteous anti-Americanism began to creep into the *NYR*'s reports on Vietnam, especially those of Noam Chomsky, Mary McCarthy, and I. F. Stone. The war seemed increasingly to provide the occasion for an extreme and bitter repudiation, marked by an unmistakable touch of *Schadenfreude*, of a great deal more in American life than the Johnson administration's foreign policy, the Pentagon, the military-industrial complex, and the wretched clichés of cold-war propaganda.

The May 1971 *Esquire* went even further, predicting in a press note that "from among [*The New York Review*'s] authors the next Stalin, and his speechwriters, will emerge." In Philip Nobile's phrase, what began as "a literary proposition . . . infused with liberal politics" had become a "politicized platform of the radical Left."

As Dennis Wrong suggested, although the Vietnam War occasioned much of *The New York Review*'s radicalism, the real target was not America's policy about Vietnam but America itself. Indeed, anti-Americanism — a prominent feature in almost all countercultural rhetoric — became a major leitmotif, almost a unifying theme, in *The New York Review* within a few years of its birth. For example, when Mary McCarthy traveled to Vietnam early in 1967 for *The New York Review*, she began the first installment of her report — the cover story for April 20 — with this acknowledgment: "I confess that when I went to Vietnam early in February I was looking for material damaging to the American interest and that I found it, though often by accident or in the process of being briefed by an official." In the course of her reports, McCarthy naturally places the phrase "Free World" in scare quotes and consistently portrays Americans as venal monstrosities. (When she converses with a CIA agent, his "lips flexed as he spoke like rubber bands.") Glorifying the industry and pluck of the North Vietnamese, she tells her readers that the "sense of fair play . . . has atrophied in the Americans here from lack of exercise."

At the beginning of her second installment, McCarthy famously declared that "the worst thing that could happen to our country would be to win this war." Years later, in 1979, after the horrific spectacle of the Vietnamese boat people and similar phenomena consequent on America's losing that war, she was asked if she had changed her views on Vietnam. Noting that her ideal was still "socialism with a human face" (one might as well wish for wooden iron), she nevertheless acknowledged that

> as for my current views on Vietnam, it's all rather daunting. I've several times contemplated writing a letter to [the Vietnamese premier] Pham Van Dong (I get a Christmas

card from him every year) asking him can't you stop this, how is it possible for men like you to permit what's going on? . . . I've never written that letter, though.

The combination of arrogance and naïveté implicit in Mary McCarthy's retrospective musings about Vietnam was a staple of *The New York Review*'s anti-Americanism. Jason Epstein provided a truly vertiginous example in an essay called "The CIA and the Intellectuals" (April 20, 1967). Following up on the revelation that the CIA had provided covert funding to some student and cultural organizations (including, most famously, *Encounter* magazine in England), Epstein's piece was a meditation on how "organized anti-Communism had become as much an industry within New York's intellectual life as Communism itself had been a decade or so earlier." Among other things, "The CIA and the Intellectuals" was an early masterpiece of what came to be called "moral equivalence." In one remarkable passage, Epstein writes that Stalin

> not only purged and tortured his former comrades, killed millions of Russians, signed the pact with Hitler, and suppressed the writers and artists. He had also done something which directly affected their own lives, much as the CIA and the State Department have not only burned the crops and villages and peoples of Vietnam, but have also brought so much anguish into the lives of so many young people today. What Stalin did to the generation of intellectuals who came of age between the Thirties and Fifties was to betray the idealism and innocence of their youth. By perverting revolutionary Marxism, he cheated them, as it were, in their very souls.

Epstein concludes sadly that certain radical intellectuals,

robbed of their Communist ideals by nasty Joe Stalin, devoted "the rest of their energies to retribution." Hence, you see, the birth of Neoconservatism. It's not simply that Epstein transforms a principled rejection of Communism into a psychological tic; he also insinuates an equivalence between the murderous behavior of Stalin and the activities of the American CIA. What Epstein does not see is that his friends who turned against Communism did so not because Stalin *perverted* "revolutionary Marxism" but because they finally understood that Stalinism was the natural *fulfillment* of revolutionary Marxism.

Epstein's essay is notable for its exhibition of the way liberal disillusionment can be elevated into a kind of metaphysics of anti-Americanism:

> The facts are clearer now than they were ten years ago. Then it surprised us to find that the country seemed to have fallen into a frenzy of self-destruction, tearing its cities apart, fouling its landscapes, poisoning the streams and skies, trivializing the education of its children, and not for any substantial human happiness, . . . but for higher profits and rapidly increased economic growth. . . . What we were experiencing was the familiar philistine expansionism (of which the Vietnamese are only the latest victims), this time attached to a formidable technology whose alarming possibilities were as yet unclear, but which was even then depressingly out of human scale and growing larger and more autonomous every day.

Now at last, Epstein concludes, it is clear that "pursuit of money and power became openly America's main, if not its only, business."

Which is worse, Epstein's moralism, or his hypocrisy? By psychologizing politics and attempting to replace basic political commitments with a melodrama of virtue, Epstein is really engaged in a species of moral blackmail. As Diana Trilling observed in a withering response to "The CIA and the Intellectuals," Epstein would have us believe that "depending on how we respond to the poisoning of our streams and skies we will take either a Left- or a Right-Wing position on—say—the Vietnam War. Whoever abhors polluted air and desecrated landscapes will have adequate grounds on which to judge American foreign policy. He will recognize it in all its 'philistine expansionism.' What further guide to decision in foreign affairs does anyone need?"

Stealing the youth of America

In the end, *The New York Review*'s anti-Americanism has to be seen as part of a larger project of political, intellectual, and moral delegitimation. For example, over the years, the *Review* has run some distinguished pieces on science. But it has also been prey to a kind of countercultural technophobia that borders on irrationalism. Consider, for example, John McDermott's "Technology: The Opiate of the Intellectuals," a special supplement that appeared in July 1969. The amazing conclusion of this long and tedious piece is that the spirit of scientific curiosity and the promotion of technology

> should be frankly recognized as a conservative or right-wing ideology. . . . It succeeds in identifying and rationalizing the interests of the most authoritarian elites within this country, and the expansionism of their policies overseas. Truly it is no accident that the leading figures of *laissez innover* . . . are among the most unreconstructed cold warriors in American intellectual life.

Truly, it is no accident, either, that this sort of politicized attack on science and technology became a prominent item on the menu of academic radicalism in the decades to come.

Although the Yippie leader Jerry Rubin made only one appearance in *The New York Review*, his "Emergency Letter to My Brothers and Sisters in the Movement" (February 1969), written while he was in custody, is nonetheless significant as a reminder of the kinds of views Silvers and his colleagues were willing to countenance in its pages. Rubin begins by boasting that, although the forces of repression are on the rise, "We are stealing the youth of America right out of the kindergartens and elementary schools." After some remarks about how "America's courts are colonial courts," her jails "black concentration camps," he goes on to declare that "smoking pot is a political act, and every smoker is an outlaw. The drug culture is a revolutionary threat to plasticwasp9-5america [*sic*]."

> Who the hell wants to "make it" in America anymore? The hippie-yippie-SDS movement is a "white nigger" movement. The American economy no longer needs young whites and blacks. We are waste material. We fulfill our destiny in life by rejecting a system which rejects us.

Accordingly, Rubin calls for widespread demonstrations near jails and courthouses to "demand immediate freedom for Huey P. Newton, Eldridge Cleaver, Rap Brown, all black prisoners, Timothy Leary, the Oakland Seven, all drug prisoners, all draft resisters, Benjamin Spock, . . . me," etc. Of course, Rubin was always something of a buffoon. And his later conversion from Yippie freak to Wall Street investment counselor makes his adolescent antics seem even more puerile than they perhaps were. Today, it is tempting to look back on erstwhile countercultural heroes like Jerry Rubin as comic figures, more preposterous than menacing. But it is a great mistake to believe that the preposterous is the enemy of the malign. On the contrary, such qualities often feed upon and abet each other.

In any event, if Rubin's appearance in *The New York Review* was something of an aberration, the same cannot be said about Andrew Kopkind's many appearances in its pages. Perhaps his most notorious contribution was "Soul Power," which was published as the lead essay in the Molotov cocktail issue. Ostensibly a review of Martin Luther King's *Where Do We Go from Here: Chaos or Community?*, it was really a guerrilla manifesto. Arguing that America was "a society infused with racism," Kopkind declared that King's policy of nonviolence was obsolete and that King himself (whom he described as "shuffling [!] between Chicago and Cleveland") was now "an irrelevancy." In an oft-repeated and oft-castigated phrase, Kopkind announced that "morality, like politics, starts at the barrel of a gun." (The echo of *Der Stürmer*—"When I hear the word 'culture,' I reach for my gun"—was not lost on the *Review*'s critics.) Even more troubling than Kopkind's sentimental fondness for the thuggish was his embrace of revolutionary anarchy. It is worth quoting the opening of his exhortation at length (note the allusions to *A Tale of Two Cities*, one of the most sentimentalizing portraits of the French Revolution extant):

> The Movement is dead; the Revolution is unborn. The streets are bloody and ablaze, but it is difficult to see why, and impossible to know for what end. Government on every level is ineffectual, helpless to act either in the short term or the long. The force of Army and police seems not to suppress violence, but incite it. . . . Mediators have no

space to work; they command neither resources nor respect, and their rhetoric is discredited in all councils, by all classes. The old words are meaningless, . . . the old explanations irrelevant, the old remedies useless. It is the worst of times.

It is the best of times. The wretched of this American earth are together as they have never been before, in motion if not in movement. No march, no sit-in, no boycott ever touched so many. . . . The social cloth which binds and suffocates them is tearing at its seamiest places. The subtle methods of co-optation work no better to keep it intact than the brutal methods of repression; if it is any comfort, liberalism proves hardly more effective than fascism. Above all, there is a sense that the continuity of an age has been cut, that we have arrived at an infrequent fulcrum of history, and that what comes now will be vastly different from what went before.

It is not a time for reflection, but for evocation. The responsibility of the intellectual is the same as that of the street organizer, the draft resister, the Digger: to talk *to* people, not *about* them. The important literature now is the underground press, the speeches of Malcolm, the works of Fanon, the songs of the Rolling Stones and Aretha Franklin.

"Liberalism proves hardly more effective than fascism"; "it is not a time for reflection, but for evocation"; the works of Frantz Fanon and Malcolm X, the pseudo-Dionysiac drivel of the Rolling Stones: by publishing this screed, *The New York Review* made itself party to the sanctimonious, anticultural nihilism preached by the worst elements of Sixties radicalism.

It did nothing to redeem itself with Tom Hayden's long report on the 1967 Newark riots later in the same issue.

This future California assemblyman reported on the looting, arson, shooting, and mayhem that swept over the city with a mixture of glee and revolutionary amoralism. He clearly loved every minute of it and was proud of his role in the street action. The riots were sparked by an incident of police brutality against a black taxicab driver; over the next couple of days, tensions mounted inexorably: "regardless of what the Mayor did, regardless of what civil-rights leaders did, regardless of what planners of the demonstration did, the riot was going to happen. The authorities had been indifferent to the community's demand for justice; now the community was going to be indifferent to the authorities' demand for order."

Once the riots got under way, Hayden provided a steady stream of equivocating patter: the looting was "spirited"; "many missiles were thrown at cars driven by whites but not often with murderous intent"; whites were stopped and intimidated, but "very few, if any, were shot at."

> People voted with their feet to expropriate property to which they felt entitled. . . . A common claim was: this is owed me. But few needed to argue. People who under ordinary conditions respected law because they were forced to do so now felt free to act upon the law as they thought it should be.

Moreover, Hayden said, "most of the people were taking only for themselves. One reason there was so little quarreling over 'who gets what' was that there was, for a change, enough for all." Besides, "most of the rage" was directed at white store owners, not at "schools, churches, or banks," which—Hayden assures us in one extraordinary aside—are "oppressive" but "contain little that can be carried off."

Clearly, Silvers and his colleagues experienced a frisson

of excitement at Hayden's endorsement of violence and illegality, for they allowed it to be used in an advertising campaign for *The New York Review* that fall: "If you want to bring a Molotov cocktail to your next cocktail party, arm yourself with Tom Hayden's 'The Occupation of Newark,' in which the Establishment's version of what went on there is blown to bits."

Philip Nobile believed that *The New York Review*'s flirtation with the radical Left was brief, aberrant, and basically harmless. In fact the journal's sudden jerk leftward revealed something essential not only about its politics but also about its attitude toward ideas and the life of the mind. In brief, *The New York Review* was a journal of blithe political opportunism, ready at the first hint of a change in the public mood to embrace extreme, even revolutionary, ideas that were totally at odds with its ambition to be (as the editors declared in their first issue) "a responsible literary journal." In "Radical Chic," his brilliant 1970 dissection of high-end radical posturing, Tom Wolfe mentions the *New York Review*'s Molotov cocktail issue. The journal, he notes,

> was sometimes referred to good-naturedly as *The Parlour Panther*, with the *-our* spelling of *Parlour* being an allusion to its concurrent motif of anglophilia. The *Review*'s embracing of such apparently contradictory attitudes—the nitty-gritty of the ghetto warriors and the preciosity of traditional Leavis & Empson intellectualism—was really no contradiction at all, of course. It was merely the essential double-track mentality of Radical Chic—*nostalgie de la boue* and high protocol—in its literary form.

It has often been pointed out that there was plenty about the Sixties counterculture that *The New York Review* did not endorse—the fatuousness of Pop Art, for example, or, in the Seventies and Eighties, the intellectual swamp of deconstruction and its offshoots. This is true enough. It is also true that *The New York Review* in later years has run plenty of articles sharply critical of the kind of radicalism espoused by Hayden. One thinks, for example, of Hannah Arendt's reflections on left-wing violence or Christopher Lasch's brilliant dissection of the narcissistic elements of the counterculture (later reprinted in his book *The Culture of Narcissism*).

But such pieces are not really exculpatory. *The New York Review*'s mandarin posture has naturally made it wary of much that is meretricious. What matters has been its willingness to let radical politics trump its commitment to high culture and the liberal humanistic tradition. Quite apart from the irresponsibility of the politics, there was an *intellectual* irresponsibility at work here, a preening, ineradicable frivolousness toward the cultural values that the journal was supposedly created to nurture. That is why, as one looks back over the course of *The New York Review*, it seems less an intellectual than a sociological phenomenon: not so much a distinguished literary review as, in Tom Wolfe's perfect phrase, "the chief theoretical organ of Radical Chic." What Leszek Kolakowski said about Sartre applies to *The New York Review* as well: "He oscillated . . . between identification with the Communists and violent hostility towards them. . . . At every stage, however, he endeavored to preserve his own reputation as a 'Leftist,' and even to represent himself and his philosophy as the embodiment of 'Leftism' *par excellence*." As a result, *The New York Review of Books*, more than any other journal, made the long march of America's cultural revolution seem like an intellectually respectable enterprise.

Chapter 11
What the Sixties Wrought

"One is clever and knows everything that has ever happened: so there is no end of derision. One still quarrels, but one is soon reconciled—else it might spoil the digestion.

"One has one's little pleasure for the day and one's little pleasure for the night, but one has a regard for health.

"'We have invented happiness,' say the last men, and they blink."
—Friedrich Nietzsche, *Thus Spoke Zarathustra,* 1883

We have here the peculiarly American way of digesting continental despair. It is nihilism with a happy ending.
—Allan Bloom, *The Closing of the American Mind,* 1987

Where's the outrage?
—Bob Dole, 1996

Of the privileged, by the privileged, for the privileged

"The Sixties," it seems, has become less the name of a decade than a provocation. As a slice of history, the purple decade actually encompasses nearly twenty years. It began some time in the late 1950s and lasted at least until the mid-1970s. By then it had triumphed so thoroughly that its imperatives became indistinguishable from everyday life:

they *became* everyday life. The Sixties mean—what? Sexual "liberation," rock music, chemically induced euphoria— nearly everyone would agree with that, even though some would inscribe a plus sign, others a minus sign beside that famous triumvirate. The Sixties also mean free-floating protest and political activism, a "youth culture" that never ages, a new permissiveness together with a new affluence: Dionysus with a credit card and a college education.

Whatever else it was, the long march of America's cultural revolution was a capitalist, bourgeois revolution: a revolution of the privileged, by the privileged, and for the privileged. In the twentieth century, almost all political revolutions have resulted in oppression (I count phenomena like Solidarity in Poland and the "Velvet Revolution" in Czechoslovakia as counter-revolutionary movements). By contrast, the cultural revolution in the West really has resulted in a form of liberation—but one must still ask: liberation from what? And liberation for what? The answers to those questions tell us whether the promised liberation is genuine or fraudulent. A dose of heroin may induce the feeling of freedom; in reality, that feeling signals the onset of enslavement.

The socialist economist Joseph Schumpeter was wrong when he predicted, in a postscript to *Capitalism, Socialism, and Democracy* (1950), that the collapse of capitalism and a triumphant "march into socialism" would occur in America in the near future. What we have seen instead is an explosion of capitalist energy in the marketplace shadowed by a steady creep into nanny-state socialism. But Schumpeter was uncannily right about the dangers bourgeois capitalist societies harbor within themselves. Perhaps he overstated the case when he asserted, in 1942, that "capitalism is being killed by its achievements." But he was clearly on to something when he observed that capitalism creates a critical frame of mind which, after having destroyed the moral authority of so many other institutions, in the end turns against its own; the bourgeois finds to his amazement that the rationalist attitude does not stop at the credentials of kings and popes but goes on to attack private property and the whole scheme of bourgeois values.

Rising standards of living, far from increasing allegiance to the regime that provides them, often paradoxically turn out to have the opposite effect: what Schumpeter calls the "*emotional* attachment to the social order" begins to disintegrate. In this sense, the cultural revolution is not so much anticapitalist as a toxic by-product of capitalism's success: not so much antibourgeois as an expression of what Allan Bloom described as "the bourgeois' need to feel that he is not bourgeois, to have dangerous experiments with the unlimited."

Samuel Taylor Coleridge once famously remarked that a "willing suspension of disbelief" was essential to maintaining "poetic faith." Anyone who has looked back dispassionately at the founding documents and personalities of America's cultural revolution knows what Coleridge was talking about. The "faith" in question may have been more spurious than "poetic." But there can be no doubt that America's counterculture—like all utopian movements—has exacted prodigies of credulousness from its myriad adherents, fellow travelers, and promoters.

Utopian movements succeed because they tell people something they wish desperately to hear. Whether or not the message is true is beside the point. It speaks to a deeply felt need, and that is enough. As we all know, "utopia" literally means "nowhere." This fact seldom depresses the price of its real estate because, although the down-payment for belief is steep, there are no monthly payments. The housing tracts in utopia remain glitteringly inviolable—that they are also uninhabitable is cheerfully overlooked. For the adepts of the Free Spirit in the fourteenth century, the good news was that they, the elect, were godlike creatures incapable of sin. For Karl Marx, a Communist paradise was waiting for that society brave enough to abolish private property and centralize the means of production. For Norman O. Brown, "the real world, which is not the world of the reality-principle, is the world where thoughts are omnipotent, where no distinction is drawn between wish and deed." For the cultural revolutionaries of the Sixties, the domiciles of utopia always have numerous vacancies.

Emotions of virtue

Variations on such themes are as plentiful as they are preposterous. Wilhelm Reich, Allen Ginsberg, Norman Mailer, Susan Sontag, Timothy Leary, Abbie Hoffman, Tom Hayden, the Black Panthers, Paul Goodman, Charles Reich, The Beatles: the list of agents for utopia is long and varied. It includes artists and intellectuals, entertainers, political activists, blatant poseurs, and professional gurus. In their different ways, these people pandered to a generation's vanity, ambition, cowardice, and lust for sensation; increasingly they pandered to a generation whose vanity *was* its lust for sensation. They also served, as Susan Sontag illustrated in her campy meditations on Camp, as a defense against the alarming assaults of ennui. Many promulgated —like Rousseau before them—that insatiable greed for the *emotion* of virtue which makes the actual practice of virtue seem superfluous and elevates self-infatuation into a prime spiritual imperative.

The cultural and moral results of these developments were alternately sad and comic; politically and socially, they were destructive if sometimes risible. When Fredric Jameson, the celebrated Marxist professor of literature at Duke University, waxed nostalgic about the 1960s, he spoke of the "widely shared feeling" that "everything was possible," that "universal liberation" was nigh. He explained the situation in terms that require not simply the willing suspension but the outright obliteration of disbelief. "Mao Zedong's figure for this process," Jameson wrote,

> is . . . most revealing: "Our nation," he cried, "is like an atom. . . . When this atom's nucleus is smashed, the thermal energy released will have really tremendous power!" The image evokes the emergence of a genuine mass democracy from the breakup of older feudal and village structures. . . . Yet . . . we now know that Mao Zedong himself drew back from the ultimate consequences of the process he had set in motion, when, at the supreme moment of the Cultural Revolution, . . . he called a halt to the dissolution of the party apparatus and effectively reversed the direction of this collective experiment as a whole. . . . In the West, also, the great explosions of the 60s have led, in the worldwide economic crisis, to powerful restorations of the social order and a renewal of the repressive power of the various state apparatuses.

Let us agree that Mao's image of an atomic explosion was "most revealing." What did it reveal? The prospective "emergence of genuine mass democracy"? Or an obsession with absolute power cultivated by the man who was probably the greatest mass-murderer of the twentieth century? Jameson faults Mao not for the homicidal "cultural revolution" he had set in motion in 1966, but for drawing back from its "ultimate consequences." According to Jameson, in other words, the Great Helmsman was guilty primarily of a failure of imagination. And what was the nature of that revolution whose "supreme moment" he had betrayed? At Mao's instigation, Leszek Kolakowski writes, "the universities and schools began to form Red Guard detachments, storm troops of the revolution which were to restore power to the 'masses' and sweep aside the degenerate party and state bureaucracy."

> Mass meetings, processions, and street fighting became a feature of life in all the bigger cities . . . . For several years the schools and universities ceased functioning altogether, as the Maoist groups assured pupils and students that by virtue of their social origin and fidelity to the Leader they were the possessors of a great truth unknown to "bourgeois" scholars. Thus encouraged, bands of young people bullied professors whose only crime was their learning, ransacked homes in search of proofs of bourgeois ideology, and destroyed historical monuments as "relics of the past." Books were burnt wholesale.

Et cetera. And note, finally, how Jameson compares Mao's betrayal of his "collective experiment" with the reassertion of order in the West following the assaults of Sixties radicalism and the Vietnam War. Jameson has been declaring a "worldwide economic crisis" and a "renewal" of repressive state power for as long as anyone can remember. It is safe to assume, however, that neither has intruded much on his prerogatives or remuneration as the William A. Lane, Jr., Professor of Comparative Literature, Professor of Romance Studies (French), and Chair of The Literature Program at Duke University.

Of course, Fredric Jameson was quite right to discern a "widely shared feeling" in the Sixties that "everything was possible." The conviction of unlimited possibility—credulousness reborn as policy—is another characteristic of utopian movements. It is what gives them their momentum and allows them to present naïveté as idealism, narcissism as enlightenment, chaos as freedom. It is also what makes utopian movements so susceptible to ideological manipulation. To the extent that one endorses the apotheosis of possibility, one will tend to treat the real world and its occupants with cavalier disregard. Hence the utopian element in all totalitarian political movements. "What binds these men together," Hannah Arendt observed in *The Origins of Totalitarianism*, "is a firm and sincere belief in human omnipotence. Their moral cynicism, their belief that everything is permitted, rests on the solid conviction that everything is possible."

The glow of grand ideas

For all its garishness, however, the spirit of the Sixties tends to live on and to reveal itself most clearly in a negative not a positive sense: not in what it champions so much as in what it undermines, what it corrodes. In many respects, the Sixties really did amount to a *counter*-culture: a repudiation, an inversion of the Fifties—another period that lives on as a provocation. As we enter a new century and a new millennium, the question of what the Sixties wrought is far from settled. Indeed, it has lately assumed a new urgency as it becomes ever clearer that American culture is deeply riven along fault lines first defined by the reverberations of that long, percussive decade.

This emerges clearly in a huge compendium on the

period published in 1998, *The Sixties: Cultural Revolution in Britain, France, Italy and the United States, c.1958–c.1974*. Written by the British social historian Arthur Marwick, the tome offers a kind of international sourcebook of exemplary texts, trends, and events from about 1958 through about 1974—Marwick's definition of the "long decade" that constituted the Sixties. It is an odd book. There is nearly as much about the evolution of English laws regulating the sale of alcoholic beverages as there is about the Beatles and rock music. The social-science apparatus is wheeled on early and often. The reader encounters sixteen "Characteristics of a Unique Era" ("the formation of new subcultures and movements," "upheavals in race, class, and family relationships," etc.) as well as numerous statistical summaries and charts. There is, for example, a chart indicating the percentage of Italian families who owned television sets, refrigerators, and washing machines in 1965 as compared with 1975 (more later than earlier) and a chart comparing the relative popularity in France of watching television and going out in the evening in 1967 and 1973 (ditto). Eight hundred pages of such stuff are reinforced by one hundred pages of notes and index. If nothing else, *The Sixties* provides a kind of running illustration for Schumpeter's thesis about the self-consuming nature of successful bourgeois-capitalist society.

Marwick makes a great show of being the careful, "scientific" historian, concerned with sources and evidence, not "metaphysical" theories. He begins with a good deal of methodological throat-clearing: just what counts as an historical period? What really constitutes historical influence? —that sort of thing. One might have had more faith in Marwick's scientific aptitude had the left-wing journalist Paul Berman not appeared as Professor Paul Bearman on page four of *The Sixties*, endowed not only with a new name and a professorship but also with "a strongly hostile view of the radicals of the sixties." Hostile? "We ourselves," Berman wrote in *A Tale of Two Utopias*, the book to which Marwick refers in his notes,

> —the teenage revolutionaries, freaks, hippies, and students, together with our friends and leaders who were five or ten years older and our allies around the world—stood at the heart of a new society . . . of spiritual grandeur. . . . Something soulful. A moral advance. And in the glow of the very grand and utopian idea, a thousand disparate events from around the world—the student uprisings, the hippie experiments, the religious transformations, the rise of Communism in some places and the first signs of its fall in other places, the Black Power movement, and onward through feminism and every insurrectionary impulse of the age— seemed to merge into a single tide.

If Paul Berman's book expresses "a strongly hostile view of the radicals of the sixties," what would a flattering view sound like?

Marwick provides both a mood and an argument in *The Sixties*. The mood is captured by the montages of the Fifties and the Sixties that appear in the book's opening pages. It is not all that different from the mood evoked by Berman. The Sixties, Marwick writes, prominently featured

> black civil rights; youth culture and trend-setting by young people; idealism, protest, and rebellion; the triumph of popular music based on Afro-American models and the emergence of this music as a universal language; . . . the search for inspiration in the religions of the Orient; massive changes in personal relationships and sexual behaviour; a general audacity and frankness in books and in the media,

and in ordinary behaviour; gay liberation; the emergence of "the underground" and the "counterculture"; optimism and genuine faith in the dawning of a better world.

All of which is to be contrasted with the Fifties, a dark, un-creative time whose "key features" include, among many other abominations,

> rigid social hierarchy; subordination of women to men and children to parents; repressed attitudes to sex; racism; un-questioning respect for authority in the family, education, government, the law, and religion, and for the nation-state, the national flag, the national anthem; Cold War hysteria; a strict formalism in language, etiquette, and dress codes; a dull and cliché-ridden popular culture, most obviously in popular music, with its boring big bands and banal ballads.

Marwick is quick to add that "of course" a conservative would regard the Fifties quite differently. And he admits along the way that much of what was done in the name of the Sixties "was downright stupid" (the violence, the "mindless" drug use). But in mood, *The Sixties* adheres closely to the standard left-wing account: Sixties good, Fifties bad. Toward the end of the book, in a few sentences remarkable as much for their baldness as for their naïveté, Marwick sums up his attitude:

> Life became more various and enjoyable. With less rigid conceptions of marriage and new opportunities for divorce, with changing attitudes to fashion and to education, with the abandonment of comfortable fictions about the nature of beauty and the arrival of informal, body-hugging cloth-ing, there was a healthier openness to ordinary living, less need for lies. . . . Gone was the stuffy conservatism of

previous decades, while the radical, divisive, philistine conservatism of Reagan and Thatcher was yet to come.

It is an excellent thing that Marwick early on warned us that "it is very important not to get into the position of idealizing, reifying, or anthropomorphizing periods or decades, attributing personalities to them, singling out 'good' decades from 'bad' decades." The unsuspecting reader must be grateful for that warning: otherwise he might think Marwick was doing just that.

The old hope of reorganizing the world

There is, however, another side to *The Sixties*. If in many respects it embodies the established liberal clichés about the delights of the Age of Aquarius and the depredations of the years before and after, it also challenges at least two important elements of the received story. For one thing, Marwick has no patience with what he calls the Great Marxisant Fallacy. He describes this as "the belief that the society we inhabit is the bad bourgeois society, but that, fortunately, this society is in a state of crisis, so that the good society which lies just around the corner can be easily attained if only we work systematically to destroy the language, the values, the culture, the ideology of bourgeois society."

As Marwick notes, "practically all the activists, student protesters, hippies, yippies, Situationists, advocates of psychedelic liberation, participants in be-ins and rock festivals, proponents of free love, members of the underground, and advocates of Black Power, women's liberation, and gay liberation believed that by engaging in struggles, giving witness, or simply doing their own thing they were contributing to the final collapse of the bad bourgeois society." Or so they said. Revolution in *this* sense was never more than a pipe dream—partly because, as Marwick notes, modern liberal societies are not the monolithic entities that the radicals and would-be radicals pretended they were. Liberal society—it is part of its genius—tends to absorb opposition instead of rejecting it outright. This does not mean that the cultural revolution did not happen, only that in the end it succeeded by insinuation rather than insurrection. As Marwick puts it, "the various counter-cultural movements and subcultures, being ineluctably implicated in and interrelated with mainstream society" did not so much confront that society as they *"permeated* and *transformed* it."* Exactly. In the 1960s, radicals continually bemoaned the specter of "co-optation." What they failed to see was that this process would result in the ultimate success of the values they held dear.

And this brings us to Marwick's second challenge. The counterculture of the Sixties is often described as idealistic, utopian, and anti- or non-materialistic. Marwick introduces a salutary dollop of skepticism into the discussion. As we have seen, the counterculture of the Sixties brought us a great deal of rhetoric about the evils of materialism. Marwick shows that there had never been a generation so blissfully immersed in consumerism. The 1980s and 1990s may have perfected the process. But it was the counterculture of the Sixties—supported by the unprecedented abundance the mainstream economy provided—that succeeded in first spreading the gospel. As Marwick notes, "most of the movements, subcultures, and new institutions which are at the heart of sixties change were thoroughly imbued with the entrepreneurial, profit-making ethic." All those boutiques, experimental theaters, art galleries, discothèques, nightclubs, light shows, head shops, pornographic outlets, and underground films may have challenged the morals, manners, and standards of taste and accomplishment of bourgeois capitalist society. But they did so while profiting generously from its largess.

Marwick is quite happy about all this. In his view, the international movement that "permeated" and "transformed" society constituted a "mini-Renaissance," with The Beatles, miniskirts, and the art of Andy Warhol having contributed "their mite to the people's liberation." Everywhere, people were richer, "franker" (a favorite commendation of Marwick's), and more intent upon pursuing pleasure:

> All the statistical evidence suggests that permissive attitudes and permissive behaviour continued to spread at accelerating rates, with only the utterly unforeseen occurrence of AIDS to bring any kind of caution; single parent families proliferated, the terms "husband" and "wife" became almost quaint, giving place to "lover" and "partner." . . . The appearance, also, of moralistic crusades simply testifies to the strength of the by now well-established behaviour patterns which the crusades, vainly, hoped to eliminate. The cultural revolution, in short, had continuous, uninterrupted, and lasting consequences.

Of course, Marwick is right. The only question is whether we should be as optimistic about the result as he is. Again, Marwick sounds various cautionary notes: he is disturbed by the phenomenon of political correctness; he notes that the Sixties brought various undesirable excesses. But overall Marwick is a cheerleader for the "multicultural societies" that "exhibit to the full the vibrancy and creative potential which first bloomed in the sixties."

Marwick makes two basic mistakes. One is equating "more" with "better"—equating, that is, material abundance with what the Greeks called "the good life." For most people, the good life *presupposes* a certain level of material abundance; but that is not to say that affluence *guarantees* or is identical with achievement of the good life.

Marwick's second mistake is to take the self-evaluation of the Sixties at its own estimation. You cannot step a foot into the literature about the 1960s without being told how "creative," "idealistic," and "loving" it was, especially in comparison to the 1950s. In fact, the counterculture of the Sixties represented the triumph of what the art critic Harold Rosenberg famously called the "herd of independent minds." Its so-called creativity consisted in continually recirculating a small number of radical clichés; its idealism was little more than irresponsible utopianism; and its crusading for "love" was largely a blind for hedonistic self-indulgence.

What Allan Bloom said in comparing American universities in the 1950s to those of the 1960s can easily be generalized to apply to the culture as a whole: "The fifties," Bloom wrote, "were one of the great periods of the American university," which had recently benefitted from an enlivening infusion of European talent and "were steeped in the general vision of humane education inspired by Kant and Goethe." The Sixties, by contrast, "were the period of dogmatic answers and trivial tracts. Not a single book of lasting importance was produced in or around the movement. It was all Norman O. Brown and Charles Reich. This was when the real conformism hit the universities, when opinions about everything from God to the movies became absolutely predictable." Notwithstanding Marwick's contemptuous remark about the music of the "boring big bands," stultifying conformism did not become rife in virtually every department of intellectual and cultural life until the Sixties were well advanced.

They did, however, see an astonishing explosion of material prosperity. Marwick alludes regularly to that fact, he pets and caresses it, he produces it whenever he attempts to justify his claims on behalf of the achievements of the period. To be sure, material prosperity is a nice thing, a very nice thing. But it does not guarantee cultural health or moral vigor. The culture of the 1990s has served as a vivid reminder of this home truth. We—the industrialized, technologized world—have never been richer. And yet to an extraordinary extent we in the West continue to inhabit a moral and cultural universe shaped by the hedonistic imperatives and radical ideals of the Sixties. Culturally, morally the world we inhabit is increasingly a trash world: addicted to sensation, besieged everywhere by the cacophonous, mind-numbing din of rock music, saturated with pornography, in thrall to the lowest common denominator wherever questions of taste, manners, or intellectual delicacy are concerned. Marwick was right: "The cultural revolution, in short, had continuous, uninterrupted, and lasting consequences."

A special nuttiness

Paul Berman's *A Tale of Two Utopias* (1996) provides a good illustration of just how "continuous, uninterrupted, and lasting" those consequences have been. Berman worked very hard in his book to memorialize the supposed idealism of the counterculture. He himself is a disappointed radical. But his disappointments have not led him to abandon his radicalism. On the contrary, his disappointments have in a curious way *become* his radicalism. Perhaps it was this skillful feat of political alchemy that led the MacArthur Foundation to confer upon him one of its famous (left-wing) "genius" awards.

A Tale of Two Utopias is instructive for anyone wishing to understand the long march of America's cultural revolution. Berman knows that things have not worked out as he hoped, that the utopian schemes he once cherished have, all of them, soured and turned rancorous. The adjectives he employs to describe them now range from "kooky," "loony," and "mad" to "criminal"; nevertheless, he comes not to bury the cultural revolution but to praise it. If things haven't developed according to plan, well, it is not his fault. Beginning at least in 1965, when (he tells us) he went as a "wide eyed" high-school student to Washington, D.C., to join in an anti-war march, Berman has been an absolute sucker for what might be called Westchester radicalism. On that occasion in 1965, the American Socialist leader "Norman Thomas spoke. Joan Baez sang. It was a glorious April afternoon." Obviously, to be young then was very heaven.

In due course, Berman graduated to Columbia College and joined the Students for a Democratic Society (SDS) in its period of decline, finding that this organization, despite its "special nuttiness," delivered on its promise "to take young people who felt empty of identity and give them a sense of control over their own destiny." For people who felt "offended by the soft life that was their own," Berman explains, participation in the SDS and similar organizations filled an existential void. Politics in the ordinary sense was only part of the equation. The deliberately outlandish dress, music, and behavior that radical organizations in the 1960s fostered were also important: they all "generated an atmosphere of confrontation, which turned giddy and hot, which created a festival atmosphere." Which led to the sit-ins, occupation of buildings, and charges of criminal trespassing. Then "off you went to jail, where for once you felt morally at peace." And here we come to the emotional core of *A Tale of Two Utopias*. For out of that same festival atmosphere "came a few tiny indications that a new society, organized on novel principles, might at any moment burst into view. . . . Sheer madness, those mass meetings were. Yet they took place, and the superdemocratic utopia flickered into reality before your eyes."

In proposing to trace "the political journey of the generation of 1968," Berman was at the same time tracing his own political itinerary. But only rarely did he speak *in propria persona*. When he alluded, say, to a "vague new sensibility" that "managed to be trembly with expectation" or conjured "the dream of a genuine socialism, uncorrupted, untyrannical, de-Stalinized, ultra-democratic," he did so in the third person. In fact, *A Tale of Two Utopias* is a kind of spiritual-political credo disguised as a piece of intellectual history. Berman drew upon a motley agglomeration of persons and events in an effort to define a sensibility, the sensibility of a Sixties radical who is thoroughly disabused but not disillusioned. This imparts a certain schizoid quality to the book: Berman's evidence points in one direction, all his rhetoric in the opposite direction. Ostensibly, he set out to investigate the unhappy logic of revolutionary utopianism, which always begins in moralistic self-infatuation and infallibly ends in disaster.

The basic argument of *A Tale of Two Utopias* is as simple as it is preposterous: namely, that the fall of Communism and the still tenuous rise of liberal democracy in parts of Eastern Europe and elsewhere are the adult rerun of the radical movements of the 1960s. In the aftermath of 1989, Berman wrote, it suddenly became "obvious that those long-ago utopian efforts to change the shape of the world were a young people's rehearsal, preparatory to adult events that only came later. Suddenly it was obvious that the authentic political revolution of our era was now, not then; liberal and democratic, not radical leftist in the '68 style;

real, not imaginary." Obvious to him, that is. How would the people actually living under Communist tyranny regard this feeble effort to establish a moral equivalence between the "liberation" brought by the counterculture of the 1960s and their own political liberation in the 1990s?

Contemplating the triumph of Václav Havel in Czechoslovakia (Havel is one of Berman's heroes), Berman wrote that

> the old hope of reorganizing the world on a drastically new and infinitely more democratic basis, the universal project, the grand aspiration for the poor and the downtrodden, *that* hope, the forbidden utopian dream, once again seemed, in its newly liberal and anti-grandiose version— well, thinkable.

What we have here is utopianism on a fake diet. The moral is: Sixties radicals never die; they just fade away into the pages of *The New Yorker* and the comfort zone of munificent "genius" awards.

Such, finally, is the burden of *A Tale of Two Utopias*: to show that liberal democracy, rooted though it is in capitalism and shot through with a suspicion of utopian enthusiasm, is somehow, really, at bottom, in its fundamental impulse—the latest version of utopia (though we mustn't call it that) and, moreover, a utopia that depends crucially on the "exhilaration" of a Sixties-style radicalism accoutered in the wariness of the 1990s.

This of course is putting it much more baldly than Berman deigned to do. In his introduction, "The Dream of a New Society," Berman provided an insider's sketch of the "utopian exhilaration" that, he rightly noted, "swept across the student universe and across several adult universes as well" in and around 1968:

the student uprisings, the building occupations, marches, strikes, battles with the police, the insurrections that were sexual, feminist, and gay, the bursts of ecological passion, the noisy entrance of the first mass of African-American students into the previously segregated American universities, the slightly crazy effort to raise insubordination into a culture, to eat, dress, smoke, dance differently. . . .

Berman's enthusiasm for what he accurately described as "an insurrection in middle-class customs" is patent in every phrase. He was equally upbeat about the other Sixties revolutions he describes, the upsurge in pseudospirituality (*not* Berman's term)—the "bits and pieces of Buddhism, Beat poetry, transcendentalism, Mexican folklore, psychedelic mind expansions, and God knows what else"—as well as various more overt political agitations against "Western imperialism" and, in a few scattered places, Communist tyranny.

Consider Berman's ambitiously titled first chapter, "The Moral History of the Baby Boom Generation." It ought to have been called "The Immoral History of the Baby Boom Generation." "Every few decades," Berman wrote, "a pure flame of political rebellion shoots up somewhere and with amazing speed spreads in all directions, until half the countries on earth have been scorched." It happened in 1776; it happened in 1789; it happened in 1848; it happened in 1917; and, according to Berman, it happened again in 1968. The student rebellions of 1968, he said, were "one more instance of the same mysterious phenomenon, except on a bigger geographical scale than before." What is really mysterious is how someone with a college education could actually believe that the triumph of the countercultural revolution in 1968 was morally equivalent to the triumph of the American Revolution in 1776 (to take just that one instance). Or perhaps this is the sort of thing that, these days, *only* someone with a college education could believe?

A Whitmanian critic

For the rest, Berman meanders among familiar signposts of the Sixties. He revisits the Port Huron statement ("longer than the *Communist Manifesto*" but "not as good") and the career of Tom Hayden, that one-time admirer of North Korea's Kim Il Sung whom some people—friends, too —referred to as "the next Lenin." The Weather Underground and other such criminal groups get some attention. Berman lets us know that he also read some books about the student movements in Europe and Latin America, and he treats readers to a similar digest of events and personalities there: Pierre Goldman, André Glucksmann, Régis Debray; the Red Brigades, the Baader-Meinhof gang, the Sandinistas. Berman is far from uncritical of these people and movements; he speaks of "childish lives," of "criminal leftism," of movements going "mad." But all his criticism is advanced in an exonerating context of supposed "idealism." "Faraway solidarity became their religion. They said in effect: I struggle on behalf of others, therefore I am. . . . It was a grand idea, morally."

Berman's long last chapter, "A Backward Glance at the End of History," begins by pondering some very large questions, to wit: Is there some "larger meaning" (i.e., utopian impulse) that can be discerned in the liberal and national revolutions that broke out in and after 1989 in Eastern Europe? Some "crucial truth about the nature of man and the shape of history"? Berman reveals that his labors yielded the following insight into the philosophy of history: that some people think that things change without order or meaning, while others believe that there is a discernible meaning in events and even progress to the pattern of history. Of course, it sounds preposterously simplistic when put like that. Alas, that is precisely how Berman *does* put it. *Ipse dicit*: "There was the idea that things change . . . but without ever arriving at any kind of order or final shape. . . . And there was the idea that things change, and eventually the chaos adds up to progress."

Berman spends approximately one hundred pages mulling over this profound thought, drawing on works by André Glucksmann (a former Maoist who advocates the history-is-chaos theory) and Francis Fukuyama (the famous neo-Hegelian who discerns a pleasing shape to the course of history). He treats readers to a great deal of pointless biographical detail about both authors, and he then attempts a summary of their relevant works, Glucksmann's book *The 11th Commandment* and Fukuyama's *The End of History and the Last Man*. I am no fan of Fukuyama's Hegelian fantasia. But to say, as Berman does, that his idea of progress charts "the same direction in world events that Whitman has invoked in his poetry and prose" is woefully to misunderstand both Whitman and Fukuyama. And what, finally, does Berman make of all this? He expresses a slight preference for the lively chaos espoused by André Glucksmann, but concludes thus: "The messages from these two authors . . . are at odds with one another, but since I am a critic and not a philosopher, I see no reason not to say that both messages seem true enough." No one will accuse Berman of being a philosopher. But even a critic might be expected to stop short of embracing blatant contradiction—unless, of course, he is a "Whitmanian" critic, in which case contradiction need be no bar to affirmation.

At the end of his chapter on the baby boom generation, Berman spoke of his "bafflement" that "a movement so grand and touching in its motives as the student leftism of the 1960s could have degenerated and disappeared so quickly." He needn't have been puzzled. The reason is not far to seek. The crucial thing to understand about the student (and faculty) leftism of the 1960s and 1970s is its combination of hedonism and bourgeois antibourgeois animus. That is the real explanation of its attack on middle-class values, its surrender to drugs and promiscuous sex, its infatuation with bogus forms of "spirituality," and its destructive dabbling in insurrectionary politics. Nor need Berman have waxed elegiac. Students may rarely stage sit-ins today. But the emancipatory ethos that he longingly evoked in these pages has not disappeared; it has been woven into the fabric of American life: bureaucratized, as successful revolutions always are. It has transformed not only the university, but the media and every major cultural institution in this country. It has, in fact, succeeded beyond the wildest dreams of many of its early partisans. It is perhaps debatable whether, as Berman insists, "the left-wing idea . . . is a permanent feature of any reasonably modern society." But it is undeniably an ingrained feature of *our* society. Berman writes about the Sixties the way left-wing intellectuals write about Communism: as if it were a noble idea that somewhere, somehow went wrong. But neither Communism nor the radicalism of the 1960s went wrong: they were born wrong. Berman's failure to face up to that fact makes his utopian tale just that: a tale about nowhere.

Is the revolution over?

Charles Dickens's sentimental portrayal of the French Revolution in *A Tale of Two Cities* continues to speak deeply to the left-wing imagination. Andrew Kopkind and Paul

Berman were not the only ones to have adapted its title. In May 1998, Mark Lilla, a political philosopher (then at New York University, now at the University of Chicago) also adapted it for "A Tale of Two Reactions," his reflections on the dynamics of America's cultural revolution that were published in *The New York Review of Books*. The fact that the essay appeared in *The New York Review* had a certain poignancy, of course, since *The Review* contributed so conspicuously to the counterculture in the 1960s. Lilla's general point was that when a cultural revolution is finally successful, continued opposition is merely "reactionary," that is, bootless and intellectually undignified. He gives two examples. The first is the countercultural revolution of the Sixties. Unlike many people on the Left, Lilla has no interest in denying that this revolution actually took place. Indeed, he not only argues that the cultural revolution happened but also that it has been wildly successful in its effect on public authority, the family, and individual morality (and, he might have added, on cultural and intellectual life). In fact, the cultural revolution has been so successful that conservative resistance—and here he cites my own essays on the cultural revolution in *The New Criterion* as exhibit A—long ago became completely otiose and reactionary. Lilla's second example is the so-called "Reagan revolution" of the 1980s. This, too, he says, has been so successful in altering our view of certain economic and political matters that left-wing attacks on "Reaganism"—he cites a series in *The Nation* as an example—are now beside the point or, worse, merely reactionary. (Such attacks, he says, are examples of "progressive reaction.")

· In the end, Lilla's basic message is not far from the old advice: "If you can't beat them, join them." But connoisseurs of cultural polemic will see that its effectiveness depends less on its message than its method. Lilla offers his readers two patently unacceptable extremes and then endeavors to place himself not so much between them as above them: a *tertium quid* of sweet reasonableness—Lilla invokes "a small stream of liberal thought"—uncontaminated by any "reactionary" sentiments. William Hazlitt long ago described the essence of this strategy in his essay on "the common-place critic" who, Hazlitt observed, "believes that truth lies in the middle, between the extremes of right and wrong." What makes Lilla's essay of particular interest is the subtle way he goes about occupying that middle—or, more accurately, "middle"—ground.

One device is a generous deployment of . . . well, let us call it "smoke." Lilla says that conservatives "romanticize the affluent Fifties" and so "are reticent to seek the causes of the cultural revolution there." In fact, many conservative discussions of the counterculture locate its origins in the Beat sensibility of the middle Fifties. That is the reason that so much space is devoted in this book (and in the original articles Lilla was addressing) to figures like Allen Ginsberg, Jack Kerouac, William S. Burroughs, Norman Mailer, Herbert Marcuse, and Wilhelm Reich, all of whom made their reputations in the Fifties or earlier.

Then there is the question of causes. Lilla says that "to judge by the essays of Roger Kimball and other conservatives, the cause of the Sixties was quite simply . . . the Sixties. They just happened, as a kind of miracle, or anti-miracle" (ellipsis in the original). "Why," he asks, "did such a profound revolution take place in America when it did? Let us call this the Tocqueville question." Well, part of what we may call "the Tocqueville answer" is quoted in the Introduction to *The Long March*: "When great revolutions are successful," Tocqueville wrote in his book on the *ancien régime* and the French Revolution, "their causes cease to exist, and the very fact of their success has made them incomprehensible." All manner of sociological, technological, and demographic phenomena have been adduced to "explain" the rise of the counterculture: a new-found affluence together with the postwar population explosion together with an unprecedented number of people in college; the birth-control pill; increased mobility brought about by the widespread private ownership of cars; the Vietnam War. . . . The list is a long one, always pertinent, never conclusive. For the truth is, as Irving Kristol observed, "the counterculture was not 'caused,' it was born. What happened was internal to our culture and society, not external to it." In this respect, anyway, Schumpeter was right. Accordingly, the real task for a cultural critic is not etiological—there are a never-ending series of incomplete answers to the question "Why?"—but diagnostic and, ultimately, therapeutic. The pathology is real; the problem is to assay its nature and severity and then decide what to do about it.

The strategy of splitting the difference always depends on a bit of conceptual legerdemain. In Lilla's scheme, the key evasion comes in his contention that America's cultural revolution and the policies of the Reagan administration count as "complementary" phenomena. Lilla speaks—as many before him have spoken—of a Reagan "revolution." But that is a publicist's (or a polemicist's) misuse of language. Reagan's policies were important; they were far-reaching; in my judgment, most of them were beneficent. But they did not constitute a revolution. If anything, they were an attempt to undo or palliate a set of social and fiscal policies that have a much greater claim to being described as revolutionary: I mean the "welfare state" ideology that began under Franklin Roosevelt and reached its final, malodorous flowering in the "Great Society" of Lyndon Johnson and the sclerotic "nanny state" ideology of Jimmy Carter and Bill Clinton.

But it is quite wrong to see in Reagan's policies a revolutionary departure from the past. On the contrary, they count as a small step in the direction of regaining a foothold in the body of American political and economic tradition. Lilla tells his readers that, "thanks to Reagan, most Americans now believe (rightly or wrongly) that economic growth will do more for them than economic redistribution, and that to grow rich is good." Note in passing Lilla's parenthetical remark, which allows him to play both sides of the ideological fence he has erected. The main point, however, is that most Americans are clever enough to have figured out this message all on their own: they didn't need Ronald Reagan to tell them that economic growth is a good thing or that, given the choice, they would just as soon be well off as taxed into poverty, thanks very much. Nor is this a recent development. Lilla wheels on Tocqueville early and often in his essay. But already in 1835, in the first volume of *Democracy in America*, Tocqueville observed that he knew "of no country . . . where the love of money has taken stronger hold on the affections of men and where a profounder contempt is expressed for the theory of the permanent equality of property." I really do not think we can blame Ronald Reagan for Alexis de Tocqueville.

Perhaps the greatest challenge for the reader of Lilla's essay is trying to determine where exactly he stands. As with Berman, Lilla's arguments tend to point in one direction, his rhetoric in another. The tone, the atmosphere, the *weather* of "A Tale of Two Reactions" was orthodox left-liberal. But many of the substantial points Lilla raises would seem to support the conservative indictment of the cultural revolution. Lilla even provides detailed summaries of how the cultural revolution has had a devastating effect on everything from private morality to social policy.

When drug pushers and vagrants are permitted to set the tone in public parks, it is not the police who lose. It is poor urban families who lose their backyards. When children are coddled and undisciplined in the schools, they are the first to suffer, their families next. When universities cater to the whimsical tastes of their students and the aggressive demands of political interests, they cease to be retreats for serious cultivation of the self. When pornography is readily available on cable TV or the World Wide Web, the sleaze merchants profit and we are all demeaned.

Lilla offers these and similar observations as "commonplaces in conservative cultural literature today," and so they are. He says that he thinks that they are "largely correct."

But Lilla also says that the cultural revolution represents a "plausible metamorphosis" rather than an "alien distortion" of the American tradition. What can this mean? What can it mean when he says that, because "the revolution is over," it is useless to criticize its effects? Lilla correctly notes that "the moral views of 'ordinary Americans' are approaching those" of the "new class" shaped by the cultural revolution. He cites this as a reason to abandon criticism. But isn't it rather grounds for even deeper alarm? Lilla observes that many Americans today "see no contradiction in holding down day jobs in the unfettered global marketplace . . . and spending weekends immersed in a moral and cultural universe shaped by the Sixties." He is quite right. But is this really a reason for complacency?

Lilla's position is a sophisticated variation on the "but everyone does it" defense. Properly brought up children know that that argument doesn't hold much water, and one must assume that deep down Lilla knows it as well.

In the early years of this century, John Fletcher Moulton, a British judge, observed in a speech that there is a widespread tendency to regard the fact that [one] can do a thing as meaning [one] may do it. There can be no more fatal error that this. Between "can do" and "may do" ought to exist the whole realm which recognizes the sway of duty, fairness, sympathy, taste, and all the other things that make life beautiful and society possible.

One of the most destructive effects of America's cultural revolution has been to exacerbate this tendency to the point where the "sway of duty, fairness, sympathy, taste," and all the rest—everything that Lord Moulton congregated under the memorable category of "obedience to the unenforceable"—has been rendered nugatory. This has plunged our culture into a moral crisis whose dimensions we are only now beginning to reckon. Lilla complained that reactionary sentiment on the Left and the Right has "brought serious political reflection down to absolute zero" and left "the field of common political deliberation" vacant. But as long as he sides with those who "see no contradiction in holding down day jobs in the unfettered global marketplace . . . and spending weekends immersed in a moral and cultural universe shaped by the Sixties," Lilla will find that there is nothing to deliberate about.

The survivalist option

To an extent scarcely imaginable thirty years ago, we now live in that "moral and cultural universe shaped by the Sixties." The long march of America's cultural revolution has succeeded beyond the wildest dreams of all but the most starry-eyed utopians. The great irony is that this victory took place in the midst of a significant drift to the center-Right in electoral politics. The startling and depressing fact is that supposedly conservative victories at the polls have done almost nothing to challenge the dominance of left-wing, emancipationist attitudes and ideas in our culture. On the contrary, in the so-called "culture wars," conservatives have been conspicuous losers.

One sign of that defeat has been the fate of the culture wars themselves. One hears considerably less about those battles today than in the early and mid-1990s. That is partly because, as Robert Novak notes in his book *Completing the Revolution* (2000), "moral issues tend to exhaust people over time." Controversies that only yesterday sparked urgent debate today seem, for many, strangely beside the point. There is also the issue of material abundance. For if the Sixties were an assault on the moral substance of traditional culture, they nonetheless abetted the capitalist culture of accumulation. Yes, there are exceptions, but they are unimportant to the overall picture. Indeed, it happened that the cultural revolution was most damaging precisely where, in material terms, it was most successful. This put many conservatives in an awkward position. For conservatives have long understood that free markets and political liberty go together. What if it turned out that free markets plus the cultural revolution of the Sixties added up to moral and intellectual poverty? This unhappy thought has lately been the subject of much discussion and disagreement. Among those identified as conservatives, the two most popular responses at the moment seem to be retreat and denial. Both are mistaken.

Probably the most vivid example of the counsel of retreat is "A Moral Minority?," the now-notorious open letter written by the conservative activist Paul Weyrich to his friends and supporters. Dated February 16, 1999, this heartfelt, eighteen-hundred-word document is clearly the product of profound disillusionment bordering on despair.

Over the last few decades, Weyrich has done an enormous amount to promote the conservative agenda. He has been instrumental in helping many conservative candidates get elected. It was he who popularized the phrase "moral majority." And yet the impressive political victories he helped to win have clearly not translated into moral or cultural victories. If anything, the culture today is in worse shape than in 1980 when Ronald Reagan was elected: "our culture," Weyrich argued, "has decayed into something approaching barbarism." The reason? "Politics itself has failed. And politics has failed because of the collapse of the culture. The culture we are living in becomes an ever-wider sewer. In truth, I think we are caught up in a cultural collapse of historic proportions, a collapse so great that it simply overwhelms politics."

Weyrich began with a faith in the moral wisdom of the majority of American people. That faith has been broken.

> Let me be perfectly frank about it. If there really were a moral majority out there, Bill Clinton would have been driven out of office months ago. It is not only the lack of political will on the part of Republicans, although that is part of the problem. More powerful is the fact that what Americans would have found absolutely intolerable only a few years ago, a majority now not only tolerates but celebrates. Americans have adopted, in large measure, the MTV culture that we so valiantly opposed just a few years ago, and it has permeated the thinking of all but those who have separated themselves from the contemporary culture.

Weyrich may have overstated his case. The MTV culture that he rightly deplores may not have permeated the thinking of quite "all" who have failed to exempt themselves from contemporary culture. And it should be noted that he issued various qualifications and expressions of tentativeness ("I don't have all the answers or even all the questions"). But by and large, I think it must be admitted that his unhappy diagnosis is right. At the deepest level—at the level of the culture's taken-for-granted feelings and assumptions about what matters—the hedonistic, self-infatuated ethos of cultural revolution has triumphed to an extent unimaginable when it began.

What is the appropriate response? Weyrich's "frankly rather radical" proposal was what we might call the survivalist option: opt out, take to the hills. "What seems to me a legitimate strategy," he wrote, "is to look at ways to separate ourselves from the institutions that have been captured by the ideology of Political Correctness, or by other enemies of our traditional culture." Some of Weyrich's suggestions are more plausible than others. Homeschooling, for example, has proven to be an attractive alternative for many families around the country who are appalled by the extent to which both public and private schools have been dumbed-down and have been captured by the ideology of political correctness. But what about his praise for those "setting up private courts, where they can hope to find justice instead of ideology and greed"? Do we really want to encourage efforts to establish a "private" judiciary?

In the last year or so, certain liberals have adopted the strategy of attacking conservatives for aping the radical tactics and anti-Americanism of the 1960s. Although the attack is often ludicrously wide of the mark, it has been enormously popular. Liberals understandably enjoy beating conservatives with the stick that only yesterday was wielded so effectively against them. Regrettably, Weyrich has given his enemies plenty of ammunition for such attacks. Rhetorically and substantively, the most ill-judged part of his letter comes in the peroration advocating adopting a "modified version" of the radical slogan "turn on, tune in, drop out." It doesn't matter that Weyrich wants us to turn *off* our television sets rather than turn on with drugs, or that he advises us to "tune out" the ambient noise of cultural degradation. What catches everyone's attention is his endorsement in any form of Timothy Leary's infamous slogan and his final plea that we "drop out of this culture."

As could have been predicted, Weyrich's letter created a journalistic firestorm. Liberals savored the evidence of capitulation it seemed to suggest; conservatives for the most part shrank back in appalled silence from the spectacle of political suicide. For his part, Weyrich later declared that "we're not surrendering—we're opening a different front." And in "Creating a New Society," a response to the storm of criticism "A Moral Minority?" had prompted, he said that his letter had been "misread" and that what he proposed was "nothing less than [what] the early Christians did within the Roman Empire: creating a new society within the ruins of the old." It remains to be seen how effective his protestation will be.

A brigade of moral ostriches

Even if one strenuously disagrees with Weyrich's prescriptions, his seriousness and the pathos of his response made his letter a moving document. Here is a man who has fought long and hard for values he believes in deeply. He may be mistaken; he is not supercilious. I wish I could say the same about the conservatives who have adopted the strategy of denial. If Weyrich erred on the side of petulance —threatening to go home and take his marbles with him if the game was not played his way—the happy conservatives neither see nor hear nor speak any evil so long as there is a game going and they are allowed to play. Looking around at our astonishing prosperity, they respond (in answer to Bob Dole's plaintive question) "Who needs outrage? We're doing fine, thanks."

A recent salvo from the camp of contentment was "Good & Plenty: Morality in an Age of Prosperity," the cover story for the *The Weekly Standard* of February 1, 1999. It is an extraordinary performance. Written by David Brooks, a senior editor at the *Standard*, "Good & Plenty" is an unashamed paean to philistinism. It seems entirely appropriate that its title recalls a popular brand of candy. Brooks is an intelligent critic and a beguiling writer. But he has nothing except sweet things to say about our cultural situation in this essay. He begins by recounting a trip he made to a small town in northeast Connecticut. "I asked some of the older residents whether the cultural upheavals of the 1960s had affected the town much. They didn't know what I was talking about. They remember the sixties as a golden age when jobs were plentiful and the factories were buzzing." Doubtless they did. But so what?

One of Brooks's main points is that "we shouldn't leap to conclusions about the supposed degradation of our culture." That little town he visited was up in arms about a porn shop that had opened down the street. But the town's newfound prosperity came largely from a local gambling casino: so they are tough on smut but welcome gambling. According to Brooks, the situation in our culture is like a mixed day in the stock market: some issues are up, some are down. It is "hard to tell whether the aggregate effect is positive or negative." Besides, we shouldn't ignore "all the social indicators that are moving in the right direction: abortion rates are declining, crime is down, teenage sexual activity is down, divorce rates are dropping."

Possibly. But as the historian Gertrude Himmelfarb pointed out in *The Wall Street Journal*,

> for almost every favorable statistic, an ornery conservative can cite an unfavorable one. He can even go beyond the statistics to point to the sorry state of the culture: the loss of parental authority and of discipline in the schools, the violence and vulgarity of television, the obscenity and sadism of rap music, the exhibitionism and narcissism of talk-shows, the pornography and sexual perversions on the Internet, the binge-drinking and "hooking up" on college campuses.

And so on. If none of that made much of an impression on Brooks, it is because he wants to scrap all such moral considerations anyway and replace them with pragmatic, "utilitarian" tests. He notes with approval the extent to which society has recast moral—his word is "moralistic" —language in terms of health and safety. Today, he writes, "we regulate behavior and control carnal desires with health codes instead of moral codes. Today in mainstream society, people seldom object to others' taking the Lord's name in vain—but watch out if they see a pregnant woman smoking or drinking." Note the use of "mainstream"—we reasonable people, you understand, do not worry about morals per se: that's for those poor fanatics who still get worked up about something as outmoded as blasphemy. We enlightened pragmatists are beyond all that.

Brooks acknowledges that many people might consider "morality as mere healthism . . . meager, superficial." But really, he says, in these "happy, prosperous times" "people" —i.e., people like Brooks—have decided that they "want a lower-case morality that will not arouse passions or upset the applecart." So what if we have a moral pygmy in the

White House? Those good folks from Connecticut agreed that "personal behavior has no connection with public performance." What about the continuing depredations of the culture revolution? "No cause for alarm," Brooks says: "the counterculture has nothing to do" with contemporary life in America. The counterculture of the 1960s, he assures us, was "utopian" whereas "today's moral attitudes are anti-utopian. They are utilitarian. They are modest. They are, in fact, the values of the class the counterculture hated most. They are the values of the bourgeoisie." If we are looking for the origin of today's spirit, Brooks tells us that we should not look to Abbie Hoffman or Gloria Steinem but to . . . Benjamin Franklin, "the quintessential bourgeois." Well, Benjamin Franklin was a libertine, it is true. But that is not what Brooks means. He wants to enlist Franklin in his brigade of moral ostriches.

What the Sixties wrought

A lot of nasty things have been said about the bourgeoisie over the years. But few people can hold that class in deeper, if unwitting, contempt than does Brooks, for all his praise. According to him, the bourgeois doesn't want to bother with "grand abstractions," he is "never heroic" and "has no grandeur," he "never seem[s] to look up from quotidian concerns to grapple with great truths or profound moral issues." At most this modern Polonius is "modest, useful, and reliable." If this is "utilitarian," no wonder Russell Kirk described utilitarianism as "a philosophy of death." Brooks wants us to celebrate this stunted caricature because, after all, conservatives have always championed the bourgeoisie. ("Well, my fellow right-wingers, you wanted bourgeois values? You got 'em.")

What Brooks neglects is the fact that what conservatives have traditionally championed are bourgeois *values* not bourgeois vices. And those values are rooted deeply in a God-fearing Protestant ethic that emphasizes church, community, country, family, and moral honor. The bourgeois ethic is not a form of Romanticism, true enough; its ideal is moderation, not excess. There is a deep sense in which Schumpeter was right that "capitalist civilization is rationalistic and 'anti-heroic.'" But that does not mean that bourgeois capitalism need embrace the vacuous, feel-good, "I've-got-mine" philosophy Brooks apparently wants us to embrace. "Anti-heroism" need not exclude passionate commitments or steadfast loyalty to transcendent values. Irving Kristol once wrote that "if you believe that a comfortable life is not necessarily the same thing as a good life, or even a meaningful life, then it will occur to you that efficiency is a means, not an end in itself."

Perhaps Brooks would scoff at such distinctions, branding them merely "grand," "abstract," or "heroic." If so, what he espouses is not conservatism but a cheerful, buttoned-down version of the moral vacancy that Weyrich rightly lamented. It is both ironical and dispiriting to realize that the counterculture may have won its most insidious victories not among its natural sympathizers on the Left but, on the contrary, among those putatively conservative opponents who can no longer distinguish between material affluence and the moral good. In other words, it may be that what the Sixties have wrought above all is widespread spiritual anesthesia. To a degree frightening to contemplate, we have lost that sixth sense that allows us to discriminate firmly between civilization and its discontents. That this loss goes largely unlamented and even unnoticed is a measure of how successful the long march of America's cultural revolution has been.

Acknowledgments

I t is with pleasure and gratitude that I dedicate *The Long March* to my friend and colleague Hilton Kramer. It was he who, several years ago, first suggested that I write a book about America's cultural revolution. When a decent interval elapsed and nothing happened, he then suggested that I write a series on the subject for *The New Criterion*, thus inducing me to produce the basis for the present book. I have benefited greatly from his astute criticism.

I am also most grateful to Peter Collier, my editor at Encounter Books. Peter knows as much about the subject of this book as anyone, and he did for my manuscript what editors of old are reported to have done: he read through it carefully and made dozens of substantive suggestions for improvement.

I am extremely grateful as well to Erich Eichman, who snatched time from his own labors to read and comment with his usual insight on the entire manuscript. I would also like to thank Jonathan Cohen, Donald Kagan, and Carl Rollyson for their help and expertise in commenting on various parts of the book. I am particularly in debt to Alexandra Kimball, who, among other things, cheerfully read and re-read this book as it evolved and who neverthe-less consented to read through it once more to compile the index. I am also grateful to my colleagues, past and present, at *The New Criterion*—Sara E. Lussier, Robert Messenger, Robert Richman, Maxwell Watman, and David Yezzi—for their help and encouragement along the way.

Finally, I would like to express my special thanks to the John M. Olin Foundation and the W. H. Brady Foundation, both of which helped make it possible for me to write this book. I am profoundly grateful to them.

With so much help, one might reasonably expect perfection; alas, I am only too aware of the many imperfections that remain: they are poor things, but my own.

A word about references: In order not to interrupt the flow of the argument, I decided against including superscripts for routine citations. There are a few substantive footnotes in the text, but references, identified by a brief quotation and the page to which they refer, are gathered at the end of the book.

RK
January 2000

Notes

Introduction: What is a Cultural Revolution?

4   "moral center . . . ," "had been an intelligent . . ." Sandra Blakeslee, "Old Accident Points to Brain's Moral Center," *The New York Times*, May 24, 1994, pages C 1, C 14.

5   "great revolutions . . ." Alexis de Tocqueville, *The Old Regime and the Revolution*, Vol. I, edited by François Furet and Françoise Mélonio (Chicago: University of Chicago Press, 1998), page 95.

5   "the most total . . ." David Frum, *How We Got Here: The 1970s: The Decade That Brought You Modern Life (For Better or Worse)* (New York: Basic Books, 2000), page xxii.

6   "We have witnessed . . ." Paul Oskar Kristeller, "A Life of Learning," *The American Scholar*, Summer 1991, page 348.

6   "in or about December 1910, . . ." Virginia Woolf, "Mr. Bennett and Mrs. Brown," *Collected Essays*, Vol. I (New York: Harcourt, Brace & World, 1967), pages 320–321.

8   "A revolution is not . . ." Jean-François Revel, *The Totalitarian Temptation* (Garden City: Doubleday, 1977), page 8.

8   "The images of Orpheus . . ." Herbert Marcuse, *Eros and Civilization: A Philosophical Inquiry into Freud* (Boston: Beacon Press, 1966, orig. pub. 1956), page 164.

9   "the bourgeois' need . . ." Allan Bloom, *The Closing of the American Mind: How Higher Education Has Failed Democracy and Impoverished the Souls of Today's Students* (New York: Simon and Schuster, 1987), page 78.

9   "We're permanent . . ." Jerry Rubin, *Do It! Scenarios of the Revolution* (New York: Ballantine Books, 1970), page 89.

10   "Satisfy our demands . . ." Rubin, *Do It!*, page 125.

10   "Though it may appear . . ." José Ortega y Gasset, *The Revolt of the Masses* (New York: W. W. Norton, 1932 [1930]), page 189.

11   "the triumph of babydom . . . ," "Two decades . . ." Alain
       Finkielkraut, *The Undoing of Thought*, translated by Dennis O'Keeffe
       (London: The Claridge Press, 1988), pages 129, 127–128.

12   "like Monteverdi . . ." Richard Poirier, "Learning From the Beatles,"
       Partisan Review, Vol. 34, No. 4, 1967, page 527.

12   "It is not just . . ." Finkielkraut, *Undoing*, pages 114, 115.

13   "value vacuum . . ." Hermann Broch, *Hugo von Hofmannsthal and
       His Time: The European Imagination 1860–1920*, translated by Michael
       P. Steinberg (Chicago: University of Chicago Press, 1984), page 55.

13   "battle between elitism . . ." William A. Henry, III, *In Defense of
       Elitism* (New York: Doubleday, 1994), page 12.

14   "social indicators . . ." Francis Fukuyama, *The Great Disruption:
       Human Nature and the Reconstitution of Social Order* (New York:
       The Free Press, 1999).

14   "The Sixties . . ." Robert Bork, *Slouching Towards Gomorrah: Modern
       Liberalism and American Decline* (New York: Regan Books, 1996),
       page 13.

15   "the long march . . ." Herbert Marcuse, *Counterrevolution and Revolt*
       (Boston: Beacon Press, 1972), page 55.

16   "the nasty things . . ." Harvey Mansfield, "The Legacy of the Late
       Sixties," *Reassessing the Sixties: Debating the Political and Cultural
       Legacy,* edited by Stephen Macedo (New York: W. W. Norton,
       1997), page 23.

16   "neither morals, nor riches . . ." Quoted in Hannah Arendt,
       On Revolution (New York: The Viking Press, 1965), page 142.

17   "I think I know man . . ." Quoted in Carol Blum, *Rousseau and the
       Republic of Virtue: The Language of Politics in the French Revolution*
       (Ithaca: Cornell University Press, 1986), page 84.

17   "drunk on virtue . . ." Quoted in Blum, *Rousseau*, page 49.

17   "Those who dare . . ." Jean-Jacques Rousseau, *The Social Contract*
       (New York: Hafner, 1947), page 36 (Book II, Chapter vii, "Of the
       Legislator").

17   "the revolutionary consciousness . . ." Roger Scruton, "Man's
       Second Disobedience: Reflections on the French Revolution,"
       The Philosopher on Dover Beach: Essays (New York: St. Martin's Press,
       1990), page 200.

17   "born free . . ." Rousseau, *Contract*, page 5 (Book I, Chapter i,
       "Subject of the First Book").

18   "general will . . ." Rousseau, *A Discourse on Political Economy*, in
       The Social Contract and Discourses (New York: Dutton, 1973),
       pages 127–128.

18   "virtue and its emanation . . ." Quoted in Blum, *Rousseau*, page 30.

19   "The moral revolution . . ." Edward Shils, "Dreams of Plenitude, Nightmares of Scarcity," *The Order of Learning: Essays on the Contemporary University*, edited by Philip G. Altbach (New Brunswick: Transaction, 1997), page 199.

19   "The highest ideal . . ." Edward Shils, "Totalitarians and Antinomians," *Political Passages: Journeys of Change Through Two Decades 1968–1988*, John H. Bunzel, editor (New York: The Free Press, 1988), page 15.

20   "one has often been struck . . ." Arendt, *On Revolution*, page 79.

22   "something admirable in violent emotion . . ." T. S. Eliot, *After Strange Gods: A Primer of Modern Heresy* (New York: Harcourt, Brace, and Company, 1934), pages 59–60.

22   "the virtues have gone mad . . ." G. K. Chesterton, *Orthodoxy: The Romance of Faith* (New York: Doubleday, 1990, orig. pub. 1908), page 30.

23   "will bring down . . ." Irving Kristol, "Countercultures," *Neo-Conservatism: The Autobiography of an Idea* (New York: The Free Press, 1995), page 146.

24   "commentary about the 1960s . . ." For example, Myron Magnet's *The Dream and the Nightmare: The Sixties' Legacy to the Underclass* (Encounter Books, 2000; orig. pub. 1993) deftly shows how aspects of the ideology of emancipation from the 1960s were translated into social policies that encouraged a disastrous culture of dependence. David Horowitz's and Peter Collier's *Destructive Generation: Second Thoughts About the Sixties* (Summit, 1990; new edition 1997) provides an impassioned chronicle of disillusionment by two former radicals. Allan Bloom's *The Closing of the American Mind* (Simon and Schuster, 1987) analyzes how an unthinking commitment to relativism and "openness" in the Sixties corrupted higher education and stunted the emotional and spiritual lives of college students at even the best colleges and universities. On the other side of the ideological spectrum, there are books like Todd Gitlin's *The Sixties: Years of Hope, Days of Rage* (Bantam, 1987), which both offers a history and attempts an exoneration of its subject, and his later volume *The Twilight of Common Dreams: Why American is Wracked by Culture Wars* (Metropolitan Books, 1995), which attempts to explain why the grandiose "idealism" of the Sixties failed. Also from a left-liberal perspective is Morris Dickstein's *Gates of Eden: American Culture in the Sixties* (Basic Books, 1977), which locates the rise of Sixties radicalism essentially in a reaction to Cold War politics. I should also mention the huge omnibus history by Arthur Marwick, *The Sixties* (Oxford, 1998), a 900-page sociologicohistorical grab-bag that extols the Sixties as a period of "optimism and genuine faith in the dawning of a better world." I discuss Marwick's book in detail in Chapter 11.

24   "widely shared . . ." Fredric Jameson, "Periodizing the 60s," *Ideologies of Theory, II: Syntax of History* (Minneapolis: University of Minnesota Press, 1988) page 207.

24   "the world wide . . ." Jameson, *ibid.*

24   "In Praise of the Counterculture," *The New York Times*, December 11, 1994, page A 14.

25   "the way we think . . ." Marilynne Robinson, *The Death of Adam: Essays on Modern Thought* (Boston: Houghton Mifflin, 1998), page 153.

25   "Only a few periods . . ." "In Praise of the Counterculture," page A 14.

29   "life of complete . . ." Shils, "Totalitarians," page 15.

29   "the totalitarian tissues . . ." This and the following quotations from "The White Negro" can be found in Norman Mailer, *Advertisements for Myself* (Cambridge: Harvard University Press, 1992, orig. pub. 1959), pages 337–358.

30   "one of the best things . . ." Mailer, *Advertisements*, page 335.

30   "the white race . . ." "Against Interpretation" and "Notes on 'Camp'" were published in *Against Interpretation* (New York: Dell, 1964). The quotation about the white race appears in "What's Happening in America (1966)," *Styles of Radical Will* (New York: Farrar, Straus and Giroux, 1969), page 203.

30   "America is a cancerous . . . ," "rock, grass . . ." Susan Sontag, "Some Thoughts on the Right Way (for us) to Love the Cuban Revolution," *Ramparts*, April 1969, pages 6, 18.

32   "merely a Negro . . ." James Baldwin, "The Discovery of What it Means to Be an American," *Nobody Knows My Name: More Notes of a Native Son, Collected Essays* (New York: The Library of America, 1998), page 137.

32   "an insurrectionary act . . ." Eldridge Cleaver, *Soul on Ice* (New York: McGraw-Hill, 1968), page 14.

34   "jump, jam & party . . ." Diana West, "Before Their Time," *The Wall Street Journal*, December 3, 1999, page W 17.

34   "the path of sublimation . . ." Norman O. Brown, *Life Against Death: The Psychoanalytic Meaning of History*, second edition, with an introduction by Christopher Lasch (Hanover: Wesleyan University Press, 1985, orig. pub. 1959), page 307.

35   "La contrerévolution . . ." Arendt, *On Revolution*, page 18.

Chapter 1: A Gospel of Emancipation

38 "startling oases of creativity . . ." James Campbell, writing about Burroughs, in *This is the Beat Generation: New York–San Francisco–Paris* (London: Secker & Warburg, 1999), page 285.

39 "depth and seriousness . . ." Lisa Phillips, et al., *Beat Culture and the New America: 1950–1965* (New York: Whitney Museum of American Art, 1995), pages 12, 13.

39 "politicians looking . . ." Phillips, et al., *Beat Culture and the New America*, page 13.

40 Lisa Phillips, "Beat Culture: America Revisioned," Phillips, et al., *Beat Culture and the New America*, pages 23–40. All quotations from Lisa Phillips are from this essay.

42 "I don't know exactly . . ." Norman Podhoretz, "At War With Allen Ginsberg," *Ex-Friends: Falling Out With Allen Ginsberg, Lionel and Diana Trilling, Lillian Hellman, Hannah Arendt, and Norman Mailer* (New York: The Free Press, 1999), page 54.

42 "in later life . . ." Podhoretz, *Ex-Friends*, page 31.

43 "one of America's most celebrated . . ." Wilborn Hampton, "Allen Ginsberg, 70, Master Poet of Beat Generation," *The New York Times*, April 6, 1997, page 1.

43 "PBS television documentary . . ." "The Life and Times of Allen Ginsberg," directed by Jerry Aronson, aired in September 1997 as part of the PBS American Masters series.

43 "great gifts . . ." Helen Vendler, "Two Poets," *Harvard Magazine*, September–October 1997, pages 62–66. The other poet Vendler discusses, incidentally, is Shakespeare.

43 "Bill was never keen . . ." Barry Miles, *William Burroughs: El Hombre Invisible* (London: Virgin, 1992), page 13.

43 "Addict, killer, pederast . . ." David Ulin, "William S. Burroughs, 1914–1997," *The Village Voice*, August 12, 1997, page 51.

43 "a sweet, funny, and lonely man . . ." Legs McNeil, "Mouse Hunting," *New York*, August 18, 1997, page 14.

44 "a seminal figure . . ." Tony Perry, "Beat Icon William S. Burroughs Dies at 83," *Los Angeles Times*, August 8, 1997, page A1.

44 "experimenting with drugs . . ." Richard Sevro, "William S. Burroughs Dies at 83," *The New York Times*, August 3, 1997, page B5.

45 "honored him with . . ." Jack Kerouac, *The Portable Jack Kerouac*, edited by Ann Charters (New York: Viking, 1995).

45 "edition of his letters . . ." Jack Kerouac, *Selected Letters: 1940–1956*, edited by Ann Charters (New York: Viking, 1995).

45 "sort of church . . ." David Streitfeld, "William Burroughs: Shooting Star," *The Washington Post*, August 4, 1997, page C 1.

47 "disaster-area . . ." David Stove, "A Farewell to Arts: Marxism, Semiotics, and Feminism," *Cricket versus Republicanism and Other Essays*, edited by James Franklin and R. J. Stove (Sydney: Quakers Hill Press, 1995), page 14.

47 "Bill's sixteenth birthday . . ." Miles, *William Burroughs*, page 25.

48 "Bill continued . . ." Miles, *William Burroughs*, page 37.

48 "$200 a month . . ." Miles, *William Burroughs*, page 40.

50 "LAG IN PROCEDURE. . ." Kerouac, *The Portable Jack Kerouac*, pages 484–5.

50 "We drove to Terry's . . ." Jack Kerouac, *On the Road* (New York: Penguin, 1991), page 98.

52 "Whom bomb . . ." Allen Ginsberg, *Collected Poems: 1947–1980* (New York: Harper & Row, 1984), page 568.

52 "Come on go down . . ." Ginsberg, *Collected Poems*, page 613.

54 "heartless nonsense . . ." Podhoretz, *Ex-Friends*, page 37.

54 "shared a passionate desire . . ." Miles, *William Burroughs*, page 38.

54 "an illusion . . ." Harvey Mansfield, "The Legacy of the Sixties," *Reassessing the Sixties: Debating the Political and Cultural Legacy*, edited by Stephen Macedo (New York: Norton, 1997), pages 31, 32.

55 "Allen, completely naked . . ." Michael Schumacher, *Dharma Lion: A Biography of Allen Ginsberg* (New York: St. Martin's Press, 1992), pages 345, 347.

55 "reemergence in the twentieth . . ." Lee Bartlett, editor, *The Beats: Essays in Criticism* (Jefferson, N.C.: McFarland, 1981), page 181.

56 "I'm violently anti-Christian . . ." Miles, *William Burroughs*, page 91.

56 "take a tip . . ." Miles, *William Burroughs*, page 119.

56 "I think love . . ." Miles, *William Burroughs*, page 123.

56 "exterminate all the women . . ." Miles, *William Burroughs*, page 119.

57 "Bill opened his travel bag . . ." Miles, *William Burroughs*, page 48.

57 "a lifelong struggle . . ." Miles, *William Burroughs*, page 48.

57 "A horde of . . ." William S. Burroughs, *Naked Lunch* (New York: Grove Press, 1990; orig. pub. 1959), page 75.

58 Burroughs, *Naked Lunch*, pages 69–70.

58 "the sex and sadism . . ." Bartlett, *The Beats*, page 31.

58 "a religious writer . . ." Burroughs, *Naked Lunch*, page xvii.

58 "like a classical satirist . . ." Mary McCarthy, "Burroughs' *Naked Lunch*," *The Writing on the Wall and Other Literary Essays* (New York: Harcourt, Brace & World, 1970), page 50.

59 "liberated them . . ." Norman Cohn, *The Pursuit of the Millennium: Revolutionary Millenarians and Mystical Anarchists of the Middle*

Ages (New York: Oxford University Press, 1970, orig. pub. 1957), pages 150, 151.

59 "It was a world . . ." Podhoretz, *Ex-Friends*, page 34.

60 "its flight . . ." Immanuel Kant, *Critique of Pure Reason*, translated by Norman Kemp Smith (New York: St. Martin's Press, 1965), page 47.

60 "short spasms . . ." Walter Bagehot, *Physics and Politics: Or, Thoughts on the Application of the Principles of "Natural Selection" and "Inheritance" to Political Society*, edited by Roger Kimball (Chicago: Ivan R. Dee, 1999), page 102.

60 "We'll get you . . ." Podhoretz, *Ex-Friends*, page 40.

Chapter 2: Norman Mailer's American Dream

61 "worship of juvenile values. . ." Alain Finkielkraut, *The Undoing of Thought*, translated by Dennis O'Keeffe (London: The Claridge Press, 1988), page 128.

62 "perpetual *enfant terrible*. . ." The best biography of Mailer is Carl Rollyson, *The Lives of Norman Mailer: A Biography* (New York: Paragon House, 1991). *Mailer: A Biography* by Mary V. Dearborn (New York: Houghton Mifflin, 1999) brings the story up to the present but adds little that is essential.

62 "a nice Jewish boy. . ." Richard Poirier, *Norman Mailer* (New York: The Viking Press, 1972), page 18.

62 "Mailer would spend . . ." Norman Podhoretz, "A Foul Weather Friend to Norman Mailer," *Ex-Friends: Falling Out With Allen Ginsberg, Lionel and Diana Trilling, Lillian Hellman, Hannah Arendt, and Norman Mailer* (New York: The Free Press, 1999), page 190.

62 "big sacrifice . . ." Rollyson, *Norman Mailer*, page 13.

63 "a stopover at Marx . . ." Diana Trilling, "The Radical Moralism of Norman Mailer," *Norman Mailer: A Collection of Critical Essays*, Leo Braudy, editor (Englewood Cliffs: Prentice-Hall, 1972), pages 65, 64.

63 "mate the absurd . . ." Norman Mailer, "Advertisement for 'The Homosexual Villain,'" *Advertisements for Myself* (Cambridge: Harvard University Press, 1992, orig. pub. 1959), page 221.

64 "first royalty check . . ." James Wood, "Mailer: A New Biography Captures This Vexing Creature," *The New York Observer*, December 6, 1999, page 1.

64 "there is no doubt . . ." Philip D. Beidler, *Scriptures for a Generation: What We Were Reading in the '60s* (Athens: University of Georgia Press, 1994), page 133.

65   "Mailer has opened . . ." Richard Gilman, "What Mailer Has Done,"
     Braudy, *Norman Mailer*, page 160.

65   "Mailer has won . . ." Nat Hentoff, jacket copy for *The Armies of the
     Night: History as a Novel, The Novel as History* (New York: Signet,
     1968).

66   "I wonder . . ." Peter Manso, *Mailer, His Life and Times* (New York:
     Simon and Schuster, 1985), pages 462–463.

66   Mailer, *Armies*, page 58.

67   Norman Mailer, *An American Dream*, page 269.

67   "jousting tournaments . . ." Podhoretz, *Ex-Friends*, page 213.

68   "God, I wish . . ." Rollyson, *Norman Mailer*, page xvii.

68   "Among 'uptown intellectuals' . . ." Manso, *Mailer*, page 327.

68   "Artists get away . . ." Dawn Powell, *The Golden Spur* (New York:
     Vintage, 1990, orig. pub. 1962), page 18.

69   "infinitely more pretentious . . ." Stanley Edgar Hyman, "Norman
     Mailer's Yummy Rump," Braudy, *Norman Mailer*, page 104.

69   "I have a slight . . ." Quoted in Wood, "Mailer: A New Biography,"
     page 1.

70   "Let me tell you again . . ." Norman Mailer, *Ancient Evenings*
     (Boston: Little, Brown, 1983), page 66.

70   "Even in the first . . ." Mailer, *Evenings*, page 390.

71   John Simon, "Mailer's Mystic Marriage," *The Sheep From the Goats:
     Selected Literary Essays* (New York: Weidenfeld & Nicolson, 1989),
     page 4.

71   "she was good . . ." Clive James, "Mailer's Marilyn," *At the Pillars of
     Hercules* (London: Faber & Faber, 1979), page 204.

71   "a 'superb' actress . . ." Simon, *Sheep*, page 5.

71   "she had learned . . ." Norman Mailer, *Marilyn: A Biography*
     (New York: Grosset & Dunlap, 1973), page 43.

72   "it is a rule . . ." Mailer, *Marilyn*, page 54.

72   "it is a sign . . ." Joseph Epstein, "Mailer Hits Bottom," *Plausible
     Prejudices: Essays on American Writing* (New York: W. W. Norton,
     1985), page 204.

72   Mailer, *Advertisements*, page 492.

72   "the power of . . ." Norman Mailer, *The Prisoner of Sex* (Boston:
     Little, Brown, 1971), page 212.

73   "This 6th note . . ." Elizabeth Hardwick, "The Sixth Vice
     Presidential Note," quoted in Philip Nobile, *Intellectual Skywriting:
     Literary Politics and "The New York Review of Books"* (New York:
     Charterhouse, 1974), page 202.

73   "the only revolution . . ." Mailer, "A Public Notice on Waiting for
     Godot," *Advertisements*, page 325.

74 "a man is . . ." Norman Mailer, "Papa & Son," *Pieces and Pontifications* (Boston: Little, Brown, 1982), page 93.

74 "the American . . ." Mailer, *Advertisements*, page 339.

74 "to be an existentialist . . . ." Mailer, *Advertisements*, page 341.

74 "we find ourselves . . ." Mailer, *Pontifications*, page 84.

75 "I think when . . ." Mailer, *Pontifications*, page 101.

75 "a minor artist . . ." Mailer, *Advertisements*, page 325.

76 "another major . . ." Rollyson, *Norman Mailer*, page 287.

76 "an intellectual . . ." Norman Mailer, Introduction to Jack Henry Abbott, *In the Belly of the Beast: Letters From Prison* (New York: Random House, 1981), page xi.

77 "I'm willing . . ." Rollyson, *Mailer*, page 315.

77 "the totalitarian tissues . . ." This and all quotations in the following two paragraphs are from Mailer, "The White Negro: Superficial Reflections on the Hipster," *Advertisements*, pages 337–358.

79 "the seminal manifesto . . ." David Horowitz, *Radical Son: A Journey Through Our Times* (New York: The Free Press, 1997), pages 385, 386.

80 "one of the key men . . ." Epstein, "Mailer Hits Bottom," page 191.

80 "settle for nothing less . . ." Mailer, *Advertisements*, page 341.

Chapter 3: Susan Sontag & the New Sensibility

82 "perhaps the foremost . . ." Susan Sontag, "Some Thoughts on the Right Way (for us) to Love the Cuban Revolution," *Ramparts*, April 1969, page 6.

82 "whatever bears . . . ," "Poetry, . . ." Matthew Arnold, "Wordsworth," *The Portable Matthew Arnold*, edited by Lionel Trilling (New York: Viking, 1949), pages 342, 343.

82 "*a disinterested endeavour* . . ." Arnold, "The Function of Criticism," *Portable Arnold*, page 265.

83 "only a piece . . ." John Simon, *Partisan Review*, Winter 1965, page 157.

83 "in place of a hermeneutics . . . ," "to dethrone the serious . . . , " ". . . the Matthew Arnold notion of culture . . ." Susan Sontag *Against Interpretation and Other Essays* (New York: Dell, 1966), *seriatim*, pages 14, 288, 299.

84 "reactionary, impertinent . . ." Sontag, *Interpretation*, page 7.

84 "He was standing . . ." Sohnya Sayres, *Susan Sontag: The Elegiac Modernist* (New York: Routledge, 1990), page 27.

84 "You know, I think . . ." Leland Poague, editor, *Conversations with*

Susan Sontag (Jackson: University Press of Mississippi, 1995), page 115.

86 "The satisfactions of *Paradise Lost* . . ." Sontag, *Interpretation*, page 22.

86 "a critic whose . . . ," "Has silence or . . ." Marvin Mudrick, "Susie Creamcheese Makes Love Not War," *Harper's*, February 1983, pages 64, 63.

87 "in black trousers . . ." Poague, *Conversations*, page ix.

87 "Norman Podhoretz suggested . . ." Norman Podhoretz, *Making It* (New York: Harper & Row, 1967), pages 154–155.

87 "I believe that . . ." Sayres, *Elegiac Modernist*, page 25.

88 "a couple of women . . ." and other quotations about *Flaming Creatures*, Sontag, *Interpretation*, pages 226–229.

89 "nothing succeeds better . . ." John Simon, "From Sensibility Toward Sense," *The Sheep From the Goats: Selected Literary Essays* (New York: Weidenfeld & Nicolson, 1989), page 24.

89 "Camp is . . ." and other quotations about camp, Sontag, *Interpretation, seriatim*, pages 287, 290, 292.

90 "O is an adept . . ." Susan Sontag, "The Pornographic Imagination," *Styles of Radical Will* (New York: Farrar, Straus and Giroux, 1969), page 55.

90 "the traumatic failure . . ." Sontag, *Styles*, page 70.

91 "not everyone . . ." Sontag, *Styles*, pages 71–72.

92 "Nietzsche was a . . ." "Writing Itself: On Roland Barthes," Sontag, *Reader*, page 441.

92 "the AIDS epidemic . . . ," "risk-free sexuality . . ." Susan Sontag, AIDS *and its Metaphors* (New York: Farrar, Straus and Giroux, 1989) page 62, 77.

92 "if art is understood . . ." Sontag, *Interpretation*, page 303.

92 "Dearest M. . . ." Susan Sontag, *I, etcetera* (New York: Anchor Books, 1991, orig. pub. 1978), page 25.

93 "acclaimed beyond . . ." Sontag, "Camus' *Notebooks*," *Interpretation*, page 53.

93 "The task of the writer . . ." Quoted in Paul Hollander, *Anti-Americanism: Irrational & Rational* (New Brunswick: Transaction, 1995, orig. pub. 1992), page 63.

94 Quotations about the Cuban revolution are from Sontag, "Some Thoughts on the Right Way (for us) to Love the Cuban Revolution," *Ramparts*, April 1969, pages 6–19.

95 "Hollander quotes . . ." Paul Hollander, *Political Pilgrims: Western Intellectuals in Search of the Good Society*, fourth edition (New Brunswick: Transaction, 1998), pages 266–267.

95   "aren't good enough haters . . ." Sontag, "Trip to Hanoi," *Styles*, page 231.

96   "They genuinely care . . ." Sontag, "Trip to Hanoi," *Styles*, page 258.

96   "in many respects . . ." Sontag, "Trip to Hanoi," *Styles*, page 259.

96   "The Vietnamese are . . ." Sontag, "Trip to Hanoi," *Styles*, page 263.

96   "A small nation . . ." Quoted in Hollander, *Anti-Americanism*, page 67.

97   "deserves . . . ," "the truth is that Mozart . . ." Sontag, "What's Happening in America (1966)," *Styles*, pages 195, 203.

97   "Imagine, if you will, . . ." A version of Sontag's comments was reprinted in *The Nation*, February 27, 1982, pages 229–231, from which these quotations are taken.

98   "transcend the categories . . ." Sontag, *Interpretation*, page 26.

98   "negates the possibility . . ." Sontag, "Fascinating Fascism," *Reader*, page 308.

98   "tourists of reality" Susan Sontag, *On Photography* (New York: Farrar, Straus and Giroux, 1977), page 110.

98   "perils of over-generalizing . . ." Sontag, *Reader*, page 61.

98   "it is not that Sontag . . ." Hilton Kramer, "Susan Sontag: The Pasionaria of Style," *The Twilight of the Intellectuals: Culture and Politics in the Era of the Cold War* (Chicago: Ivan R Dee, 1999), page 229.

98   "the relation between boredom . . ." Sontag, "Notes on 'Camp'," *Interpretation*, page 289.

99   "one important consequence . . ." Sontag, "One Culture and the New Sensibility," *Interpretation*, page 303.

Chapter 4: The Liberal Capitulation

102   "the Matthew Arnold . . ." Susan Sontag *Against Interpretation and Other Essays* (New York: Dell, 1966), page 299.

102   "the totalitarian tissues . . ." Norman Mailer, "The White Negro: Superficial Reflections on the Hipster," *Advertisements for Myself* (Cambridge: Harvard University Press, 1992, orig. pub. 1959), pages 337–358.

103   "Rock, grass, better . . ." Susan Sontag, "Some Thoughts on the Right Way (for us) to Love the Cuban Revolution," *Ramparts*, April 1969, page 6.

103   "from the first . . ." John Silber, "Poisoning the Wells of Academe," *Encounter*, August, 1974, page 30.

104   "After the Vietnam War . . ." Quoted in Dinesh D'Souza, *Illiberal*

Education: The Politics of Race and Sex on Campus (New York: The Free Press, 1991), page 18.

106 "Those of us who watched . . ." Nathan Glazer "What Happened at Berkeley." This essay was first published in *Commentary* in February 1965. I have cited the reprinted version that appears in *The Berkeley Student Revolt: Facts and Interpretations*, a collection edited by Seymour Martin Lipset and Sheldon S. Wolin (New York: Doubleday, 1965), page 286.

107 "the student demand . . ." Lipset and Wolin, *The Berkeley Student Revolt*, page 301.

107 "racial injustice . . ." Quoted in Lipset and Wolin, *The Berkeley Student Revolt*, page 217.

107 "politics and education . . . ," "main purpose . . . " Lipset and Wolin, *The Berkeley Student Revolt*, pages 211, 214.

107 "excessive greed . . ." Lipset and Wolin, *The Berkeley Student Revolt*, page 215.

108 "A high incidence . . ." Lipset and Wolin, *The Berkeley Student Revolt*, page 9.

108 Silber, "Poisoning the Wells," page 34.

108 Silber, "Poisoning the Wells," page 38.

109 Kennan's essay, first delivered as a speech at Swarthmore College, was published in *The New York Times Magazine* on January 21, 1968, where it generated enormous controversy. It was reprinted, with thirty-odd responses, as *Democracy and the Student Left* (Boston: Little, Brown, 1968).

109 "There is an ideal . . ." George F. Kennan, et al., *Democracy and the Student Left*, page 3.

109 Kennan, *Democracy and the Student Left*, page 7.

110 "the human being . . ." Kennan, *Democracy and the Student Left*, pages 10, 11.

110 "There is . . ." Kennan, *Democracy and the Student Left*, pages 13, 14.

111 "a revolution in the name . . ." quoted in Jerry L. Avorn, et al., *Up Against the Ivy Wall: A History of the Columbia Crisis*, (New York: Atheneum, 1969), page 281.

111 "deplorable custom . . ." "Harvard and Beyond: The University Under Siege," *Time*, April 18, 1969, page 47.

111 "was established . . ." Silber, "Poisoning the Wells," page 32.

112 "the liberal president . . ." "It Can't Happen Here—Can It?," *Newsweek*, May 5, 1969, page 27.

112 "no one personified . . ." Donald Alexander Downs, *Cornell '69: Liberalism and the Crisis of the American University* (Ithaca: Cornell University Press, 1999), page 6.

112 "175 points . . ." Walter Berns, "The Assault on the Universities: Then and Now," *Reassessing the Sixties: Debating the Political and Cultural Legacy,* edited by Stephen Macedo (New York: Norton, 1997), page 158.

113 "create the tools . . ." Berns, "The Assault on the Universities," page 158.

113 "There is nothing . . ." Berns, "The Assault on the Universities," page 158.

114 "quickly became an assault . . ." Berns, "The Assault on the Universities," page 161.

114 "You better . . ." "The Bitter Spring of 1969," *The Cornell Daily Sun,* April 19, 1979, page 17.

115 "if any more whites . . ." "The Bitter Spring," page 21.

115 "when black students . . ." Allan Bloom, "The Democratization of the University," *Giants and Dwarfs: Essays 1960–1990* (New York: Simon and Schuster, 1990), page 368.

115 "the resemblance . . ." Quoted in Homer Bigart, "Faculty Revolt Upsets Cornell," *The New York Times,* April 25, 1969, page 30.

116 "complete capitulation . . ." "The Bitter Spring," page 23.

116 "The presence of arms . . ." "The Bitter Spring," page 25.

116 "Cornell has three hours . . ." "The Bitter Spring," page 25.

117 "if we had a good reason . . ." James John as quoted in Charles S. Williams, "Some Professors Fight Back," *Cornell Alumni News,* June 1969, page 27.

117 "I don't need to be intimidated" "The Bitter Spring," page 26.

117 "That decision was . . ." "The Bitter Spring," page 26.

118 "one of the most positive . . ." "It Can't Happen Here—Can It?," *Newsweek,* May 5, 1969, page 30.

118 "pompous teachers . . ." Quoted in Berns, "The Assault on the Universities," page 160.

119 "By surrendering . . ." Berns, "The Assault on the Universities," page 163.

119 "the Cornell crisis . . ." Downs, *Cornell '69,* page 19.

120 "Hillary was not . . ." David Brock, *The Seduction of Hillary Rodham* (New York: The Free Press, 1996), page 31. For additional details, see "Hillary for the Defense," by John McCaslin, *The Washington Times,* June 12, 1998. This sotry is available online at http://www.offduty.org/html/politics/communist.html.

121 "one of the biggest pig . . . ," "Basically, what we . . ." John Taft, *Mayday at Yale: A Case Study in Student Radicalism* (Boulder: Westview, 1976), page 19. Where I have "either" the text has "even," which I take to be a misprint.

122 "There's no reason . . . ," "Why don't we . . . ," "Do you know . . ." Taft, *Mayday, seriatim*, pages 36, 68, 69–70.

122 "white oppressors . . . ," "legally right but . . ." Taft, *Mayday*, page 31.

123 "three full professors . . . ," "it would not be proper . . . ," "I am skeptical . . ." Taft, *Mayday, seriatim*, pages 32, 37, 87.

123 "thunderous applause . . ." Taft, *Mayday*, page 87.

123 "suspension of normal . . ." Taft, *Mayday*, page 92.

123 "A compromise was absurd . . ." Taft, *Mayday*, page 93.

124 "voted overwhelmingly . . ." Taft, *Mayday*, pages 96–7.

124 "Those students . . ." Quoted in Taft, *Mayday*, page 102.

125 "The violation of law . . ." Kennan, *Democracy and the Student Left*, page 18.

126 "Where authority abdicates . . ." Edward Shils, "Dreams of Plenitude, Nightmares of Scarcity," *The Order of Learning: Essays on the Contemporary University*, edited by Philip G. Altbach (New Brunswick: Transaction, 1997), page 215.

126 "the liberal university . . ." Bloom, *Giants*, page 387.

Chapter 5: The Politics of Delegitimation

127 "the decisive feature . . ." Roger Scruton, *The Philosopher on Dover Beach: Essays* (New York: St. Martin's Press, 1990), page 203.

128 "Utopians . . ." Leszek Kolakowski, "The Death of Utopia Reconsidered" *Modernity on Endless Trial* (Chicago: University of Chicago Press, 1990), page 139.

128 "to be a revolutionary . . ." Quoted by Morris I. Liebman, William Sloane Coffin, Jr., and Morris I. Liebman, *Civil Disobedience: Aid or Hindrance to Justice?* (Washington: American Enterprise Institute for Public Policy Research, 1972), page 22.

129 "uncovered, but did not create . . ." Michael Lind, *Vietnam: The Necessary War. A Reinterpretation of America's Most Disastrous Military Conflict* (New York: The Free Press, 1999), page 215.

129 "Vietnam offered . . . ," "If there had . . . ," "more a catalyst . . ." Paul Hollander, *Political Pilgrims: Western Intellectuals in Search of the Good Society*, fourth edition (New Brunswick: Transaction, 1998), page 198.

130 "the frivolous elevation . . ." David Stove, *Anything Goes: Origins of the Cult of Scientific Irrationalism* (Sydney: Macleay Press, 1998), page 185.

130 "institutions of higher . . ." Paul Hollander, *Anti-Americanism:*

Irrational & Rational (New Brunswick: Transaction, 1995, orig. pub. 1992), page 149.

133 "shamelessly bypass[ing] . . . ," "as much of God as . . . ," "National security . . ." William Sloane Coffin, Jr., *Once to Every Man* (New York: Atheneum, 1977), *seriatim*, pages 80, 89, 113.

133 "a form of moral jiu-jitsu . . ." Charles Evans Whittaker and William Sloane Coffin, Jr., *Law, Order, and Civil Disobedience* (Washington: American Enterprise Institute for Public Policy Research, 1967), page 39.

133 "If we are to . . ." Coffin and Liebman, *Civil Disobedience*, page 4.

133 "a very special feeling . . ." Coffin, *Once to Every Man*, page 316.

134 "legally right but . . . ," "To those who say . . ." Quoted in John Taft, *Mayday at Yale: A Case Study in Student Radicalism* (Boulder: Westview, 1976), page 31.

134 "his best to guarantee . . ." Quoted in Taft, *Mayday*, pages 31–32.

134 "the universal conscience . . ." Coffin and Liebman, *Civil Disobedience*, page 1.

135 "in democratic societies . . ." Coffin and Liebman, *Civil Disobedience*, page 12.

135 "the day that men . . ." Coffin and Liebman, *Civil Disobedience*, page 21.

135 "The advocates of civil disobedience . . ." Coffin and Liebman, *Civil Disobedience*, page 21.

136 "'liberal' but not 'reactionary' . . ." Zinn as quoted in Coffin and Liebman, *Civil Disobedience*, page 22.

136 "Liberating tolerance . . ." Herbert Marcuse, "Repressive Tolerance," *A Critique of Pure Tolerance*, Robert Paul Wolff, et al. (Boston: Beacon Press, 1965), page 109.

137 "had become a holy man . . ." Murray Polner and Jim O'Grady, *Disarmed and Dangerous: The Radical Lives and Times of Daniel and Philip Berrigan* (New York: Basic Books, 1997), page 350.

138 "are small but purified . . ." Quoted in Francine du Plessix Gray, *Divine Disobedience: Profiles In Catholic Radicalism* (New York: Alfred A. Knopf, 1970), page 77.

138 "moral fundamentalism . . ." Gray, *Divine Disobedience*, page 79.

138 "one had to go to jail . . ." Daniel Berrigan, *Night Flight to Hanoi: War Diary with 11 Poems* (New York: Macmillan, 1968), page xiii.

138 "I have a great fear . . ." Quoted in Hollander, *Anti-Americanism*, page 87.

139 "the American ghetto . . ." Daniel Berrigan, *Night Flight*, page xiv.

139 "here we begin to understand . . ." Hayden quoted in Paul Hollander, *Political Pilgrims*, page 273.

139 "Our apologies . . ." Daniel Berrigan, *Night Flight*, page xvi.

140 "anyone who works for the draft board . . ." Quoted in Walter Berns, "The Assault on the Universities: Then and Now," *Reassessing the Sixties: Debating the Political and Cultural Legacy,* edited by Stephen Macedo (New York: W. W. Norton, 1997), page 181.

140 "the time has arrived . . ." Daniel Berrigan S.J., "Letter from the Underground," *The New York Review of Books*, August 30, 1970, pages 34, 35.

141 "the biography of the white Westerner . . ." Daniel Berrigan, *Night Flight*, page 27.

141 "like stepping out upon the threshold . . ." Daniel Berrigan, *Night Flight*, page 40.

142 "They seemed eager . . ." Daniel Berrigan, *Night Flight*, pages 86–87.

142 "Six of them entered . . ." Polner and O'Grady, *Disarmed and Dangerous*, page 346.

142 "a small but stubborn . . ." Polner and O'Grady, *Disarmed and Dangerous*, page 347.

143 "of course [Daniel Berrigan] violated . . ." Daniel Berrigan, *Night Flight*, page xii.

143 "in a society where . . ." Montesquieu, Book 11, Chapter 3, "What Liberty Is," *The Spirit of the Laws*, translated by Anne M. Cohler, et al. (Cambridge: Cambridge University Press, 1989), page 155.

143 "The violation of law . . ." Georg F. Kennan, et al., *Democracy and the Student Left* (Boston: Little, Brown, 1968), page 18.

144 "It seems to me . . ." Kennan, et al., *Democracy and the Student Left*, page 167.

144 "Men are qualified . . ." Quoted in John Silber, "Poisoning the Wells of Academe," *Encounter*, August, 1974, page 30.

Chapter 6: The Marriage of Marx & Freud

146 "to make the anatomical . . ." Lionel Trilling, "The Kinsey Report," *The Liberal Imagination: Essays on Literature and Society* (New York: Scribner's, 1950), page 233.

146 "a moral revolutionary . . ." Joseph Epstein, "The Secret Life of Alfred Kinsey," *Commentary*, January 1998, page 39.

147 "'Sexual liberation' is . . ." Irving Kristol, "Countercultures," *Neo-Conservatism: Selected Essays 1949–1995* (New York: The Free Press, 1995), pages 141–142.

148 "with the vague sense . . ." David Allyn, *Make Love, Not War: The*

Sexual Revolution: An Unfettered History (Boston: Little Brown, 2000), page 3.

148 "For all its faults . . ." Allyn, *Make Love, Not War*, page 293.

148 "in the late seventies . . ." Allyn, *Make Love, Not War*, page 5.

149 "defining new possibilities . . ." Allyn, *Make Love, Not War*, page 233.

149 "smash monogamy . . ." Allyn, *Make Love, Not War*, page 220.

149 "Sexual intercourse began . . ." Philip Larkin, "Annus Mirabilis," *Collected Poems* (New York: Farrar, Straus and Giroux, 1988), page 167.

149 "For all its faults . . ." Allyn, *Make Love, Not War*, page 300.

149 "the price of . . ." Rochelle Gurstein, *The Repeal of Reticence: A History of America's Cultural and Legal Struggles Over Free Speech, Obscenity, Sexual Liberation, and Modern Art* (New York: Hill and Wang, 1996), page 52.

150 "The more people . . ." Gurstein, *The Repeal of Reticence*, page 112.

151 "'How,' he asked . . ." Jerry Rubin, *Do It! Scenarios of the Revolution* (New York: Ballantine Books, 1970), page 111.

152 "his work . . ." Hal Cohen, "A Secret History of the Sexual Revolution: The Repression of Wilhelm Reich," *Lingua Franca*, March 1999, page 30.

152 "the sexual question . . . ," "a satisfactory genital sex life . . . ," " . . . sex was everything." Richard King, *The Party of Eros: Radical Social Thought and the Realm of Freedom* (Chapel Hill: University of North Carolina Press, 1972), *seriatim*, pages 69, 66, 51.

153 "he watched his tutor . . ." Hal Cohen, "A Secret History of the Sexual Revolution," page 25.

153 "It's color . . . ," " . . . *present everywhere*," "*it charges living tissue* . . ." Wilhelm Reich, *Selected Writings: An Introduction to Orgonomy* (New York: Farrar, Straus and Giroux, 1979), *seriatim*, pages 219, 198, 237.

154 "Our orgone therapy experiments . . ." Reich, *Selected Writings*, pages 233, 234–5.

154 "boxes ranged from . . ." Hal Cohen, "A Secret History of the Sexual Revolution," pages 28, 31.

155 "not into the ground . . ." Reich, *Selected Writings*, pages 435, 444.

155 "If I were ever to look . . ." Norman Mailer, *Advertisements For Myself* (Cambridge: Harvard University Press, 1992, orig. pub. 1959), page 301.

155 "have been assigned . . ." Mildred Edie Brady, "The Strange Case of Wilhelm Reich," *The New Republic*, May 26, 1947, page 20.

155 "Brady believes . . ." Quoted in Hal Cohen, "A Secret History of the Sexual Revolution," pages 29–30.

156 "the ultimate regulator . . ." Howard J. Chavis, M.D., Letter to the Editor, *The New Criterion*, March 1998, pages 79–80.

156 "an illicit, forced . . ." Harvey Mansfield, "The Legacy of the Late Sixties," *Reassessing the Sixties: Debating the Political and Cultural Legacy*, edited by Stephen Macedo (New York: W. W. Norton, 1997), page 24.

157 "sought to combine . . ." King, *The Party of Eros*, page 50.

157 "we knew that . . ." Morris Dickstein, *Gates of Eden: American Culture in the Sixties* (New York: Basic Books, 1977), pages 70, 81.

158 "the very incarnation . . ." Norman Podhoretz, *Making It* (New York: Harper & Row, 1967), page 297.

159 "masterwork . . . ," "Like Allen Ginsberg . . ." Dickstein, *Gates*, pages 77, 75.

159 "pathetically . . ." Kingsley Widmer, *Paul Goodman* (Boston: Twayne, 1980), page 106.

160 "My purpose . . ." Paul Goodman, *Growing Up Absurd: Problems of Youth in the Organized System* (New York: Random House, 1960), page 14.

160 "Is it possible . . . ," "the young men who conform . . ." Goodman, *Growing Up Absurd*, pages 133, 13.

161 "a man is a fool . . . ," "pacific, artistic . . . ," "the kind of sex . . ." Goodman, *Growing Up Absurd*, *seriatim*, pages ix, 165, 185.

161 "reveal a man . . ." King, *The Party of Eros*, page 81.

161 "I distrust women . . ." Paul Goodman, *Five Years* (New York, Brussel & Brussel, 1966), page 8.

161 "There have been . . ." Goodman, *Five Years*, page 247.

161 "The gonad theory . . ." King, *The Party of Eros*, page 84.

161 "the good society . . ." Joseph Epstein, "Paul Goodman in Retrospect," *Commentary*, February 1978, page 73.

162 "My own view . . ." *Commentary*, April 1978, page 13.

162 "intrinsic connection . . . ," "demands a union . . ." Norman O. Brown, *Life Against Death: The Psychoanalytic Meaning of History*, second edition (Hanover: Wesleyan, 1985, orig. pub. 1959) pages 10, 307.

162 "I can recall no . . ." Dickstein, *Gates*, page 81.

163 "end of its tether . . ." Norman O. Brown, "Apocalypse: The Place of Mystery in the Life of the Mind," *Harper's*, May 1961, pages 46–49.

163 "neurosis. . . ," "all sublimations . . . ," "the compulsion to work . . . ," "all thinking . . . ," "The work of constructing . . ." Brown, *Life Against Death*, *seriatim*, pages 19, 128, 237–238, 163, 176.

164 "We may therefore . . ." Brown, *Life Against Death*, page 321.

164 "Freud presented . . ." John Passmore, "Paradise Now: The Logic of the New Mysticism," *Encounter*, February 1970, page 4.

164 "The unconscious . . . ," Norman O. Brown, *Love's Body* (New York: Random House, 1966), pages 217, 63.

165 "subversive of civilization . . ." Brown, *Life Against Death*, page 63.

165 "quantifying rationality," "nonmorbid science . . ." Brown, *Life Against Death*, page 236.

167 "the gradual undermining . . ." Herbert Marcuse, *Eros and Civilization: A Philosophical Inquiry into Freud* (Boston: Beacon Press, 1966, orig. pub. 1956), page xxiv.

168 "the horrors . . . ," "the fall . . ." Herbert Marcuse, *Counterrevolution and Revolt* (Boston: Beacon Press, 1972), pages 1, 2.

168 "Love Mystified: A Critique of Norman O. Brown," together with Brown's response, appears in Herbert Marcuse, *Negations: Essays in Critical Theory* (Boston: Beacon Press, 1968), pages 227–247.

168 "the body in its entirety . . . ," "protests against . . . ," "the redemption of pleasure . . ." Marcuse, *Eros and Civilization*, *seriatim*, pages 201, 171, 164.

169 "This change . . . ," "The brute fact . . . ," "the instinctual value . . ." Marcuse, *Eros and Civilization*, *seriatim*, pages 201, 231, 235.

169 "the necessity of death . . ." Marcuse, *Eros and Civilization*, page 237.

170 "Under the rule . . . ," "a rising standard . . ." Herbert Marcuse, *One-Dimensional Man: Studies in the Ideology of Advanced Industrial Society* (Boston: Beacon Press, 1964), pages 7, 49.

170 "Liberating tolerance . . ." Herbert Marcuse, "Repressive Tolerance," *A Critique of Pure Tolerance*, Robert Paul Wolff, et al. (Boston: Beacon Press, 1965), page 109.

171 "*more* representation . . . ," "extreme suspension . . ." Herbert Marcuse, "Repressive Tolerance," pages 109–111.

171 "depends on . . ." Leszek Kolakowski, *Main Currents of Marxism*, Vol. III, *The Breakdown* (Oxford: Oxford University Press, 1978), page 418.

172 "ideas are *all*-important . . ." Kristol, *Neo-Conservatism*, page 198.

172 "the dissipation . . ." Roger Scruton, *Sexual Desire: A Moral Philosophy of the Erotic* (New York: The Free Press, 1986), page 347.

Chapter 7: The Greening of America

175 "the culture's infatuation . . ." Midge Decter, "Rome Burns," *The Wall Street Journal*, July 30, 1999, page W 15.

177 ". . . a life of surfing . . ." This and other quotations in this extract are from Charles A. Reich, *The Greening of America* (New York: Random House, 1970), *seriatim*, pages 219, 348, 240, 100, 136.

177 "a degree in surfing . . ." An overview of the story is available in "Endless Summer School" by Alex Salkever in the online magazine *Salon* at http://www.salon.com/books/it/1999/07/14/surfing. Plymouth University's catalog is available online at http://www.plymouth.ac.uk/plymouth/maincourse.htm.

177 " 'Oh, wow!' . . ." Reich, *Greening*, page 263.

177 "*benefits* . . ." Thomas Mallon, "Charles Reich's Con Job," *The American Spectator*, October 1990, page 38.

177 "*The New Yorker* . . ." *The Greening of America* was excerpted in *The New Yorker*, September 26, 1970, pages 42–60.

178 Among the pieces on Reich in *The New York Times* were Op-Eds by Galbraith (October 26, 1970), Kennan (October 28), and Marcuse (November 6); *The Greening of America* was reviewed in the daily *Times* by Christopher Lehmann-Haupt on October 22, 1970, and in the Sunday *Book Review* on November 8.

178 "the genuine strengths . . ." Peter Caws, "Stage V and Con III," *The New Republic*, November 14, 1970, page 21.

179 "Since machines . . ." Reich, *Greening*, pages 352, 376.

179 Roger Starr, "The Counter-Culture and Its Apologists: 2," *Commentary*, December 1970, pages 46–54.

179 "the communal we . . ." L. E. Sissman, "I-Less in Gaza," *The Atlantic Monthly*, June 1971, page 30.

179 "a bag . . ." Stuart Alsop, "A Bag of Scary Mush," *Newsweek*, November 9, 1970, page 102.

180 "There is a revolution coming . . ." Reich, *Greening*, page 4.

181 ". . . anti-community." Reich, *Greening*, page 8.

181 "vast apparatus . . ." Reich, *Greening*, page 253.

181 "work and living . . ." Reich, *Greening*, page 8.

182 "the majority . . . ," "beginning with school . . ." Reich, *Greening*, pages 274, 9.

183 "farmers, owners . . ." Reich, *Greening*, pages 25–6.

183 "inhuman structure . . . ," "aircraft employees . . . , " "ethic of control . . ." Reich, *Greening*, *seriatim*, pages 58, 82, 83.

183 "has been persuaded . . ." Reich, *Greening*, page 85.

183 "It is not the misuse . . ." Reich, *Greening*, page 125.

184 "a few individuals . . . ," "Authority, schedules . . ." Reich, *Greening*, pages 217, 362.

184 "antagonistic or . . . ," "I'm glad . . ." Reich, *Greening*, pages 226, 219.

185 "One of the few . . . ," "conversions," "In a brief span . . ." Reich, *Greening*, *seriatim*, pages 388, 222, 224.

186 "The most constant presence . . ." Charles Reich, *The Sorcerer of Bolinas Reef* (New York: Random House, 1976), pages 68–69.

186 "What the new generation . . ." Reich, *Greening*, page 252.

187 "a higher, transcendent . . ." Reich, *Greening*, page 5.

187 "the hard questions . . ." Reich, *Greening*, page 357.

187 ". . . restoring dulled consciousness," "Beethoven seems . . ." Reich, *Greening*, pages 258, 246.

188 "Nothing is more singular . . ." Allan Bloom, *The Closing of the American Mind: How Higher Education Has Failed Democracy and Impoverished the Souls of Today's Students* (New York: Simon and Schuster, 1987), pages 68ff.

188 "farmers, owners of small . . ." Reich, *Greening*, page 226.

189 "Someone may . . ." Reich, *Greening*, pages 227–228.

189 "highly impressionistic . . . ," "any and all experience . . . ," "engage in actions . . ." Reich, *Greening*, *seriatim*, pages 17, 233, 257.

190 "deny the importance . . . ," "Bell bottoms . . ." Reich, *Greening*, pages 238, 311.

190 "see effortlessly. . ." Reich, *Greening*, page 261.

190 "He does not 'know' . . ." Reich, *Greening*, page 261.

190 ". . . perfection so absolute . . ." Norman Cohn, *The Pursuit of the Millennium: Revolutionary Millenarians and Mystical Anarchists of the Middle Ages* (New York: Oxford University Press, 1970, orig. pub. 1957), pages 150–151

191 "totalitarian movements' . . ." Hannah Arendt, *The Origins of Totalitarianism* (New York: Harcourt Brace Jovanovich, 1973, orig. pub. 1951), page 336.

191 "are 'whole' human . . ." Susan Sontag, "Trip to Hanoi," *Styles of Radical Will* (New York: Farrar, Straus and Giroux, 1969), page 263.

191 "The earnest . . ." Evelyn Waugh, *Black Mischief* (Boston: Little, Brown, 1932), page 195.

Chapter 8: The Project of Rejuvenilization

193 "promoter, apologist . . ." Theodore Roszak, *The Making of a Counterculture: Reflections on the Technocratic Society and its Youthful Opposition* (New York: Doubleday, 1969), page 164.

194 "one of the most . . ." Charles A. Reich, *The Greening of America* (New York: Random House, 1970), page 258.

194 "planned and scripted . . . ," "to satisfy a deep . . . ," "believers in capital . . ." Martin A. Lee and Bruce Shlain, *Acid Dreams: The Complete Social History of* LSD: *The* CIA, *the Sixties, and Beyond*

THE LONG MARCH

(New York: Grove Press, 1992, orig. pub. 1985), *seriatim*, pages xx, 294, xv.

195 "capable of rendering . . ." Quoted in Timothy Leary, *Flashbacks: A Personal and Cultural History of an Era* (New York: Putnam, 1990, orig. pub. 1983), page 391.

195 "On the basis of his claim . . . ," "mystics on the spot . . ." Leary, *Flashbacks*, pages 116, 117.

196 "I gave way to delight . . ." Leary, *Flashbacks*, page 32.

196 "the world was divided . . ." Leary, *Flashbacks*, page 342.

196 "the most shattering . . ." Leary, *Flashbacks*, page 118.

196 "I have never recovered . . ." Leary, *Flashbacks*, page 119.

197 "it may become possible . . ." Leary, *Flashbacks*, page 373.

198 "with the expectation . . ." Leary, *Flashbacks*, page 383.

198 "counterfeit infinity . . ." Roszak, *Making of a Counterculture*, pages 155ff.

198 "the LSD trip . . ." Quoted in Philip D. Beidler, *Scriptures for a Generation: What We Were Reading in the '60s* (Athens: University of Georgia Press, 1994), page 132.

199 "your advertising . . ." Leary, *Flashbacks*, page 252.

199 "Laws are made . . ." Quoted in Beidler, *Scriptures for a Generation*, page 132.

199 "student of altered . . ." Leary, *Flashbacks*, page 46.

200 "the four of us . . ." Leary, *Flashbacks*, page 55.

200 "My eyes connected . . ." Leary, *Flashbacks*, page 113.

200 "Ever since my Easter Sunday . . ." Leary, *Flashbacks*, page 222.

201 "new age gospel . . ." Beidler, *Scriptures for a Generation*, page 35.

201 "the Judeo-Christian . . ." Leary, *Flashbacks*, page 109.

201 "Drugs Are the Origin . . ." Leary, *Flashbacks*, page 91.

201 "an orthodox, psychedelic religion . . ." Text available online at http://www.leary.com/archives/text/books/religion.

202 "euphoric downer . . ." Leary, *Flashbacks*, page 323.

202 "Training centers like ours . . ." Leary, *Flashbacks*, page 71.

203 "The bowl of pills . . ." Leary, *Flashbacks*, pages 85–86.

203 "I was at that time . . ." Leary, *Flashbacks*, page 113.

204 "During the thirteen . . ." Leary, *Flashbacks*, pages 39–40.

205 "For two years . . ." Leary, *Flashbacks*, page 177.

205 "After thirty minutes . . ." Leary, *Flashbacks*, page 108.

205 "The national headquarters . . ." Leary, *Flashbacks*, page 160.

206 "jet-setters, celebrities . . ." Leary, *Flashbacks*, page 190.

206 "I had become . . ." Leary, *Flashbacks*, page 260.

206 "We partied until . . ." Leary, *Flashbacks*, pages 263–4.

207 "to shoot a genocidal robot . . ." Shlain, *Acid Dreams*, page 265.

207 "a battle of egos . . ." Shlain, *Acid Dreams*, page 267.

208 "I was . . ." Leary, *Flashbacks*, page 10.

208 "quietly cooperated . . ." "Timothy Leary Aided FBI, Records Show," *The New York Times*, July 1, 1999, page A 17.

208 "good behavior . . ." Shlain, *Acid Dreams*, page 292.

208 "now permeate . . ." Shlain, *Acid Dreams*, page xv.

209 "With the aid . . ." Leary, *Flashbacks*, page 66.

209 Harvey Mansfield, "The Legacy of the Late Sixties," *Reassessing the Sixties: Debating the Political and Cultural Legacy,* edited by Stephen Macedo (New York: W. W. Norton, 1997), pages 31–32.

210 "'Pleasure,' he candidly . . ." Shlain, *Acid Dreams*, page 292.

210 "currently involved . . ." Leary, *Flashbacks*, page 66.

Chapter 9: Eldridge Cleaver's Serial Extremism

211 "Panthers are . . ." Quoted in Martin A. Lee and Bruce Shlain, *Acid Dreams: The Complete Social History of* LSD: *The* CIA, *the Sixties, and Beyond* (New York: Grove Press, 1992, orig. pub. 1985), page 267.

212 "They intimidated . . ." *Flashbacks: A Personal and Cultural History of an Era* (New York: Putnam, 1990, orig. pub. 1983), page 305.

212 "the Panthers had killed . . ." David Horowitz, "Who Killed Betty Van Patter?," December 13, 1999, on-line article in *Salon*, http://www.salon.com/news/col/horo/1999/12/13/betty.

212 "nothing made . . ." Todd Gitlin, *The Sixties: Years of Hope, Days of Rage* (New York: Bantam, 1987), page 348.

213 "The black movement itself . . ." Tom Wolfe, *Radical Chic & Mau-Mauing the Flak Catchers* (New York: Farrar, Straus and Giroux, 1970), pages 8, 40.

214 "the fact remains . . ." Horowitz, "Who Killed Betty Van Patter?"

214 "We are all . . ." Jerry Rubin, *Do It! Scenarios of the Revolution* (New York: Ballantine Books, 1970), page 241.

214 "metamorphosed into . . ." John Kifner, "Eldridge Cleaver, Black Panther Who Became G.O.P Conservative, Is Dead," *The New York Times*, May 2, 1998, pages B 8ff.

215 "If Eldridge Cleaver . . ." Kifner, pages B 8ff.

217 "Desire for the white . . . ," "we shall have our . . . ," "let me drink . . ." Eldridge Cleaver, *Soul on Ice* (New York: McGraw-Hill, 1968), *seriatim*, pages 160, 61, 207.

217 "Cleaver is simply . . ." Cleaver, *Soul on Ice*, page xii.

217 "I'd like to . . ." Cleaver, *Soul on Ice*, page 19.

217 "grand, old-fashioned . . ." Richard Gilman, "White Standards and Negro Writing," *The New Republic*, March 9, 1968, page 28.

218 "Each half of . . ." Cleaver, *Soul on Ice*, pages 177, 178.

218 "the drama of . . ." Norman Mailer, "The White Negro," *Advertisements for Myself* (Cambridge: Harvard University Press, 1992, orig. pub. 1959), page 347.

219 "Rape was an . . . " Cleaver, *Soul on Ice*, page 14.

219 "slit some . . ." Cleaver, *Soul on Ice*, page 14.

219 "could not approve . . ." Cleaver, *Soul on Ice*, page 15.

219 "an extremist by nature . . ." Cleaver, *Soul on Ice*, page 16.

219 "the style throughout . . ." David Evanier, "Painting Black Cardboard Figures," *The New Leader*, March 25, 1968, page 23.

219 "Original and disturbing . . ." This and other reviews cited in this paragraph are collected in the article on Cleaver in *Contemporary Literary Criticism*, Vol. 30 (Detroit: Gale Research, 1973), pages 53–69.

219 "has a rare honesty . . ." Jack Richardson, "The Black Arts," *The New York Review of Books*, December 19, 1968, pages 12–13.

220 "unsparing . . ." Quotations in this paragraph are from Gilman, "White Standards," pages 25–30.

221 "they haven't had . . ." Interview with Nat Hentoff, *Playboy*, December 1968, pages 89–108, 238.

222 "I fell . . ." Cited in the article on Cleaver in *Contemporary Authors: New Revision Series*, Vol. 16 (Detroit: Gale Research, 1985), pages 64–66.

223 "Just as you didn't . . ." Myron Magnet, *The Dream and the Nightmare: The Sixties' Legacy to the Underclass* (New York: William Morrow, 1993), page 18.

224 "in California alone . . ." Nina J. Easton, "America the Enemy," *Los Angeles Times Magazine*, June 18, 1995, page 8.

224 "far from being peripheral . . ." David Horowitz, *Radical Son: A Journey Through Our Times* (New York: The Free Press, 1997), page 385.

224 "perhaps the most . . ." Susan Sontag, "Some Thoughts on the Right Way (for us) to Love the Cuban Revolution," *Ramparts*, April 1969, page 6.

Chapter 10: A Nostalgia for Molotovs

226 "twenty-five people . . ." David Horowitz, *Radical Son: A Journey Through Our Times* (New York: The Free Press, 1997), page 167.

226 "not in his juridical . . ." Jason Epstein, "The Trial of Bobby Seale," *The New York Review of Books*, December 4, 1969, page 35.

226 "metaphysically conceived . . ." Epstein, "The Trial of Bobby Seale," page 36.

227 "had been invited to . . . ," "barbecue some pork . . ." Epstein, "The Trial of Bobby Seale," page 35.

227 "If a pig comes . . ." Quoted in Horowitz, *Radical Son*, page 167.

227 "make sure . . ." Quoted in Horowitz, *Radical Son*, page 167.

228 "Sweet, bland . . ." Elizabeth Hardwick, "The Decline of Book Reviewing," *Harper's*, October 1959, page 139.

229 "everybody talked . . ." Philip Nobile, *Intellectual Skywriting: Literary Politics and "The New York Review of Books"* (New York: Charterhouse, 1974), page 18.

229 "the disappearance . . ." Edmund Wilson, "Every Man His Own Eckermann," *The New York Review of Books*, Summer 1963, page 1.

229 Nobile, *Intellectual Skywriting*, page 111.

230 Nobile, *Intellectual Skywriting*, page 111.

230 "designed to provoke . . ." Paul Johnson, *Modern Times: The World from the Twenties to the Nineties*, revised edition (New York: HarperCollins, 1991), page 498.

230 "a competition of terror . . ." Johnson, *Modern Times*, page 499.

230 "support Algerian fighters . . ." Quoted in Annie Cohen-Solal, *Sartre: A Life*, translated by Anna Cancogni (New York: Pantheon, 1987), page 391.

231 "an interview with 'David Burg' . . ." Robert B. Silvers, "The Voice of a Dissenter: An Interview with a Graduate of Moscow University," *Harper's*, May 1961, pages 122–131.

231 "Silvers has disputed . . ." Personal communication, dated September 10, 1998.

233 "*Partisan Review* on butcher . . ." Dennis H. Wrong, "The Case of 'The New York Review,'" *Commentary*, November 1970, page 49.

233 "as might be expected . . ." Dwight Macdonald, *The New York Review of Books*, December 26, 1963, page 7.

234 "Negro *in extremis* . . . ," "how *The Fire* . . ." F. W. Dupee, "James Baldwin and the 'Man,'" *The New York Review of Books*, Winter, 1963, pages 1, 2.

234 Tom Hayden, "The Occupation of Newark," *The New York Review of Books*, August 24, 1967, page 24.

234 "the most hideous . . ." Noam Chomsky, "On Resistance," *The New York Review of Books*, December 7, 1967, page 4.

235 "massive retaliation . . ." Todd Gitlin, *The Sixties: Years of Hope, Days of Rage* (New York: Bantam, 1987), page 401.

236 "a link between campus . . ." Quoted in Nobile, *Intellectual Skywriting*, page 4.

236 Wrong, "The Case of 'The New York Review,'" page 52.

236 "from among [*The New York Review's*] authors . . ." Quoted in Nobile, *Intellectual Skywriting*, page 5.

236 "a literary proposition . . ." Nobile, *Intellectual Skywriting*, page 4.

237 "I confess . . ." Mary McCarthy, "Report From Vietnam, I: The Home Program," *The New York Review of Books*, April 20, 1967, page 5.

237 "lips flexed as he spoke . . . ," "sense of fair play . . ." Mary McCarthy, "Report From Vietnam, II: The Problems of Success," *The New York Review of Books*, May 4, 1967, page 4.

238 "socialism with a human face . . ." Mary McCarthy quoted in Paul Hollander, *Political Pilgrims: Western Intellectuals in Search of the Good Society*, fourth edition (New Brunswick: Transaction, 1998), page xcv.

238 "organized anti-Communism . . ." Jason Epstein, "The CIA and the Intellectuals," *The New York Review of Books*, April 20, 1967, page 16.

238 "not only purged . . ." Epstein, "The CIA and the Intellectuals," page 17.

239 "The facts are clearer . . ." Epstein, "The CIA and the Intellectuals," page 18.

239 "pursuit of money . . ." Epstein, "The CIA and the Intellectuals," page 19.

240 "depending on how we respond . . ." Diana Trilling quoted in Nobile, *Intellectual Skywriting*, page 45.

240 John McDermott, "Technology: The Opiate of the Intellectuals," *The New York Review of Books*, July 31, 1969, page 35.

241 "We are stealing the youth . . ." Jerry Rubin, "An Emergency Letter to My Brothers and Sisters in the Movement," *The New York Review of Books*, February 13, 1969, page 27.

241 "America's courts . . ." Rubin, "An Emergency Letter," page 27.

242 "a society infused with racism . . ." Andrew Kopkind, "Soul Power," *The New York Review of Books*, August 24, 1967, page 3.

243 Kopkind, "Soul Power," page 3.

244 "regardless of what the Mayor did . . ." Hayden, "The Occupation," page 16.

244 "many missiles . . . ," "very few, if any . . ." Hayden, "The Occupation," page 18.

244 "People voted with . . ." Hayden, "The Occupation," page 17.

245 "If you want to bring . . ." Nobile, *Intellectual Skywriting*, page 55.

245 "was sometimes referred to . . ." Tom Wolfe, *Radical Chic &*

Mau-Mauing the Flak Catchers (New York: Farrar, Straus and Giroux, 1970), page 86.

246 "He oscillated . . ." Leszek Kolakowski, *Main Currents of Marxism*, Vol. III, *The Breakdown* (Oxford: Oxford University Press, 1978), page 179.

Chapter 11: What the Sixties Wrought

248 "march into socialism . . ." Joseph A. Schumpeter, *Capitalism, Socialism, and Democracy*, third edition (New York: Harper & Brothers, 1950, orig. pub. 1942), pages 415ff.

248 "capitalism is being . . ." Schumpeter, *Capitalism, Socialism, and Democracy*, page xiv.

249 "capitalism creates . . .," "*emotional* attachment . . ." Schumpeter, *Capitalism, Socialism, and Democracy*, pages 143, 145.

249 "the bourgeois' need . . ." Allan Bloom, *The Closing of the American Mind: How Higher Education Has Failed Democracy and Impoverished the Souls of Today's Students* (New York: Simon and Schuster, 1987), page 78.

249 "willing suspension . . ." Samuel Taylor Coleridge, *Biographia Literaria*, Vol. II (Oxford: Oxford University Press, 1907, orig. pub. 1817), Chapter 14, page 6.

250 "the real world . . ." Norman O. Brown, *Love's Body* (New York: Random House, 1966), page 151.

251 "widely shared feeling . . ." Fredric Jameson, "Periodizing the 60s," *Ideologies of Theory, II: Syntax of History* (Minneapolis: University of Minnesota Press, 1988), pages 207–208.

252 "the universities and schools . . ." Leszek Kolakowski, *Main Currents of Marxism*, Vol. III, *The Breakdown* (Oxford: Oxford University Press, 1978), page 508.

253 "What binds these men . . ." Hannah Arendt, *The Origins of Totalitarianism* (New York: Harcourt Brace Jovanovich, 1973, orig. pub. 1951), page 387.

254 "Characteristics . . ." Arthur Marwick, *The Sixties: Cultural Revolution in Britain, France, Italy and the United States, c.1958–c.1974* (Oxford: Oxford University Press, 1998), pages 16ff.

255 "a strongly hostile . . ." Marwick, *The Sixties*, page 4.

255 "We ourselves . . ." Paul Berman, *A Tale of Two Utopias: The Political Journey of the Generation of 1968* (New York: W. W. Norton, 1996), pages 7, 12.

256 "black civil rights . . ." Marwick, *The Sixties*, page 3.

256 "rigid social hierarchy . . ." Marwick, *The Sixties*, page 3.

256 "was downright stupid . . ." Marwick, *The Sixties*, page 803.

257 "Life became more . . ." Marwick, *The Sixties*, pages 803, 806.

257 "it is very important . . ." Marwick, *The Sixties*, page 7.

257 "the belief that . . ." Marwick, *The Sixties*, page 10.

257 "practically all . . ." Marwick, *The Sixties*, page 10.

258 "the various counter-cultural . . ." Marwick, *The Sixties*, page 13.

258 "most of the movements . . ." Marwick, *The Sixties*, page 13.

259 "permeated . . . ," "their mite to . . ." Marwick, *The Sixties*, pages 20, 806.

259 "All the statistical . . ." Marwick, *The Sixties*, page 802.

259 "exhibit to the full . . ." Marwick, *The Sixties*, page 20.

260 "'The fifties,' Bloom wrote . . ." Allan Bloom, *The Closing of the American Mind: How Higher Education Has Failed Democracy and Impoverished the Souls of Today's Students* (New York: Simon and Schuster, 1987), pages 322–323.

261 "The cultural revolution . . ." Marwick, *The Sixties*, page 802.

262 "Norman Thomas spoke . . ." Berman, *A Tale of Two Utopias*, page 58.

263 "special nuttiness . . . ," "came a few tiny indications . . ." Berman, *A Tale of Two Utopias*, pages 59–62.

263 "vague new sensibility . . . ," "the dream of a genuine . . ." Berman, *A Tale of Two Utopias*, pages 8–9, 11.

264 "obvious that those long-ago . . . ," "the old hope of reorganizing . . ." Berman, *A Tale of Two Utopias*, pages 15, 16–17.

264 "utopian exhilaration . . ." Berman, *A Tale of Two Utopias*, page 7.

265 "the student uprisings . . ." Berman, *A Tale of Two Utopias*, page 8.

265 "bits and pieces . . ." Berman, *A Tale of Two Utopias*, page 8.

265 "Every few decades . . . ," "one more instance . . ." Berman, *A Tale of Two Utopias*, pages 21, 22.

266 "longer than the *Communist Manifesto* . . ." Berman, *A Tale of Two Utopias*, page 46.

266 "the next Lenin . . ." Berman, *A Tale of Two Utopias*, page 76.

266 "childish lives . . . ," "criminal leftism . . . ," "mad . . ." Berman, *A Tale of Two Utopias*, *seriatim*, pages 33, 92, 88.

266 "crucial truth about . . ." Berman, *A Tale of Two Utopias*, page 254.

267 "There was the idea . . ." Berman, *A Tale of Two Utopias*, page 254.

267 "the same direction in world . . ." Berman, *A Tale of Two Utopias*, page 320.

267 "The messages from . . ." Berman, *A Tale of Two Utopias*, page 338.

268 "a movement so grand . . ." Berman, *A Tale of Two Utopias*, page 121.

268 "the left-wing idea . . ." Berman, *A Tale of Two Utopias*, page 100.

269 "A Tale of Two Reactions," Mark Lilla, *The New York Review of Books*, May 14, 1998, pages 4–7. All quotations from Lilla are from this essay.

270 "the common-place critic . . ." William Hazlitt, "On Common-Place Critics," *The Collected Works of William Hazlitt*, edited by A. R. Waller and Arnold Glover, Vol. 1 (London: J. M. Dent, 1902), page 139.

270 "When great revolutions . . ." Alexis de Tocqueville, *The Old Regime and the Revolution*, Vol. I, edited by François Furet and Françoise Mélonio (Chicago: University of Chicago Press, 1998), page 95.

271 "the counterculture was not . . ." Irving Kristol, "Countercultures," *Neo-Conservatism: The Autobiography of an Idea* (New York: The Free Press, 1995), page 136.

272 "of no country . . ." Alexis de Tocqueville, *Democracy in America*, Vol. I (New York: Alfred Knopf, 1991), page 51.

274 "there is a widespread tendency . . ." John Fletcher Moulton, "Law and Manners," *The Atlantic Monthly*, July 1924, page 3.

275 "moral issues . . ." Robert D. Novak, *Completing the Revolution: A Vision for Victory in 2000* (New York: The Free Press, 2000), page 149.

275 "A Moral Minority?," Paul Weyrich, is available on line at http://www.freecongress.org/fcf/specials/weyrichopenltr.htm. Unless otherwise noted, all quotations from Weyrich are from this document.

278 "we're not surrendering . . ." Quoted in Alan Wolfe, "Look Who's Turning Off and Tuning Out This Time," *The New York Times*, February 22, 1999, page A 17.

278 "Creating a New Society," Paul Weyrich, is available on-line at http://www.freecongress.org/fcf/specials/followup.htm.

279 "Good & Plenty: Morality in an Age of Prosperity," David Brooks, *The Weekly Standard*, February 1, 1999, pages 17–20. All quotations from Brooks are from this article.

280 "The Panglosses of the Right Are Wrong," Gertrude Himmelfarb, *The Wall Street Journal*, February 4, 1999, page A 22.

281 "a philosophy of death . . ." Russell Kirk, *The Conservative Mind: From Burke to Eliot*, seventh revised edition (Washington, D.C.: Regnery, 1994, orig. pub. 1953), page 287.

282 Schumpeter, *Capitalism, Socialism, and Democracy*, page 127.

282 "if you believe . . ." Irving Kristol, "On Conservatism and Capitalism," *Neo-Conservatism: The Autobiography of an Idea* (New York: The Free Press, 1995), page 233.

Index

Only works and authors mentioned in the text are included in the index. Full references for all cited works appear in the endnotes.

Index

Index

University of California at San Diego, 166
University of Chicago, 84–85, 158, 162, 229, 269
University of Freiburg, 166
University of Wisconsin, 162
USSR, *see* Soviet Union
Utilitarianism, 280–281
Utopianism, 127–128, 147, 168–171, 191, 249–250, 255, 281

Valladares, Armando, 95
Vanity Fair (magazine), 150
Vendler, Helen, 43, 53
Vidal, Gore, 232
Vietcong, 138, 213
Vietnam, anti-war feeling about, 65, 75, 131, 133, 138–143, 151; fall of Saigon, 13; North, 93, 95–96, 133, 140–142, 191, 234, 237; war in, 31, 46, 102–104, 129, 182, 228, 234, 236–240, 252, 271
Village Voice, The (newspaper), 43, 64, 227
Vollmer, Joan, 47–48, 56–57

Walker Art Center, 38
Wall Street Journal, The (newspaper), 33, 175, 280
Warhol, Andy, 259
Warren, Robert Penn, 232
Washington Post, The (newspaper), 45
Washington State University, 204
Watergate, 206
Waugh, Evelyn, *Black Mischief*, 191
Weather Underground, 135, 149, 187, 207
Weekly Standard, The (magazine), 279
Weil, Simone, 83
Wells, H[erbert] G[eorge], 163

Wesleyan University, 162
West, Diana, 33–34
West Point, 204
Weyrich, Paul, "Creating a New Society," 278; "A Moral Minority?," 275–278, 282
White, Phil, 48
Whitman, Walt, 267; *Leaves of Grass*, 52; *Song of Myself*, 52, 164
Whitney Museum of American Art, The, 37–41
Whyte, William, Jr., *The Organization Man*, 28
Widmer, Kingsley, *Paul Goodman*, 159
Wilbur, Richard, 233
Williams, Colin, 177
Williams, Robert Franklin, 217
Williams College, 133
Wilson, Edmund, 229, 232
Wittgenstein, Ludwig, *Tractatus Logico-Philosophicus*, 58
Wolfe, Tom, *Radical Chic*, 93, 212–213, 224–225, 245–246
Woodstock Festivals, 5, 174–176, 187, 226
Woolf, Virginia, 6
Wordsworth, William, 82
Wouk, Herman, *The Caine Mutiny*, 63
Wright, Richard, 215
Wrong, Dennis, 236–237

X, Malcolm, 216–217, 243

Yale Law Review (journal), 179
Yale Law School, 190, 213, 230
Yale University, 111, 119–125, 132–136, 176, 179, 186, 215, 220
Youth culture, 9–11

Zinn, Howard, 136, 139, 141, 143

A NOTE ON THE TYPE

The Long March is set in 11-point Galliard on
14-point leading. Designed by Matthew Carter
in the late 1970s, Galliard is based on several
French Renaissance fonts cut by the great
typographer Robert Granjon (1545–1588).